PRAISE FOR
KENNY KINGSTON,
"THE *ORIGINAL* PSYCHIC TO THE STARS"...

"Kenny Kingston is one of a kind . . . a psychic par excellence."
— Robert Osborne, *Hollywood Reporter*

"To me, Kenny Kingston is the most entertaining psychic/medium in the world. He has been a guest on my radio show many times, and has always been a smash. You will have fun with his book."
— Larry Elder, KABC Radio talk show host, Los Angeles

"Kenny Kingston explodes with the power within."
— Brad Steiger, author

"The greatest . . . so very accurate!"
— Joyce Jillson, astrologer

His clients have included actors, politicians, and members of the British Royal Family. He has appeared on numerous television and radio shows, has hosted his own television program, *The Kenny Kingston Show*, and has been host of the highly-successful *Kenny Kingston Psychic Hotline* television infomercial for many years. Now famed celebrity psychic Kenny Kingston reveals what the stars have told him from beyond . . .

I STILL TALK TO . . .

Seven Locks Press
P.O. Box 25689
Santa Ana, CA 92799
(800) 354-5348

Individual Sales. This book is available through most bookstores or can be ordered directly from Seven Locks Press at the address above.

Quantity Sales. Special discounts are available on quantity purchases by corporations, associations, and others. For details, contact the "Special Sales Department" at the publisher's address above.

Printed in the United States of America

Library of Congress Cataloging-in-Publication Data
is available from the publisher
ISBN 0-929765-79-6

Cover photo by Alan Weissman
Cover & Interior Design by Sparrow Advertising & Design

I STILL TALK TO . . .

BY PSYCHIC KENNY KINGSTON
AS TOLD TO VALERIE PORTER

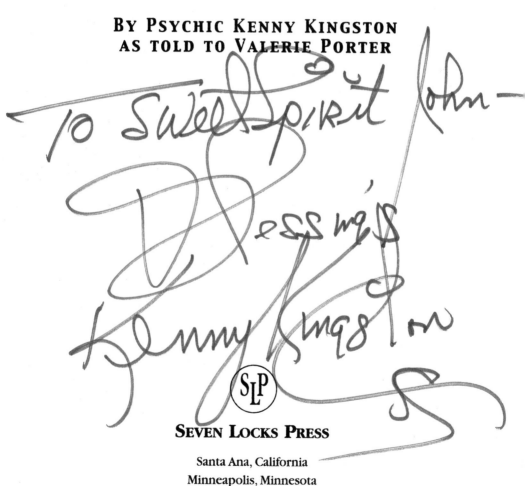

To Sweet Spirit John —
Blessings
Kenny Kingston

SLP

SEVEN LOCKS PRESS

Santa Ana, California
Minneapolis, Minnesota
Washington, D.C.

DEDICATION

For my adored mother—my pal—Catherine "Kaye" Kingston, who left this plane on July 7, 1984, but who is "here" whenever I need her.

And to Valerie's dear dad, Norman Charles Porter.

They knew that we all choose our parents and if we had it to do all over again, we'd still choose them. May a choir of angels surround and love them as we always will.

To my dear Clifton Webb . . . my guide and my friend:

Please forgive me for not holding a seance in your memory for this book, Sweet Spirit.

We make contact so often—sometimes daily—and I know you're aware that I always give you credit for providing my sense of humor during my personal appearances (while my guide Henry C. provides legal and medical advice and my third guide Chief Running Bull tickles selected audience members, providing relaxation and a sense of fun).

Syndicated columnist and author James Bacon often said in his column, which ran in 450 newspapers, "Clifton got more publicity in 'death' than in life, thanks to Kenny Kingston."

So I'm giving you a rest, Clifton. I keep you going so much that you're deserving of it. Though you're mentioned in this edition, I promise you'll be included more heavily in any future volumes.

Thank you, dear friend . . . until next time.

ACKNOWLEDGMENTS

In addition to the many people mentioned in the book who offered cooperation and information, we would like to thank most heartily the following for their contributions toward the successful completion of this project:

Steve Schiffman (Desert Inn); Marvin Paige (Motion Picture & Television Research Service); Jeffrey Leonardi; Hotel Ritz-Paris; Hotel Concorde Saint-Lazare-Paris; Copthorne Tara Hotel-London; Dorothea Bellisime; Betty Flesher; Stephanie Miller-KABC Radio; Corinne and George Sidney; Cindy Williams; Larry Elder; Vernon Scott (UPI); Jackie Zeman; Mary Higgins Clark; Carol Vitale; Kelly Lange; Rick Miramontez Public Relations; columnist James Bacon; Patte Barham; Reverend Michael Wakefield; Paul Lewis (London Weekend Television); Scott Michaels and Graham Norton (*So . . . Graham Norton* show, London); Joyce Aimee and Helen Barkan of Aimee Entertainment; Frank Skinner (Avalon Television, London, England); Peter Hill (Associate Editor *London Daily Star*); Rita Montanez; Martin Singer, Esq.; Lynne Lester and Gloria Hillard (CNN); Dan Jbara (*Hard Copy*); Gary, Carol and Melissa Gursey; Lucie Arnaz; Philip Vandervort; Steve Marraccini (Queen Mary); Joyce Jillson; Brad Steiger; Army Archerd (*Daily Variety*); Robert Osborne (*The Hollywood Reporter*); Sybil Brand; Steve and Jayne Meadows Allen; Margaret Bonfiglio; and Tresa Semer. And a very special thank you to the people who helped us bring this project to fruition: Ray Cavaleri; Stephen F. Breimer, Esq.; Michael Hamilburg; Jeremy Tarcher; and Jim Riordan.

SOME THOUGHTS ABOUT HEAVEN . . .
PAST AND PRESENT

Benjamin Franklin: "I believe that the soul of man is immortal and will be treated with justice in another life, respecting its karma in this."

Author/television personality Steve Allen (reprinted with Mr. Allen's permission from his current book *More Steve Allen on the Bible, Religion and Morality, Book Two*) : "There has long been the quite clear teaching that at the moment of physical death the spirits of human beings go either to Heaven, Hell, or—as some believe—Purgatory. Our religious instructors are not in the habit of adding, 'Oh, by the way, if your surviving spirit happens *not* to go to one of these three classic destinations it might end up just wandering around Cleveland for a few hundred years' . . . It would at least be reasonable, assuming there are free-floating spirits, that there would be some edifying purpose to their occasional encounters with human beings. A ghost, for example, might choose to say something like, 'Do not be startled, my friend; I intend you no harm. Rather I appear before you to assure you not only that there is life after physical death but that mankind must now repent, return to the Lord, and prepare for his imminent coming.' Such a message, quite aside from the question as to whether it is sound and reliable or totally out-of-touch with any sort of reality, is at least coherent and consistent with much that religious people already believe."

Daytime actress Jacklyn Zeman ("Bobbie" on *General Hospital*) : "I've always thought of the other side as a place where souls stop off for a while between lifetimes. I think it's a place of great vision where the eyes and the heart look upon one's past life and we are given an opportunity to expand our abilities for our next life. I tend to be a very positive person and I believe in the goodness of human nature. I think most souls improve with each go round."

Auto tycoon Henry Ford: "Genius is experience. Some seem to think that it is a gift or talent, but it is the fruit of long experience in many lives. Some are older souls than others, and so they know more . . . Work is futile if we cannot utilize the experience we collect in one life in the next."

Actress Barbara Hale (film actress but perhaps best known as Della Street for many years on television's "Perry Mason"): "Heaven is *not* the end . . . it's just the beginning! It's filled with beauty, joy, contentment, no pain, acceptance, peace and everlasting love for all."

Charles Dickens (from *The Old Curiosity Shop*) : (Reflecting upon Little Nell's 'death')— "It is not," said the schoolmaster, as he bent down to kiss her on the cheek, and gave his tears free vent, "it is not on Earth that Heaven's justice ends. Think what it is, compared with the world to which her young spirit has winged its early flight, and say, if one deliberate wish expressed in solemn terms above this bed could call her back to life—which of us would utter it!"

Actress Cindy Williams (from *American Graffitti, Laverne & Shirley, Getting By*): "Five years ago, I fell into a deep state of grieving over the death of a child—not my own, but one who felt like my own. Nothing seemed to comfort me. One night as I was falling asleep, a spirit came to me. He took me gently by the shoulder and led me to a garden. He pointed upward to five different and beautifully colored birds who flew down and settled in the air to my left. This gentle spirit then gestured to each bird asking each to sing its individual song for me. They did so with such beauty and love that I wept with joy. I then realized that this spirit was Saint Francis of Assisi, my patron saint. I was elated.

Saint Francis then led me down a small hill, and stepping in front of me, he reached to what I can only describe as the corner of the horizon and peeled away the darkness, revealing to me a river of light—a river of indescribable beauty. It was made of colored, dancing diamond light, a beauty so generous, so joyful, I had to approach it. I wanted to touch it, to join it.

As I moved toward the river, the hand of Saint Francis touched my shoulder gently, conveying to me that it was time to return. I did not want to return and resisted. But I heard a beautiful voice say lovingly, "It is not time yet; you must return." Reluctantly I retreated, back past the garden. With an overwhelming sense of comfort and absolute love I awoke.

I am convinced that Saint Francis had shown me some of the joys that await us all in Heaven, and to grieve for a loved one entering Heaven from this world is an empty thing."

William Shakespeare: "There are more things in heaven and earth, Horatio, than are dreamt of in your philosophy."

INTRODUCTION

"No one dies, they only have a new birthday, for that is when life really begins."

That has been my motto for many years, and my belief for all of my life. I have long believed that our time here on Earth is just one piece of the puzzle. What happens after we *leave* Earthplane is even more wonderful and fulfilling than anything we could imagine—it holds more fear, dread, confusion yet fascination than anything we encounter in so-called life.

It is my feeling, and I am joined by a multitude of others, that when our time here is completed, we do not "die," never to be seen or heard from again. Instead, I feel we merely "pass" into another dimension—like crossing a bridge or going into another room. (And "passing" is the term I much prefer to use instead of "death" or "dying").

In this new dimension, which I call "Paradise," "the other side," or simply "the spirit world," the essence of our being, the "spirit" or "soul," continues to exist—we still laugh, we still love, we see our relatives, and we make new friends.

If I seem definite about this belief, it is with good reason—I have been communicating with spirits since I was a very young child.

I was *born* psychic—to the seventh daughter of a seventh daughter (a very psychic sign in itself). At age four I was taught to read tea leaves by my grandmother, Catherine Walsh Clark. When I was seven, my mother Catherine (Kaye) Kingston taught me psychometry (this is the art of touching a personal object—a watch, ring, or earring, for example—which has been worn by someone consistently for at least two hours). I then pick up psychic vibrations emanating from the object.

The first actual encounter with a spirit which I remember came when I was 10 years old. I was taking an exam in school and struggling for the answers (I had not studied for the exam!) Suddenly I heard a kind, elderly male voice speaking in my ear, giving me the answers. The gentleman said he was my grandfather, Henry C. (for "Clark"). I had never met my grandfather, he passed before I was born, but since I had no better solution, I wrote down the answers he gave me. To my surprise and delight—I passed the exam with 86% accuracy!

Before long I found I was able to communicate not only with my grandfather's spirit but also with many others, and thus became not only a psychic who could tell people about their past, present and future, but a "medium" as well—a person with a direct link to the other side.

Surprisingly, I never questioned this ability—it seemed totally natural to me—just a wonderful gift I'd been given. My gift was the ability to communicate with those who'd passed on, and I became very fond of these entities, calling them my "Sweet Spirits," a phrase which has been associated with me throughout my life.

During my career many people have noted that while I do give psychic readings to doctors, lawyers, and people from all walks of life, nevertheless the *famous* seem to have been associated most closely with me, both as clients and as spirits I've contacted.

Again, as with the psychic ability, these celebrities have more or less always been part of my life. I recall as a child watching my family entertain politicians and performers in our New York State home. Among our neighbors were the great stage actress Katharine Cornell and her director-husband Guthrie McClintic. Once he learned of my abilities, Mr. McClintic often asked me to, in his words, "touch the script Miss Katharine should do next."

A dear friend of my mother's was legendary sex symbol Mae West; thus as a child I grew up thinking of her as my friend as well. Mae was very interested in psychic phenomena and was quite psychic herself, and she coached me in the art of clairaudio—listening to the sound of a voice and picking up psychic vibrations from it. Soon she was even calling me on the telephone and asking for my psychic advice—all of this when I was about 6 years old!

Eventually, word of mouth passed from one personality to the next and my reputation grew. I developed a roster of clients in the entertainment, political, and social worlds. As I worked with the celebrated, I began contacting their equally celebrated friends and loved ones in spirit who would come in during psychic sessions we would hold.

Thus, as my reputation grew and word of my communications with personalities both here and on the other side gained attention in the media, I found radio and television talk show hosts frequently asking me, "So, Kenny—do you still talk to . . . " followed by the name of a celebrated spirit (from Marilyn Monroe to Harry S. Truman). Today I've become accustomed to being asked, "Have you talked to Elvis lately?"

It seemed inevitable, then, that one day I would write this book—a combination of experiences regarding the famous and my communications with them after their passing.

The spirits we contacted for this book were not "forced" to appear—they came of their own free will. In fact, it is impossible to demand communication with someone from the other side. You can only request their presence and hope they have something they wish to say in return.

For most spirits, it seems they really enjoy the opportunity of communicating with those of us "alive" on Earthplane once again. This book is perhaps the chance for the spirits we contacted to relay a message to their public or their loved ones. When someone passes, often things are left unsaid because time simply runs out. This, then, is the chance for the spirits you'll encounter in our book to finish any unfinished business—to say what they may not have had a chance to say, and also to bring us up to date on their "lives" now that they've had a chance to spend some time adjusting to the spirit world.

As you read the book, I think you'll find one thing very clear—there is definitely a serious aspect to "life" on the other side. As a result, you'll find many spirits studying something they always wanted to study, but never before had the opportunity. Before you think this might become uninteresting to read, realize that here on Earthplane, if you call several homes on any given weekday looking for the adult occupants, you'll no doubt find they are at work—that's one of the primary functions in our life here. In the spirit world, one of the primary functions is to study—to learn and progress—to grow and develop as a person. In other words, they have a *purpose* in the spirit world and, for many, their favorite way of fulfilling that purpose is to learn new information which will help them perhaps overcome weaknesses or shortcomings they had in "life."

Another primary role on the other side is to become a "protector." This is another method of progressing or advancing—by helping those of us here on Earthplane. Many spirits spend time watching over a loved one or a person they particularly like or admire, for spirits are in a much better position to know what lies ahead for us and what is best for us, because they are more open to a higher level of consciousness and psychic awareness from the moment they begin their new "life."

Some spirits also spend time greeting and counseling new arrivals as they enter Paradise. These kindly spirits provide a friendly atmosphere for initiating just-arrived spirits who are confused about their new surroundings. I find it most comforting to know a loved one, friend, or kindly soul will be waiting to help us adjust following *our* passing, don't you?

I'm sure you'll also find it refreshing to learn, as you read our communications, that there is certainly time for amusement and enjoyment on the other side, and spirits can retain a keen and wonderful sense of humor.

There is plenty of time for rest and relaxation, and some spirits enjoy hobbies such as gardening amid the many lush trees and flowers, visiting friends and family members who haven't been seen for many years, or tending animals who have passed on—for yes, the spirits of dogs, cats, horses, and other creatures live on as well.

In other words, all of the good elements of our lives *here* continue on the other side; they are just heightened and improved and there are many delightful things to occupy the Sweet Spirits in Paradise. The only elements of "life" eliminated on the other side are the negative aspects—crime, illness, and that one thing which can be such a downfall here on Earthplane—jealousy.

With so many activities to choose from, making contact with us here is just one aspect of the spirit's existence. Therefore, we are very fortunate when all elements are in place and they are in a position to communicate with us, and in return we are in a position to receive them—how glorious!

As a result, when we began writing this book, we were not successful in every contact, or at least not always on the first try. In one or two cases we attempted to contact someone and found that they were not available. We were told by a spirit emissary sent by them that they were busy with another project at the moment but would come to us at a later date. Later in this book we will discuss the particulars of a few such cases.

Another reason a spirit might not appear is because this person has reincarnated, and such was the case with Humphrey Bogart, who is discussed later in the book. (Reincarnation is another philosophy I strongly believe in, where the spirit, after resting on the other side, returns to live again in another time and place and as another person. We carry some of our traits and interests with us from one lifetime to the next but also develop new ones along the way. We can pay back much of our "karma" by reincarnating. Karma is a term meaning "cause and effect." In other words, what we do in one life, good or bad, influences what happens to us in another lifetime—we are rewarded or punished accordingly).

In still another instance, a spirit might not be able to materialize because he or she is in the "screening room,"—which is not a place to watch current films while eating popcorn! It is a very serious situation where we see highlights of our last life played before us, then see what could take place in our next life if we so desire. We choose the lifestyle, environment—even the parents we wish to have. (So the next time your children complain about you, say, "Don't blame me—you chose me!").

You'll find that we chose various types of locations for our visits with spirits in this book. We went wherever we felt the vibrations, or psychic feelings of spirit, would be the strongest—thus you'll find us at former residences, the very spot of a passing, favorite nightclubs—any location which would be most likely to coax a spirit to return.

We used several methods of contact. In some cases, we held a seance, and through our transcript you'll have a chance to "relive" the experience with us as we see a spirit (called a materialization) or perhaps hear, see, and feel them (something which takes place during a seance—when the form of a spirit actually enters a room and their presence is made known by way of sound, sight, and touch).

In some cases, I actually entered into a trance (a deep meditative state) where my soul or spirit temporarily left in order to allow the soul or spirit we had contacted to enter my body. This allowed the spirit to talk and move about freely. It is a most unusual experience for the spirit, the psychic-medium, and those witnessing the event.

In a few cases in this book, where contact was made most easily, I was able to walk through a personality's former residence, pick up vibrations and relay messages, or even sit quietly in my own home and communicate directly with a spirit. You may say, as you begin reading a communication of this type, "Is it *really* that easy—can he just open his mouth and speak to spirit?" In answer to that question—what can I say? As I mentioned, I feel I've been blessed with a gift. Spirit communication doesn't always have to be the "stuff" of movies, with wild gyrations and facial contortions by the psychic and with spirits flying around the room. In answer to the question, yes, thankfully, many times I can just open my mouth, *listen*, and communicate what the spirit is saying.

As you become part of these communications, you'll notice references to many phenomena such as cool breezes, bright lights, a warmth almost like "burning up," or mists forming. These are fairly standard when a spirit is entering, especially during a seance or materialization. Remember—spirits are traveling from their world to ours—they're entering a different atmosphere, and the lights or variations in temperature reflect these changes. It's rather like the atmospheric pressure in an airplane changing as different altitudes are reached.

When we pass, we leave behind the physical flesh and bones we once had, and what remains, the soul, is much lighter in weight and almost transparent. The mist or glow which we often see is what the spirit creates in order to be seen by us. Its technical term is "ectoplasm." The ectoplasm is a substance which attaches itself to the soul and makes it more visible. Usually a spirit works hard to summon up as much ectoplasm as they can in order to be seen as clearly as possible.

Those of you who are fascinated with the legendary personalities of the world will find the following pages most unusual—just when you thought there was nothing more to learn about your favorite personality, here is *new* information—here are fresh facts about the person's existence *today*. Together we'll be exploring what this incredible group of world figures are doing now—for remember, they are not "dead"— they are still within reach.

Those of you interested in, or perhaps well-versed in, psychic phenomena will hopefully enjoy the opportunity of becoming an eyewitness to our communications with the spirit world.

And those of you who are curious about the spirit world will perhaps find some answers within these pages. Perhaps you will emerge with a better understanding of the spirit world. I believe you will *definitely* emerge with less fear of it. Through the contacts we make, we'll attempt to answer questions such as, "What does it feel like when we 'pass'?," "What does the other side look like?," and "Do we change or progress—do we atone for our sins?"

Regardless of your reasons for reading the book, I invite you to sit back, relax—be enlightened and entertained. I love the Sweet Spirits—they're a joy to me. I hope my experiences with them in this book will be a joy and a comfort to you.

TELEVISION

LUCILLE BALL

THEN

When I was growing up as a young schoolboy in Buffalo, New York, I developed an interest in the entertainment world, and my native city provided many wonderful experiences and opportunities to indulge my interest.

Among my family's neighbors were the "First Lady of the American Theater," Katharine Cornell, and her director husband Guthrie McClintic. I'd often watch Ms. Cornell from backstage during her performance at one of Buffalo's legitimate theaters, the Erlanger. Mr. McClintic, recognizing my psychic abilities, would occasionally present several manuscripts to me and ask me to "touch the script that Ms. Katharine should do next."

Many theater companies came into our area, because Buffalo served as a reliable "tryout city" for a play prior to Broadway. This gave me ample opportunities to go to the theater, mostly with my mother, or to watch at the stage door following a performance, for a glimpse of the actors and actresses.

In addition to its popular legitimate theaters, the city of Buffalo often attracted other entertainment, in the form of live stage shows in between films shown at the movie theaters. It was a common occurrence at the time, for promotional purposes and to increase attendance, to bring in musicians, singers, or actors to perform onstage before the next screening of a film. On less frequent occasions, the actual stars of the film would also appear onstage as part of a personal appearance tour.

I'd read in the newspaper that Maureen O'Hara and Lucille Ball would be appearing at a nearby theater for just such an occasion, to promote their new film, *Dance, Girl, Dance*. I knew instantly that I wanted to have a chance to see the two actresses. But rather than seeing their film or their appearance inside the theater, I decided to wait *outside*, near the stage door, in order to get a closer look at the two ladies as they left the theater.

I also felt that it would be interesting to see what psychic feelings I could get about the two women and wanted to get as close as possible to do so.

Needless to say, I was not the only person wanting to get close to Maureen O'Hara and Lucille Ball, and police had anticipated that by stationing guards at the stage door. I was content, though—I was able to get up to the front of the line of people waiting. We were rewarded shortly, when the two emerged.

Lucille Ball caught my attention immediately with her carrot-red hair. I noticed everything—her fox fur coat, a plaid skirt showing beneath the coat as she walked, and bright red shoes. She stopped for a moment, took out a package of Lucky Strike cigarettes, and actually lit a cigarette by first striking a match to the bottom of one of those red shoes. It was fascinating to me!

Maureen O'Hara emerged behind her, with flaming red hair only slightly more subdued than her fellow actress. Ms. O'Hara was draped in a black form-fitting coat, and smiled briefly not only at those of us gathered near the door, but at the working people who'd gathered at the windows of the office building across the street, and were peering out.

"Oh, Miss O'Hara!" the shop girls called down. "Hello, Miss O'Hara!" Then next I heard, "Lucille! Look over here Lucille—Hello!" Though I was young, I noticed the subtle difference—Maureen O'Hara was considered 'Miss O'Hara'—a film star, perhaps a bit aloof and untouchable, while Lucille Ball, also a film actress, was 'Lucille' to her admirers.

My eyes returned to Lucille Ball, and I became confused. I saw her in a small "box" of some type—she was laughing and smiling, but contained inside of the box. It meant nothing to me at the moment, although I recalled the incident vividly years later and realized I must have been seeing a rather primitive premonition of *television*, without even knowing yet what it *was*.

Following this brief but memorable exposure to Lucille Ball, it was perhaps 10 years before I would have a chance to see her once again in person (though I enjoyed her, in the meantime, in a film called *Dark*

Corner, ironically starring Clifton Webb, who would later become a friend and is now one of my spirit guides).

In the late '40s I relocated to San Francisco, California, after having served time in the Army. My interest in entertainment had continued and in fact heightened during the intervening years, and this particular evening I'd seen bandleader Desi Arnaz and his orchestra performing at the Orpheum Theater. Lucille Ball and Desi were married by this time, and she'd taken time off from doing films to appear onstage with him during this engagement. I felt compelled to go backstage to compliment the husband and wife on a wonderful evening of entertainment (because I'd often attended the theater, I'd become friends with several of the backstage crew at various theaters, and following a performance, they would allow me to go backstage to meet the performers—quite a treat indeed).

What transpired this particular night is a story Desi and I enjoyed telling many years afterward on Merv Griffin's popular syndicated talk show. On the air, Merv asked if Desi and I had met before. "Oh, yes," Desi smiled. "I'll never forget meeting Kenny. He came into my dressing room backstage at San Francisco's Orpheum Theater. I invited him to sit down, and he said, 'You know, you're going to become one of the greatest producer/directors in television—you'll be greatly involved in television history!' "

I continued the story: "And as Lucy stopped taking her makeup off for a moment and popped her head around the corner of the dressing room, I said, 'And of course, you'll be very much involved in the history of television, also.' " I reminded Merv that this had occurred in the late '40s while television was in its infancy, and of course before I became well known as a psychic.

"What did you think, Desi? What did you say?" Merv asked.

"I said, 'Come on, Kenny, have another drink—we'll *both* feel better!'" Desi laughed. Yet sure enough, Desi Arnaz, with Lucille Ball, formed Desilu Productions, which was one of the most important and prestigious television production houses in existence for many years, producing, in addition to *I Love Lucy*, such memorable shows as *Our Miss Brooks*, *Make Room for Daddy*, and *December Bride*.

Though Lucille and Desi divorced, the years following the San Francisco meeting were kind in many ways to them and to me, as our careers flourished. I kept in touch with Lucille sporadically, and would often give her a brief psychic message.

One day, in 1970, she asked me to do my one-man psychic performance at her daughter Lucie Arnaz's birthday party, to be held at Lucille's Roxbury Drive mansion in Beverly Hills. During the show, where I roamed throughout the audience giving psychic messages to several guests, I stopped at Lucille's table and gave her several messages.

"I'm getting these messages from a schoolteacher of yours from Jamestown, New York," I told her, and went on to describe the teacher. Tears came to Lucille's eyes and she said, "Oh yes—I remember so well! That particular teacher influenced me greatly by encouraging me to become an actress!"

At young Lucie's side during the performance stood her escort, a handsome young man whom I later learned was Philip Vandervort, a television producer. At supper following my performance, I stunned those at our table, including young Lucie, by predicting, "Do you know, you and this young man will be married within a year from today?"

The young couple grinned knowingly and I realized I'd just released their secret plans. (They made my prediction come true—by marrying exactly one year, to the day, later!)

As I prepared to leave the party, Lucille and I walked for a moment quietly around the grounds of her home. "I want to thank you again for bringing in my teacher in spirit, Kenny," she smiled. "I've read about some of the seances you've held—I always thought it would be fascinating to bring in a spirit."

Yet a contradictory side of Lucille appeared when I offered to hold a private seance for her some time. Her eyes filled with tears again momentarily, and I could tell she was tempted, yet she suddenly tensed and said, "No—I'd be afraid! No—I couldn't Kenny! But thank you!"

Perhaps it was this half-fascination, half-fear of the spirit world, but our contact was only occasional after that evening, primarily when we'd meet at a party and exchange a few words and a psychic bit of advice here and there.

My last meeting with Lucille was regrettably just three weeks before she passed away.

Singer and former M.G.M. actress Gloria DeHaven was opening an engagement at the Cinegrill night club in Hollywood. Attending the opening were many ladies she'd worked with and befriended during her career—Betty White, Bea Arthur, Jayne Meadows, Jean Simmons, Esther Williams, and of course Lucille Ball, who'd agreed to introduce Gloria on this opening night.

Before the performance began, I spotted Lucille near the bar, standing with her publicist friend Gloria Luckinbill. We greeted each other warmly and chatted about old times. Lucille, ever the protective mother, was momentarily alarmed when I said I'd run into daughter Lucie at the Playboy Mansion a few months earlier. "What was she doing there?" she frowned. "It was perfectly all right," I explained, "Lucie was there as part of a charity event to benefit homeless animals." "Oh that's different then." She sighed, obviously relieved. "Yes, that's okay—that's fine—she's a good girl." We talked a bit longer, and she once again mentioned the teacher I'd once brought in to her in spirit, and then it was showtime.

Following the performance we all attended a private party upstairs at the hotel. As I watched Lucille at a distance, I felt her aura was down—she still managed to look glamorous, yet there was an unnatural tiredness about her, and it disturbed me somewhat.

One night a couple of weeks later, I was lying in bed just before drifting to sleep and a vision of the queen of television comedy came before me. I'd actually thought of Lucille several times since our talk at the Cinegrill, but this night, just as I drifted to sleep, the question came to me, "What would happen if Lucille Ball had a heart attack? Who would take care of her children?" I knew Lucie and Desi Jr. were fully grown, but Lucille adored them with a great passion and like most mothers she still thought of them as her "babies."

As I fell asleep, I "saw" a newspaper headline—LUCILLE BALL DIES. I never use the word "die" because I feel life is ongoing, in one form or another, but of course the headline of an actual newspaper would use the word.

When I awoke I tried to abolish the thought from my mind, hoping it had been my imagination, yet knowing better deep inside.

I turned on the television news later in the day and learned Lucille Ball had suffered a heart attack that morning, soon after I awoke. I watched her doctor telling the news media that her aorta, the main artery near the heart, had ruptured but was repaired. I felt relieved at first, thinking my dream had been incorrect.

However, do remember that I read auras, and that they reflect one's mental, physical, and emotional state. The doctor's aura was not good. I feared he was not revealing his true feelings, perhaps even to himself. His aura told me he was not as confident as he hoped to appear as he spoke at the news conference.

Unfortunately, eight days later both my dream and aura reading were proven accurate. I was on a lecture tour in San Francisco and left my hotel suite to take a brief walk. I passed a newsstand and ironically one particular headline caught my attention—it said simply, LUCILLE BALL DIES.

The doctor soon revealed to the news media that the aorta had been repaired during surgery, but a nearby valve had been damaged also, and could not be repaired during the surgery, and Miss Ball was too weak to undergo a further operation to save her life.

I thought back to eight days before, when I'd had my psychic impression of Lucille Ball, and wondered if I could have done anything to help. But I realized Lucy's health had deteriorated too far. The aorta was too badly damaged and it was her time to leave us, unfortunately for all concerned. There are times when your dreams are meant as a warning and can give you guidelines to follow, and other times such as this when your psychic dreams or visions are only meant to be a glimpse at the future, perhaps to prepare you for what lies ahead.

In this case, for me, it was preparation for the loss of Lucille Ball, someone I'd known on and off since those early boyhood days in Buffalo.

LUCILLE BALL SUFFERED A RUPTURED ABDOMINAL AORTA AND PASSED AWAY FOLLOWING OPEN HEART SURGERY IN CEDARS-SINAI MEDICAL CENTER IN LOS ANGELES ON APRIL 26, 1989.

NOW

I wanted to do something special—something slightly different—for Lucille Ball, and one day the idea came to me: a seance, with a small group of people I would personally select. For the event, I chose Barbara Connor, a psychic from Orange County, California, who regularly goes into trance, teaches classes on psychic ability, and has worked with me at my psychic meetings occasionally (in addition to having appeared on NBC-TV's *Unsolved Mysteries*). Barbara's companion Doug French often acts as a "battery" for her during her trances (adding psychic energy and support); thus he was added to the group.

I was also mulling over ideas about the right location for the seance. I considered the grounds of a former home, studio, or the church where she and Desi renewed their wedding vows and their children were baptized, for example, but upon doing research, I learned that each location under consideration had been changed so drastically that few, if any, of Lucille's vibrations would still be present.

Then I thought, "The perfect place, other than a location familiar to Lucille, would be a *spiritual* setting—one with good, strong psychic vibrations, which would be conducive to bringing in spirits. But rather than using my residence again, where could this be?" And then the answer came to me. Many times I've given lectures in Claremont, California, about an hour out of Los Angeles, at a metaphysical book-and-gift shop named Merlin's Crystal Cave. The shop is owned by Annella Frantz, who, in addition to operating it (with husband David Carter), gives psychic readings in a special "nook" of the Crystal Cave.

I've come to know Annella and David, trust their vibrations, and therefore asked if we might use the shop, after hours, to hold Lucille Ball's seance. They happily agreed and were added to our select group.

In addition to Valerie and myself, the group was rounded out by Dee Hall, with whom I've been friends for many years. Dee has attended many of our seances in the past and is on the administrative staff at our regular psychic meetings. And most importantly where this particular evening was concerned, Dee was a friend of Lucille Ball and her mother DeDe for over 40 years. In fact, though I couldn't recall many of the details of the association, I had thought of Dee from the time I began organizing the seance, because her having known Lucille so well would certainly help entice Lucille's presence to be felt.

Dee's story in itself was an interesting one, and she filled us in on the details as she, Valerie, and I drove enroute to Claremont (under a large full moon!) the night of the seance. I noticed as Dee talked that she shared something with me—we both referred to the comedienne only as "Lucille" instead of "Lucy"—for some reason her personality commanded it.

"I was 19 when it began," Dee recalled. "I was waiting for a bus one day outside CBS Studios and noticed a woman watching me briefly before she entered the studio. Then the bus came along to take me home. The following week, the same woman walked over to me and said, 'You were here last week, too, weren't you?' I said yes, and before I could explain she said, 'You come with me—you don't belong out here.' The woman was DeDe, Lucille Ball's mother, and she promptly brought me backstage where Lucille was preparing to do the radio show, *My Favorite Husband*."

"After the show, DeDe said, 'Now, every week you come in with me.' This was really something for a 19-year-old, and I eventually quit the classes I was taking in order to spend more time with DeDe and Lucille."

Dee explained that she would sometimes do simple tasks like answering fan mail, but generally she just spent time with them backstage, having dinner, and watching the show being done. "They just took a liking to me," she recalled, still amazed by it to this day. "I continued to be friends with them, attended all the *I Love Lucy* tapings, met Desi, and even moved in, temporarily, with first DeDe and then Cleo (Lucille's cousin). As time went by and the children were born, I spent time with them, too, and I remember how Lucille loved those children."

When Dee married and had her own children, she lost touch with the famed comedienne and her mother for a long period of time. They became reacquainted, though, 15 years later and stayed close for another long stretch. "The last time I saw her was seven or eight years before she passed," Dee said of Lucille. "I just didn't pursue the friendship enough and lost touch. But I had a chance to see Lucie all grown up on this last visit, and I showed her baby pictures I'd taken of her out at her mom and dad's ranch in Chatsworth."

I felt that this talk of Lucille was good—talking about a spirit helps draw it near, and almost our entire drive was filled with conversation and reminiscences of Lucille.

We pulled into the parking lot and climbed the stairs to the quaint building which holds the Crystal Cave. It was once a schoolhouse, each former classroom now housing a different shop or restaurant.

When we arrived at the entrance to the Crystal Cave, we saw that Annella, David, Barbara and Doug were already gathered there. The first thing we saw was a cloud of smoke inside the cozy shop, but we realized that David was burning incense and this was what had created the smoke which swirled around the crystals, potpourri, figurines, cards, and rows of books. "I'll just put this out now," he said. "We used it to clear the vibrations so that we would be starting fresh," Annella explained. "That way there won't be any vibrations left over from customers or people who've been in today for readings."

I'm not a firm believer in incense, but I *am* all for clearing the vibrations so that the way would be clear for spirits to enter, so if David and Annella chose to burn incense, so be it.

We quickly set about preparing the room. A heavy wooden table had been placed in an area in the center of the shop, in-between glass display cases. There was just enough room for seven folding chairs to be placed around it. "We must block out the light from the hallway," I told David. "Can you hang something over the two glass panes in the shop doors?" And within moments David had hung two posters over the windows, effectively blocking out this extraneous light. We placed the Bible (for extra spiritual protection—present at all of my seances) and the red glass candle in the center of the table.

Dee had brought with her an early photo of Lucille Ball which had been lovingly autographed to Dee—we placed this facing where Dee would sit at the table. I brought a photo of myself, Lucille, Lucie, and Philip Vandervort, taken at Lucille's home when Lucie turned 19. This I placed on the table so that it would face me.

"I'll need some water in anticipation of possibly going into a trance," I told Annella, and she quickly filled not only a glass for me, but for everyone on the off chance that any one of our group could be pulled into trance at this "sitting."

Anticipation was running high. The energy in the room was almost palpable.

Presently, we positioned ourselves around the table and lit the candle. David turned out the shop lights and joined us. Valerie took notes of the proceedings:

As has become our custom over the years at my seances, we sang "In the Garden" to raise the vibrations. We held hands as we sang and with each verse our voices grew stronger. The moment we concluded the hymn a loud crack reverberated in a far corner of the shop. We dropped our hands onto the table, no longer holding one another's, but staying very close. The following then took place:

Kenny:	I feel an Eve or Evelyn here.
All:	Welcome.
Annella:	Kenny, did you know the movie actor George Raft?
Kenny:	Not really, but I had lunch with him and several other people once when I was appearing at La Costa. You know—the resort.
Annella:	He's leaning up against the door, smiling sarcastically and watching us.
Dee:	Well, Lucille knew Betty Grable . . .
Kenny:	And George Raft was one of the great loves of Betty's life. David . . . in back of you there's a Helen in spirit
David:	Welcome.
Dee:	It's cooled down in here. (It had been very warm, as though the heat had been turned on, when we began singing at the start of the seance).
Valerie:	Yes! I felt a swirl of cool air here (pointing to area to her right, in-between her chair and Kenny's).

Another loud rap resounded in a corner of the room, as though someone pounded on the wall.

Kenny: David, someone is here who talks about passing away with something like pneumonia.

(David seems unable to identify the spirit)

Annella: It's your mother, David! She passed with fluid in her lungs.

As seemingly a series of spirits began parading by:

Kenny: An Ann or Anna is trying to come in ...And why is there a Mary between David and Annella? Who's coming in around you, Dee, is someone with a 'D'—a 'D'—she's putting a box in front of you, symbolically. Who made a box lunch?

Dee: We had box lunches on the set ...

Kenny: I get a lady with glasses . . . her hair in an upsweep . . .

Dee: That's DeDe! Lucille's mother!

Annella: The Mary is from another time . . . I'll explain later . . .

At this moment a *crack* split the air directly above us, as though it came from the ceiling.

Kenny: What happened with a crack in the ceiling, or was something being done with pipes some-where regarding Lucille?

Dee: It could have been when they did add-ons to the ranch in Chatsworth—DeDe was proud of that.

Barbara began breathing heavily, then sobbing openly; tears could be seen glistening in her eyes even by candlelight.

Barbara: I'm crying . . . I want to cry.

Dee: Lucille was emotional about the add-on for her children's wing of the ranch home.

Barbara: (Sobbing) I'm very emotional now.

Kenny:	There was smoke in here when we got here, from the incense, but I feel this was also symbolic of Lucille, who used to smoke ...
Annella:	We used the incense to clear the vibrations.
Barbara:	She had a lot of sadness—she doesn't like what's going on today with her kids. Are they fighting?
Dee:	He (Desi, Jr.) is supposed to be straightened out, from the drug or alcohol problems ...
Barbara:	(Crying) I'm just so sad!
Kenny:	Anyone get a name or initial around Lucille right now?
Annella:	I feel the Helen you mentioned is with her. I see her between Dee and Doug, in spirit, but I don't know who she is.
Dee:	Oh! It was her hairdresser! She had a hairdresser named Helen!
Annella:	I also get a Grace standing near you, Dee, in spirit.
Kenny:	It could be Grace Moore, the opera diva, who perished in a plane crash. That's another reason symbolically why the smoke was important when we arrived. Lucille did a film with Clifton Webb, and Grace Moore leased her townhouse to Clifton for a time.
Dee:	Is DeDe still here?
Kenny:	Yes, she's showing herself dressed in a light blue suit. She has glasses, slender legs ...
Dee:	She wore suits a lot, had glasses, and slender legs!
Annella:	I see a vision of Lucille when she was older, in a TV show after *I Love Lucy* —about the third TV show she did. Vivian Vance was in it and Lucy's children, I believe ... I feel Lucille was able to

be more like her real self in that show. But she does look sad—at a loss—let down. She doesn't look tragic, but she seems to be saying that life hadn't been what she wanted and she was disappointed—not for lack of success . . . these were emotional disappointments.

Kenny: She was ready to go (pass away) years before—she willed herself to go.

Annella: Did she have a drinking problem?

Kenny: Well . . .

Annella: Yes, that was a shadow in her life—a sadness.

Dee: Oh! I'm warm again now.

Valerie: Yes, very warm over where we are.

Dee: The loves of her life in her later years were her grandchildren. That could be part of the sadness around her. She may be sad not to be around them physically any more.

Kenny: She shouldn't have rejected the child by Patty Duke (Sean Astin), whether it was Desi, Jr.'s son or not, whether it was her grandchild or not—she should have accepted the boy—I feel she knows that now.

Barbara: Yes.

Dee: She always regretted it, I know.

Barbara: She had mixed emotions about the drinking. It was an escape. She was deep and emotional, I feel. Smarter than people gave her credit for, too. Desi got the credit, but they were both geniuses. We all know they're together now, too.

Annella: There's anger that she feels for Desi—love and anger are mixed.

Barbara: Love-hate situation here . . . she's very proud of both children now. Oh! I have a terrible

	headache on the right side now . . . a soreness behind my ear . . . a pressure.
Kenny:	She had a stroke sometime before she passed, I believe.
Annella:	I see a vision of her young and delicate now. This is from her early years. Her beauty may have coarsened in the 1950s, but she was gorgeous when she was in her early twenties.

"I was"

All seven of us heard the delicate female whisper coming through the air, and as we looked around to see who had said it, we realized none of us had done so—it could only have been Lucille Ball materializing in voice to agree with us about her young beauty!

Kenny:	Welcome, Lucille! Welcome!
Dee:	The red hair was done to make people notice her.
Annella:	I feel water—raindrops—I don't know what that means.
Valerie:	I feel people are watching us—all around us and behind us, in spirit.
Annella:	The table is wiggling!
Barbara:	It feels like it's alive!

Indeed, the heavy wooden table actually began to move slightly from side to side—called "table tipping" by spiritualists, where spirit energy is so strong it attaches itself to an object, even a heavy object, to draw attention to its presence. It also often acts as a means of communication, as we found out as the seance proceeded:

Kenny:	The table's going up and down like it may be symbolic of Lucille's career. It's going! It's going! (The table strongly moved up and down off the floor while we struggled to keep our hands on it).

Valerie: I feel like the whole floor underneath me is moving, too—vibrating!

The table rocked back and forth.

Kenny: Give us a jolt, Lucille!

The table suddenly jerked sideways.

Kenny: That's it!

The heat in the room rose considerably. We seven tried raising our hands off the table, and could feel a vibration emanating from the table even with our hands two inches off the surface.

Kenny: If Desi, Jr. has to be careful how he spends his money or how his money is protected, rock the table, Lucille.

The table rocked wildly from side to side.

Kenny: Let us know, Lucille!

It rocked again, side to side as though an unseen force were pushing it.

Kenny: Someone close to you has told me that when the phone rang and you were told "It's your husband" you asked "Which one?"—is that right, Lucille?

The table literally danced back and forth.

Barbara: I feel physical and emotional abuse around her at one time . . . someone angry . . . she says she understands more now.

Kenny: Will you teach comedy on the other side someday?

The table rocked gently, and to keep the energy high, Kenny began singing a hymn, "It Is No Secret," which we joined him in.

Valerie: I felt swirls of cool air while we sang—all around me.

Kenny: Is it difficult to be without alcohol or cigarettes now, Lucille?

There was silence ... no rocking.

Kenny: Okay, we've established that rocking means "yes" and silence must mean "no." The amount of rocking is how strong it's a "yes," so she doesn't miss cigarettes or alcohol. Lucille, you're the only one I've contacted who didn't miss them at one time!

Barbara: She says you leaned across and whispered something to her once, about doing something ...

Kenny: Yes, about holding a seance one time. I asked if she wanted to hold a seance years ago and she said she was afraid.

The table rolled from side to side.

Valerie: You're doing well now at a seance, Lucille!

Barbara: She says you were right, Kenny. She should have done it.

Kenny: She was afraid of other things, too—to let Gary know she loved Desi so much.

The table jumped wildly up and down.

David: Did she have a problem with her right hand? Was it weakened or was there something in it, or an injury to it? I feel something with my right hand.

We didn't receive an answer to this.

Kenny: Do you go back to the house on Roxbury? (Her last home, in Beverly Hills).

The table made no move.

Kenny: You don't go back there?

Suddenly the table rocked very hard.

Kenny:	Gary Morton (her husband at the time of her passing) got the house ...
Doug:	Maybe it was all he deserved!

The table wildly jerked up and down.

Dee:	Is Cleo well?—please rock.

There was silence.

Dee:	I was afraid of that.

For a moment, perhaps to catch our breath and absorb the psychic phenomena that was happening, we were silent. No one spoke; we only sat, feeling the pulsations coming from the table.

Dee:	She'll get impatient if we don't ask her something ...
Kenny:	Do you want an unknown to play you on the big screen one day?

The table rocked from side to side.

Valerie:	My chair is vibrating!
Barbara:	Mine, too!
Kenny:	Yes!
Dee:	I just set my hands on her photo, maybe that's why we got the extra jolt of energy.

The table rocked in agreement.

Kenny:	Is your teacher with you? The one from Jamestown, New York, whom I brought back to you in spirit long ago?

We hung on as the table rocked strongly sideways.

Annella:	I see her at ... she says she was 14 years old ... skinny ... wiry, but attractive.
Kenny:	Yes, very—I see her, too.

Annella: Her whole life seems to have held disappoint-
                ments, even the good things gave her letdowns.
                There's an overpowering sadness. She's not feel-
                ing sorry for herself, but . . .

Barbara: When she had the stroke sometime before, was
                she hospitalized?

Dee: Yes.

Barbara: I feel she made the transition then, but came
                back to see how people loved her, to be shown
                that people really did love her.

Kenny: I don't like to say 'hate,' but I feel she hated
                Cedars Sinai Hospital and didn't want to 'die'
                there . . . her word . . . she wanted to 'die' at
                home.

A loud rap fell against a corner wall.

Dee: Are you worried about Lucie?

Silence, for 'no.'

Dee: Is Desi, Jr. okay?

The table wobbled slightly.

Dee: Is Desi's marriage okay?

The table shook and wobbled—a 'so-so' response.

Kenny: And Lucie's marriage?

Again, wobbly—'so-so'.

Kenny: Oh, I had a lovely picture of Lucie I should have
                brought with me tonight . . . taken a few years
                ago. I could have shown it to Lucille tonight. I'd
                told her about seeing Lucie at the Playboy
                Mansion—it was taken there.

The table wildly jumped to life.

Valerie: Sorry—sorry we didn't bring it.

Annella:	I feel she's incredibly happy to be acknowledged here.
Dee:	I think of her a lot.
Valerie:	I hope she's glad we're doing her for the book.

The table vibrated, shook, and rocked strongly.

Annella:	I get a name ... Cindy Lou ...
Kenny:	I get an Ella or Ellie Mae ...
Annella:	I think they're characters in a play.
Kenny:	No, Ellie Mae is tied into her ... she's not a character ... she's a person.
Kenny:	Who greeted you on the other side, Lucille?
Valerie:	Was it Desi?

No response.

Valerie:	Your mom?

No response.

Dee:	Vivian Vance?

There was slight movement.

Dee:	Bill Frawley?

Stronger rocking.

Kenny:	But a female was more important, in greeting you ...

Even stronger rocking.

Kenny:	A blonde ...

Again, rocking.

Kenny:	Oh, I know! Mae! Mae West! She's a greeter now!

The table rolled and jumped.

Valerie:	Well, she's surely doing her job!

Dee: Do you still play backgammon now on the other
                side?

*Surprisingly, because she was such an avid player on Earthplane, there
was no response.*

Valerie: How's Lucie's career—good?

A weak movement was felt.

Valerie: How about producing or writing for her—
                would that be good?

Again, weak movement.

Doug: I can't get over this vibrating I feel under my
                hands!

Kenny: I was vibrating this morning . . . felt my whole
                body vibrating and couldn't figure out why.

Valerie: She was probably anxious to get started!

The entire table bounced, as we did our best to "hang on."

Barbara: I feel that sadness again, now.

Kenny: I think she's sorry to quit tonight, sad to end
                this, but she's getting tired. We mustn't tire her.
                Thank you, Lucille.

All: Thank you, Lucille.

We sat quietly, very pleased and somewhat amazed by what had
taken place. Table tippings are rare, and though I've been part of such
sessions before, it was new to many in our group. Only the right combination of participants and spirit energy can produce such a
phenomenon, and we were indeed fortunate.

As David moved toward the door to turn on the lights, I blew out the
candle and we all placed our hands over the candle, getting the smoke
in the palms of our hands, marking our final connection with the
dynamic comedienne who had come through so strongly this evening.

As a footnote: Dee called me the next morning to clarify and embel-
lish upon two facts: "Kenny," she said, "last night when you said there

was someone named Ellie Mae or something close to that who was in spirit, I couldn't think. But now I remember: her maid's name was Willie Mae—that's about as close as you could get to that name! And, I remembered also that George Raft had given Lucille help when she first started in show business—he helped her financially, by lending her money for rent and so forth. I just wanted to share these things with you, Kenny, because they just further convinced me that Lucille was strongly in touch with us last night," Dee said happily.

MUSIC

★ ★ ★ ★ ★

ELVIS PRESLEY

THEN

Country singer Dottie West and I were dining together one evening in Edmonton, Alberta, Canada, after a taping of *The Tommy Banks Show*, a popular Canadian television program.

Dottie told me her friend Elvis Presley had been following my career and wanted very badly to have a private psychic reading from me.

"Well, I'm listed in the phone book, or you can feel free to give him my number," I said. "It won't be hard for him to find me."

"Kenny, why don't you call Elvis?" Dottie suggested.

I explained to her that I would be happy to call him, but that it would not be beneficial. My spirit guides have always advised me that someone *must* come to *me* for help—for me to actively "solicit" by means of calling someone or striking up a conversation and saying, "I have messages for you—you should have a psychic reading from me" would defeat the purpose.

"If Elvis wants a reading, of course I'm available," I assured her. "But he needs to take the first step toward helping himself by picking up that telephone. Once I know Elvis is truly eager to help himself, I'll be more than happy to work with him."

Dottie said, "I'll tell Elvis, Kenny. I hope he'll call you."

I asked Dottie to try to impress upon him how important reaching out could be. "If you have a stomachache, or a toothache, you don't wait for the doctor or dentist to call you and suggest treatment, do you?" I asked. "You call the doctor's office and set up an appointment. Then, once you go, they do everything they can to help you. Of course, miracles don't always occur in one visit and you may need to follow up with another visit—but the important thing is to get started. It's the same way with a psychic—reach out and you're on your way toward being helped."

Dottie listened carefully as we finished our meal, and said she'd do her best to convince Elvis.

This took place in 1975, about two years before the singing legend passed. Unfortunately, he never made the call.

During 1975 and 1976, Elvis performed several times in Las Vegas. I made a number of attempts to see him in concert, but each time had to cancel my reservations due to a change in my plans. Finally, for what was to be his last Las Vegas appearance, at the Hilton Hotel in late 1976, I made reservations and was able to keep them.

As I arrived outside the Hilton, I glanced at Elvis's name in huge letters on the marquee. Yet despite all the bright lights surrounding it, I psychically saw a dark cloud over his name. I asked my spirits what this meant, but there was only silence, so I proceeded to the main showroom. I was running a bit behind schedule and feared I would miss part of the performance unless I hurried.

Just as I greeted the maitre d' and he began showing me to my table, "the King" walked out on stage. Again, I saw the dark cloud. "I can't go down any closer to the stage" I whispered. "What's wrong, Dr. Kingston?" the maitre d' asked. "I feel such a heaviness," I said, "it's too much—I need to go back toward the exit."

"Oh, please, Dr. Kingston, can't you help him?" the gentleman pleaded. "I'll try," I said, "but I must get some distance from him." I was beginning to feel faint, and knew a thin sheen of perspiration was covering my forehead. As we approached the exit at the rear of the showroom I said, "Let me stand here—I'll do some prayerwork for him—Heaven knows the man needs it." The concerned maitre d' left me, and I glanced again at Elvis.

I saw a black aura encompassing his body. The aura is a magnetic field which surrounds the body. It reflects our physical, mental, and emotional states, with light colors representing positive traits and dark colors reflecting negative. Needless to say, black was the worst color which could surround Elvis. I wanted to get closer to him, to do prayers for him, but as I tried once more, I was overcome with a tremendous heaviness. My pulse became rapid and my stomach felt bloated. My heart felt so heavy I thought I would break into tears any moment.

I knew that this, plus the faintness and my perspiration, was something I was picking up from Elvis—my condition was psychically mimicking what he felt while gamely singing for the standing-room-only audience. I feared disaster in the future for this man, and tried desperately to visualize him well and strong again, for often psychics can visualize conditions so strongly that they can affect things and people around them.

Ultimately, I felt compelled to leave the showroom, and began walking through the casino toward my car. I trusted that Elvis had an entourage who would hopefully attend to his physical needs and knew that his spiritual condition was very personal. Again, *he* and *he* alone could decide when he needed and wanted help.

I continued to hold good thoughts for the legendary singer for the next few months, and in July of 1977 another country singer friend, Loretta Lynn, was in Hollywood to tape an appearance on *The Tonight Show* with Johnny Carson. She called me and we chatted for some time. I told Loretta that I felt Elvis really needed help, hoping perhaps she could reach him in a way Dottie had been unable to.

"I *know* he needs help, Kenny," she agreed. "I'll try my best to get through to him," she promised. "But, Loretta," I warned, "time is running out."

Again, it seems fate would have it that Elvis could not be reached, physically or spiritually. Finally, on August 4, 1977, I held my annual seance in memory of my client Marilyn Monroe's passing. During the seance, Marilyn's spirit sadly told me Elvis would be the next major celebrity to reach Paradise (or the spirit world), within two weeks. Marilyn said she feared Elvis was "giving up" in a sense, and might not fight to live.

I called a writer friend of mine, James Bacon, who had often used stories I gave him for his nationally syndicated column, which appeared in 450 newspapers at the time. "I realize you won't print this, Jim," I told him, "but I have to tell someone." I explained the feelings I'd had about Elvis, including the information just recently received at the seance. He withheld all the information I gave him—naturally, because it was too sensitive to print at the time. Unfortunately, less than two weeks later, Elvis Presley passed.

In the intervening years, James Bacon has appeared on many talk shows and has agreed that I indeed gave him the information ahead of time. However, he explained that at the time I gave it to him, he'd felt his hands were tied.

Why didn't I call Elvis after the seance? It had become obvious by then that he was choosing to refuse help. Again, I couldn't directly solicit, since he didn't request my help. At that point, what would I have said to him? I couldn't say, "You're going to pass away in two weeks," because the Master is always subject to change and people can rally and surprise everyone.

I just meditated and did prayerwork that those close to him would convince him to get help—physically as well as spiritually. I feared it was too much to ask though, as a relative stranger to him, I couldn't do much to help him at this point.

> ELVIS PRESLEY'S BODY WAS FOUND ON THE BATH-ROOM FLOOR AT HIS BELOVED GRACELAND MANSION BY HIS FIANCE, GINGER ALDEN, IN THE AFTERNOON HOURS OF AUGUST 16, 1977. CAUSE OF HIS PASSING WAS LISTED AS AN "ACCIDENTAL OVER-DOSE"—HEART CONDITION WAS ALSO SUSPECTED.

NOW

A world-famous female singer who was a friend of Elvis Presley's called me to ask if I could possibly contact Elvis for her.

I said, "I will certainly try. I'll hold a seance for him at my home, which I invite you to attend." She eagerly agreed, and asked to bring her male secretary-confidante (they are very close and feel they were husband and wife in a previous lifetime). We agreed upon a time for the seance—the following Saturday evening at 8:30.

During the day on Saturday, I meditated with a red-colored candle, which I feel encourages spirits to come in. I asked Elvis to join us at the seance that evening, saying it would be a good opportunity for him to express whatever he wanted. I believe in talking to a spirit prior to a seance—it's the same as issuing an invitation for them to attend.

As 8:30 approached, my co-author Valerie arrived. Shortly thereafter, the doorbell rang and the glamorous singer swept into the room, draped in a full-length sable coat, which she removed and handed to her secretary, who followed behind her. "Don't you look beautiful!" I commented, noticing the black silk pants, turquoise beaded sweater, and matching turquoise turban she wore. "Oh, I'm glad! I wanted to look good for Elvis!" she whispered in my ear.

I assured her Elvis would indeed find her as lovely as ever, and we moved into the den of my home, with Valerie and me sitting on one peach-colored velvet sofa and the singer and her secretary facing us on another, identical sofa.

I lit a large red candle which I'd placed on the desk to the right of me; a glass of water which would be used later sat next to the candle.

As I turned off the lamps, the candle, plus the faint glow of moonlight from the patio, became our only sources of light. As a group, we asked Elvis to join us and make his presence known.

We sat in silence for a moment, to allow ourselves a chance to get accustomed to the dimly-lit atmosphere. My co-author's notes now relay the events which transpired on that Saturday evening, for reasons which will soon become apparent. The results will be told in the third person to avoid confusion—much of what is said was transcripted from mental notes which she made that evening, though in addition she scribbled notes on a pad she held in her lap as she sat on the sofa:

Kenny felt compelled to suggest we sing "He Touched Me," a hymn he often sings at seances. Ironically, he has sensed that it was also one of Elvis Presley's favorite hymns (which Elvis's singer friend told me that evening following the seance). After our hymn concluded, Kenny asked the others to repeat after him three times, "Elvis, we ask you to join us this evening."

The candle flame began to flicker slightly. A cool breeze whirled around the room. We were all struck by the sudden change in temperature in the den. Then the breeze abruptly left us and apparently moved to the patio doorway, for the curtains moved slightly, although the door was tightly closed and no source of outside air could have entered.

Kenny saw a blue mist forming near the doorway as the curtains continued to blow gently back and forth. Valerie and the singer also saw this, yet could merely point to the door and say, "Look!"

As the mist became heavier, the curtains ceased moving, and a man began taking shape. He seemed to grow and become more clear every second and we all gasped at the sight. The blue mist had nearly disappeared now and the figure of the man appeared clearly, seen by all of us as nearly iridescent in color.

Kenny saw him clothed in a coral garment, much like a toga, with gold trim. As the image grew stronger, there was no mistaking his identity. "It's Elvis!" the singer cried. "Welcome Elvis!" we said in unison, "Welcome!"

Indeed it *was* Elvis Presley, but he was much different from the Elvis of his later years on Earth. He now had long hair and appeared almost Christ-like. Gone was the bloated, aging super-star. This Elvis was slender, yet muscular—that much was evident even with the toga he was wearing. In the image standing before us there was more of the Elvis his fans recalled most fondly.

"Welcome, Elvis, please speak," Kenny encouraged him.

The figure moved rapidly away from the doorway and toward the sofa where Kenny sat. Kenny became silent and sat quite still at this moment.

"Oh, it's freezing cold here!" Valerie said. "It's like ice!"

The figure hovered nearby as Kenny's breathing became labored. He shifted position on the sofa slightly, slumping over momentarily. The glowing figure seemed to merge with Kenny's slumped body. Kenny suddenly sat upright, his breathing back to normal once more, yet he still remained silent.

"Look, his hair seems darker! He looks more muscular and his body looks larger!" the male secretary said, and the singer and Valerie agreed.

We marveled at the changes which had taken place—in fact, Kenny no longer resembled himself in body shape and his facial features seemed to be changing, almost like melting wax being molded before our eyes. Clearly the spirit of Elvis had taken over Kenny's body.

Suddenly, Elvis, through Kenny, laughed and the singer screamed in surprise, "Elvis! Is that really you, Darling?"

In a voice totally unlike Kenny Kingston's, and with a slight Southern accent, we heard:

"It is! It is!" Then he chuckled. "So those people who think I never passed away—that I'm walkin' around Missouri or California or *anywhere*—have surely been talkin' crazy, now, haven't they? It makes me angry that some people are tryin' to make my fans believe those things."

"How are you, Elvis?" the singer asked. "Are you happy?"

His face softened then and he smiled, "Yes, Honey, I have finally found peace and happiness. And you haven't done too bad yourself. Congratulations on your new concert success!"

"Thank you! I'm so pleased you're happy, Elvis," the singer told him. "Are you with your loved ones now?" she asked.

A look of serenity came over his face and he answered, "Yes, I'm with my Momma Gladys and Daddy Vernon. Oh, Vernon and I fought about the way I spent money when we were back at Graceland, but that's been taken care of here—we don't *need* any money!"

"Was your death easy?" the male secretary asked.

Elvis walked toward the patio again, then faltered for a moment, staggering backward. Valerie ran toward him in an effort to help him gain strength and remain upright. She touched him for a moment (and is indeed the only person allowed to touch him during the seance, since she is more familiar with Kenny Kingston. The touch of a stranger while someone is in trance could be too much of a shock and could be dangerous). He stood still, then was able to resume movement again.

When he had reached the sliding glass door, he paused and answered, "There is no death. We just take on another form of existence. But yes, it was bad when I first arrived here. I took so many drugs I couldn't wake up for the longest time." He grinned and said, "When I *did* wake up I thought, 'that was the best sleep I've ever had,' but then I looked around and felt confused. Where was I? When I finally came to, I knew I wasn't in my bathroom at Graceland, the last place I remembered being. This was a strange place which I did not recognize."

The voice rose in volume as he said, "I called for help and my Momma Gladys came before me. I had seen her at Graceland for several months before—her spirit even spoke to me. It never scared me because I loved her dearly. But this time I thought, 'I'm not at Graceland anymore. Where am I and why is she here with me?' She reached out and embraced me just then and it felt warm and wonderful—like I was really home again. Then I thought, 'I never *felt* her when she visited Graceland. If she's dead and I'm with her—could *I* be gone, too?'

"Just then Momma smiled and took my hand. I felt such peace and she said to me, 'Honey, the pills you took all hit your heart at once—it was too much for it.' Then she touched my face and said, 'But I missed you and you missed me and that's why you're really here.' "

We stopped Elvis and asked, "What are you saying? Wasn't your passing just an accident—just too many pills?"

He frowned and said, "Well, it surely wasn't murder or suicide, as some people are saying. I wouldn't have done that to my little girl Lisa Marie, or to my fans."

"Then what exactly happened?" Valerie continued.

"I want to make this clear," he answered. "I was lonely. Oh, I had millions of fans, and anything I ever wanted to eat, drive, live in, or wear, but is that a life? I loved Lisa Marie, but I couldn't really talk to her— she was too young. I loved Priscilla, but that didn't work out, and it nearly broke my heart, I don't mind tellin' you. Ginger cared for me, and my buddies who protected me were always there when I needed anything, but who was I close to? No one. I forgot how to be 'me' anymore. It just got outta hand."

"What killed you, Elvis? What happened?" the singer asked.

"I took pills, yes, I did—more than most people ever take. But I'd taken them other times. *They* didn't really kill me, though I guess they kept makin' me weaker. My loneliness brought me down. My Momma watched me in spirit and came for me when I was really low. I tell you—it can happen. If you're really low or really sick, and don't care much whether you live or die, and someone misses you and loves you in spirit—they can bring you over. It happened to someone else here— Senator Robert Kennedy. But maybe he'll explain that to you one day."

"Once you realized you had passed away, how did you feel, Elvis?" the secretary asked.

"I was happy to be at peace with no pain and no loneliness," he answered. "I thought about a time when I got a death threat years ago in Las Vegas, and laughed to myself, wishing I'd known then what it was like to 'die'—I wouldn't have been so shook up by that threat at all!"

"The only thing is, I was sad to be away from my little girl. I never meant for Lisa Marie to grow up without her Daddy."

A most unusual knocking was heard on one of the den walls behind the singer and the secretary. It was almost like a tune set to rhythm. The candle flickered like a blinking light and Elvis's spirit paced back and forth in front of the patio doorway.

"I've been watching over my little Lisa Marie, though," he said proudly. "And now she has little ones of her own. She has to guard them, though. There could be a kidnapping attempt. They shouldn't let pictures be taken or released to the newspapers."

As Elvis spoke, the candle flame turned from white to a dark blue, then grew weaker, and we interpreted this as representing trouble. "Do you feel unhappiness around your daughter, Elvis?" Valerie asked.

"Danger!" he warned. "I have to protect her! I won't let her love life end up the way mine did with her mama. It'd be too hard on her, I know it would."

"How do you feel about Lisa Marie and Priscilla being involved in the Church of Scientology?" Valerie asked.

"I don't condemn or condone," he said. "Everyone has to find their own path. I was very spiritual in my own way, you know. How many people knew about the trunk of Bibles I kept? I loved giving them to special people."

He chuckled and continued, "Of course I was no angel, but many times when I had the young girls up to my room we'd just sit around and read the Bible—even if we sat on the bed in our pajamas. This didn't happen *all* the time, though," he laughed.

The knocking on the wall returned, and in the distance we heard a few notes, metallic sounding at first, then becoming clear and beautiful. They seemed to come from a piano somewhere far away. "That's Gershwin!" the singer shouted. "It's *Rhapsody in Blue*—I'm sure of it!"

Elvis paused for a moment, and we sat in silence as the piano music continued. "What does the music mean?" the singer eventually asked.

Elvis laughed, "That's a young man who was named Dan Olsson. He was here when I got here. Just a nice young fella who always wanted to play piano, but was killed in a car accident. I just took a liking to him when I got here."

"I met Oscar Levant—you remember the great composer-pianist? He's here, too. I asked him if he'd do me a favor and give Dan a few lessons. It worked—they spend a lot of time together. That happens here—people get to do what they've always wanted to do, or continue doing what they loved, if they want to." Elvis chuckled at this, obviously enjoying the musical activity around him. Then, as quickly as it appeared, the sound of the piano music disappeared.

It was silent for a moment, then Valerie asked, "What do you think of the way Graceland is being handled, Elvis?"

"I visit there often," he said. "I love it that my fans pay me respect there. 'Course, an awful lot of people are out to make a dollar there, but it's still a good thing."

He smiled and his image glowed brighter, "I loved my fans—loved singin' for them. In fact, toward the end, I only felt 'alive' when I went onstage—felt like a skeleton otherwise. Those people who thought Colonel Parker pushed me too hard and pushed for money too hard didn't understand him. He only did what I asked him to do. He helped me do what I loved—get up there and sing."

The singer asked, "Do you still sing today, Elvis?"

"Only for my friends here, Honey," he smiled. "I'm more interested in medicine now," he said happily. "I want to come back one day"—to reincarnate- "as a doctor and do lots of healing. But I want to do it with natural healing—herbs and diet and the powers of the mind. Believe me, I want to get people away from overdoing prescription medicines."

"I'm still sorry to hear you're not entertaining anymore," the singer insisted.

"Oh, Honey—you have plenty of good entertainers there now. You just think about them," he said. "I'm sorry I never hired the Oak Ridge Boys as my backup singers years ago—they're so good and we'd have done fine together. Still love to hear them today. I wish Mac Davis would get busy writin' more, too—he's wastin' his talent."

Elvis seemed to be caught up in discussing today's entertainers and continued, "You know who I admire? Patrick Swayze. Of course all of us here were happy when he did *Ghost*—it came closer to showing what it's like here than anything we'd seen so far. Swayze will go on to do a lot of good work, but what I like is he's got real 'country' in him."

"Any advice for him?" Valerie asked.

"Yes, I'd tell him to remember that the women who are throwing themselves at him won't be around forever. He should remember the wife he's got and work on keeping the marriage together. Why throw away all those years?"

"Have you seen anyone interesting on the other side?" Valerie asked.

"Lots of interesting people, Darlin'." He laughed. "But the one person I wanted to meet on Earth I still haven't met—Howard Hughes. I'm tellin' you he's not here. You might look around for him there where you are because he's not in spirit!" (This surprised us—Elvis was telling us Howard Hughes is still alive!)

Elvis's voice faded slightly and we suspected he was about to depart. "Do you have any last words to share?" Valerie questioned him.

"I surely do." He sighed. "Tell everyone to find peace and contentment where they can. I ate and ate to fill a void when I was on Earth—and it still didn't help because I didn't work on what was making me unhappy in the first place. All the money in the world can't buy you peace of mind!"

With this, Elvis stopped talking. His form staggered again near the patio door. He seemed lifeless—bouncing back and forth. Valerie ran to hold him and struggled to return him to the sofa. Elvis was leaving the body and Kenny Kingston was returning.

Kenny began breathing deeply. As Valerie briskly massaged his shoulders, the female singer and her secretary said in unison, "Thank you, Elvis, come again!" Valerie asked the singer to lead everyone in "He's Got the Whole World in His Hands" to bring up the vibrations of Earthplane and alert Kenny more strongly to his surroundings.

As the singing began, Valerie gave Kenny sips of water from the glass on the desk. Kenny choked and sputtered at first, then slowly reached shakily to grasp the glass with one hand. Valerie guided the glass with one hand, also, while continuing to massage his neck and shoulders. As the singing concluded, she whispered in his ear, "Come back, Kenny. Kenny, it's time to return. Are you there? Are you okay?"

Kenny stopped drinking water, dropped his still-shaking hand to his lap, and said faintly, "Yes, I'm back—I'm fine"—and our seance ended.

SAMMY DAVIS, JR.

★ ★ ★ ★ ★

THEN

Sammy Davis, Jr. had long since recovered from the accident which caused him to lose his eye. It was sometime in mid-1960 and his career was in high gear. I met the entertainer for the first time during this period, while staying in Las Vegas for about a week. While in Las Vegas I planned to visit a friend of mine who was working at the Sands Hotel on the set of a new film, *Oceans Eleven*, starring what was being referred to for the first time as the "Rat Pack"—Frank Sinatra, Dean Martin, Joey Bishop, Peter Lawford, and Sammy Davis, Jr.

I had noticed earlier as I drove past the Sands that a bustling activity was taking place behind the hotel. Film lighting being what it is, the area gave the illusion of looking like early morning or just before sunset.

The day I visited the set, Sammy Davis, Jr. was filming a scene which called for him to drive a truck, if I recall properly. I waited and watched with interest, and when the take was completed, my friend introduced me to Sammy. He said, "Hey, the psychic world's always intrigued me— have you got anything to say to me?" I gave him a message or two and we chatted a bit before he was called back to the set. I found him to be a "quirky" little man—full of energy and curiosity.

Later that year when *Oceans Eleven* filming had been completed, I read in the San Francisco paper that Sammy would be opening at the Geary Theater. Though we'd met, and his career was certainly in full swing, I'd never seen him perform live, and made arrangements to see the show one evening. I was impressed and amazed by his boundless enthusiasm onstage and told him so backstage afterwards. "How 'bout telling me something else?" he asked, and I gave him another couple of psychic messages.

Time passed and once again I read that Sammy would be in town to entertain, this time at San Francisco's posh Fairmont Hotel. The engagement coincided with my mom Kaye's birthday, so I arranged a dinner party in the Venetian Room prior to the show.

Shortly before showtime I excused myself from the table and went to the lobby, where I picked up the house phone and asked for Sammy Davis, Jr. I hadn't fully expected him to answer—many performers do not take calls before showtime—but before I knew it, he was on the line. I asked if he remembered me and he said, "Sure I do, Kenny, how are you?" I said, "Fine, Sammy. I wonder if you'd do me a favor." "Sure, man," he answered, "you've done them for me with your messages."

I explained about the dinner party and asked if he'd sing "Happy Birthday" to Kaye during his show. "I'd be delighted to sing it to your mother!" he happily agreed, and he said, "Let's talk in the dressing room later, too."

I returned to the Venetian Room, and moments later Sammy's show began. He'd cleared his throat a couple of times while talking between numbers, and about halfway through the show he said, "You'll have to forgive me tonight, ladies and gentlemen. I have a very bad throat— raspier than usual." When I heard this, I immediately began sending healing thoughts his way.

"But I'd like to do a special request right now," he continued. "There's a young man in the audience who's given me messages from the other world, believe it or not—Kenny Kingston. His mother Kaye is here celebrating a birthday with us, so for you, Kenny, and you, Kaye"—and he sang "Happy Birthday" to my mom.

Our time together backstage was brief, as usual. I always felt a "rush," a sense of needing to hurry around Sammy. It could have been his tremendous energy, but each of the three times we met, it seemed to be "Hiya, man, howya doin,' man? What have ya got for me? Good to talk to you," and then this "whirlwind" of a man passed by and went on to a new face and new conversation. I continued to send him healing for his throat as our party left his dressing room.

It would be nearly thirty years before I would see Sammy again. For some reason our paths had never crossed again till that evening, and this, our last encounter, was indeed memorable and almost eerie.

It was December 1, 1989, and I'd accepted an invitation to attend an exhibit of artwork by actor Jack Palance, at a gallery in Beverly Hills. I asked my friends Dr. Robert Saffian and his wife Marie to join me.

Since December 1st would also have been my mom's birthday (she passed in 1984), prior to going to the Saffian's I attended Mass at St. Cyril's, my neighborhood church, where I'd asked the Mass to be offered in memory of Kaye. Father Michael Burns handled it wonderfully, and during prayers I asked for an omen from my mom that she was safe and happy in Heaven. (I psychically knew she was, but just needed assurance, somehow).

After the service I went to Bob and Marie's hilltop home in Encino, and together we drove into Beverly Hills. Following the exhibit, Bob said, "I've made reservations at La Dolce Vita" (a nearby bistro) and we drove the short distance. As we walked in, the maitre d' said, "They're preparing your table if you'll please wait just a minute."

As we waited I looked across the room to see a man staring at me. It was Richard Pryor, with whom I'd done the *Flip Wilson Show* years before. Recognizing each other, we met halfway and embraced, exchanging "hellos" and "how are you's."

Just then the maitre d' came to show us to our table, and Richard returned to his table. Following him with her eyes, Marie said, "That's Sammy Davis, Jr. at Richard's table, with several other people."

"Sammy Davis, Jr.—that's especially important tonight," I thought, but the reason didn't quite register. I thought perhaps I would walk over later, through the celebrity-studded room, to say "hello" to Sammy, who had been through a bout with throat cancer but was supposedly doing better.

A gentleman joined us at our table, and Dr. Saffian introduced him as Dr. Grossman, the man who had worked wonders on Richard Pryor with skin grafts when Richard was burned so badly some years before. "This man is so excellent with *burns*," Bob Saffian said. I thought, "Burns—I was with *Father* Burns today at my mom's Mass—is that the omen from her?" I generally don't try the spirits—one omen and I'm content that spirit is working with me—but because Kaye's well-being was so important to me, I silently said thank you for the omen but dared ask for one more sign.

Soon, I heard a voice at a nearby table, and looked up to see Sammy Davis, Jr. leading his group in "Happy Birthday"—and my mind immediately leapt back to the Fairmont Hotel. I looked at my watch—10:30 P.M.—almost exactly the time he'd sung to Kaye those many years ago. This time the "Happy Birthday" turned out to be for Richard Pryor, but the memories flooded over me. Thirty years ago—"Please excuse me, ladies and gentlemen, I have a very bad throat"—and tonight he was dealing with *throat cancer*!

"Thank you, Kaye," I said silently, and then I rose and walked to Sammy's table. There was much talking and congratulating going on regarding Richard's birthday, but I introduced myself to Altovise, Sammy's wife, who had seen me and smiled, as the conversation went on around us. "Oh yes, you're the spirit man!" she said. "I know about you!"

I told her not to disturb Sammy, who looked very frail this close up. He was deep in conversation and had not seen me walk over. Not wanting to disrupt the private party, I said, "Just tell him hello and remind him that he sang to my mom many years ago tonight. Thank him for helping me get an omen that she's happy in Heaven," I concluded, and explained what I remembered about the Fairmont Hotel. "Oh, how sweet, sure I'll remind him, Kenny," Altovise said. "Can you stay a bit?" she asked, but I told her that my party was leaving soon.

Walking away, I thought, "Okay, that was it—that was the last sign I needed to know that Kaye is doing well. Then, excited about the results so far, I wondered, "Or *is* it the last?" Did I dare ask for more? I decided, "No, I won't ask for more confirmation—I'm satisfied."

As the Saffians and I walked out of the restaurant to retrieve the car from valet parking, I said, "You know, Bob, my current personal physician is retiring and I'll need a new doctor. Can you suggest one?" (Bob is a specialist).

"I know who he'd suggest," Marie responded quickly. "He'd like . . . " and she mentioned a doctor. "He's good," Bob said, "you would like him."

"Okay, that's fine," I said. "Is he close by? Where is his office located?"

"Clark Street," came Bob's reply, and then I knew I'd been given a special gift on my mom's birthday—an unexpected and this time unsolicited omen. For my mom's maiden name, you see, was Clark.

I was not to see Sammy Davis, Jr. again, but I carry the memory of this last, special night we shared in Beverly Hills. The Sammy I last saw was not the fireball of health and energy I'd first met, but he commanded attention till the end, and he'd once again brought the room to a hush, even thirty years to the date and exact time later, with a simple "Happy Birthday."

> SAMMY DAVIS, JR. LOST A LONG BATTLE WITH THROAT CANCER ON MAY 16, 1990, WHEN HE PASSED AWAY IN BEVERLY HILLS, CALIFORNIA.

NOW

Las Vegas, Nevada—the "bright lights" of the gambling and entertainment capital—and for a few days it was home to Valerie and me while we worked on two *planned* projects and one delightfully unexpected one.

The elegant Stars' Desert Inn Hotel played host to us so that I might hold a press conference regarding billionaire Howard Hughes (former owner of the Inn) for my magazine column, and Valerie was on assignment to write a travel article about the 200-acre resort.

We strolled the lush grounds one day prior to dressing for dinner. As we walked, our conversation turned to show business, and we recalled a conversation we'd had with entertainer Buddy Hackett earlier in the day (we'd passed one another on one of the hotel's pathways). Hackett was in residence at the hotel and performing in the showroom on a semi-regular basis.

"But I'm looking forward to Engelbert Humperdinck's show this evening," Valerie said, for Humperdinck was the current headliner in the Crystal Room (the main showroom).

I said, "It's restful here, yet there is definitely an undercurrent of excitement, as you think of the great names in entertainment who've worked and stayed here over the years."

"Yes," Valerie agreed. "The hotel's publicity director told me the names of some of those who've entertained here—Frank Sinatra, Sammy Davis, Jr . . . ." and we looked at one another.

The idea struck both of us at once—"This would be a great place to attempt to contact Sammy Davis, Jr., wouldn't it?" Valerie asked. "And I was told he stayed in the Wimbledon Building, where we are!" (There are four main buildings on the premises, each given a different name and boasting a variety of guest rooms and suites).

I said, "Tonight's the perfect time—after Engelbert Humperdinck's show." We'll be 'keyed up' from the show and we'll just come back to the suite and try to contact Sammy. After all, I'm sure many a night he came back to the building 'keyed up' and energized after performing. He should feel right at home!"

And so, later that evening, Valerie and I paid a quick backstage visit to Humperdinck. I complimented him on a stirring rendition of a duet he had done with one of his female backup singers. It was called "We Fell in Love," and he had explained to the audience that it was planned as part of a new musical based on the lives of the Duke and Duchess of Windsor. We chatted briefly in the dressing room as I told him that the Duke and Duchess were clients of mine, then Valerie and I left for our suite.

"I feel he's anxious for this to begin," I said as we entered the suite. "Sammy Davis, Jr. is definitely going to come in tonight. I feel a warmth all around me—he's almost tapping me on the shoulder and saying, 'Hurry—I'm waiting!' "

Valerie lit a candle we'd brought with us for general meditation purposes and then placed it on a coffee table in the suite's living room area. The nearby sliding glass door was left open to let the warm (but still) night air filter in.

We sat on the sofa, the candle glowing before us. The only other source of light was the moon's glow beaming in through the glass door. For reasons which will become obvious, Valerie's notes take over now:

"I feel excited," Valerie said. "It's so quiet and peaceful outside, but it's 'alive' with excitement in here."

Though at the moment there was no outside breeze at all, the candle flickered frantically back and forth, casting fast-moving shadows on the ceiling.

"There's no wind out to cause that type of movement!" Valerie said, and then realized she alone had been talking for the past couple of minutes.

"Kenny—are you there? Kenny?" she asked tentatively, but a quick look proved that though Kenny was still in a sitting position, he had slumped down some on the sofa, his head resting against the cushions. He was apparently already in a semi or full trance state—out of reach for the time being.

"Are you there, Kenny, or is this Sammy Davis, Jr., here with us now?" Valerie asked quietly.

A deep, rhythmic breathing could be heard from the body on the sofa, now apparently half inhabited by Kenny Kingston and half by Sammy Davis, Jr.

"We're asking Sammy Davis, Jr. to come in," Valerie began. "You're welcome to come in through Kenny; please come in if you're able."

Softly, from somewhere in the distance, Valerie heard the melody of the spiritual hymn "The Sweet By and By" being played. It seemed to come almost through an "echo chamber," and she realized it was being played by spirits. In the next instance, a choir began singing softly, beginning with the first verse of the hymn.

Caught up in the beauty of the words and music, and realizing that singing often helps raise the vibrations and encourages spirit energy to grow, Valerie joined them in singing. It was an unusual phenomenon—this choir which was unseen but definitely heard—and the sound it produced was soon filling Valerie's eardrums and charging the room with strength.

By the hymn's conclusion Valerie truly knew the choir had come with Sammy Davis, Jr. in spirit to give him additional spirit energy. Whatever the full explanation, the effect was that a gurgling sound could be heard, coming from the body on the sofa (Kenny and Sammy combined). Clearly progress had been made and the spirit seemed to be making efforts to speak.

The gurgling continued, then was replaced by a soft voice which said, "It was wonderful tonight . . . in the showroom . . . he really brought in the people . . . packed them in."

Just as the voice spoke, a glowing light blue mist formed around Kenny's body and off to his left side. The mist was no doubt ectoplasm—spirit energy—perhaps part of the choir which had just sung.

It obviously was caused by several spirits forming to give strength to Sammy Davis, Jr., for it seemed to envelope Kenny and even extend beyond him.

"That mist—it looks like more than one of you is here! Welcome, whoever you are, if you're good spirits you're welcome!" Valerie reassured them. "I do hope one of you gathered is the spirit of Sammy Davis, Jr.—was that you just talking to us?" she asked hopefully.

Again, the soft voice, barely a whisper, replied, "Yes . . . played that stage many times. Got that old feeling again there tonight . . . But I don't know, I'm glad I was a performer—to have had the chance to entertain the man in the street, the celebrity, royalty, the politician, but I think now I'd have been happy being a minister or man of the cloth, too."

"Really?" Valerie interrupted. "But you touched so many people's lives as an entertainer!"

The raspy whisper continued, "I was glad to reach out and touch those people with my singing, my dancing. I felt music offered a 'cure' for some folks and the 'cure' was love. I received love in return . . . what I sent out I got back. Still, would I have been better to have given myself to the cloth, maybe with a healing ministry?"

This was indeed a new side to Sammy Davis, Jr., and memories of a wild-living, fun-loving man came to mind. "Could you have lived without the wild life you led—the women you had?" Valerie asked.

"You don't miss something after a while if you don't have it anymore" came the reply. "I'm okay now without sex. I could have been loyal—to a religion or a woman. People only go from person to person because they're lonely. But you just get to know one person then change to another . . . it's hard, you know."

The blue mist glowed brightly, then seemed to pull away from Kenny's body and move toward the wooden door at the suite's entrance.

"Are the spirits leaving?" Valerie wondered, but just as quickly she heard, in a stronger voice, "Love—it was so important . . . still is important," and she knew Sammy Davis, Jr. still remained. Apparently the blue mist had been a spirit "escort" of some sort, sent to make sure he safely arrived and had enough support to begin the communication.

"So many nights in London or New York I felt warmth, even when it was bitter cold out," he continued. "The warmth and love came from the stage ... the place I felt most content. I was willing to perform for anyone; if five or six people gathered in my dressing room, I was 'on'. But I loved it then; I hope in some small way I helped people."

"You did," Valerie encouraged, "and I'm so glad you're able to be with us tonight. Would you be able to tell us how you feel now, and also what it felt like when you reached Paradise?"

Kenny/Sammy swallowed two or three times, then said, "There's still some pain in my throat. Some pain to remind me of my life as Sammy Davis, Jr.. But I get great comfort now from holding the Bible to my throat—actually I visualize that Bible and it goes to my throat automatically, because what you think of here happens, so you have to be careful. I learned that *real* fast!

"Coming here was unreal," the voice continued. "When I had my accident years ago ... "

"When you lost your eye in the car accident?" Valerie verified.

"Yes, then; I felt myself floating. It was an unreal quality—I saw the accident below me and knew I was being taken to 'Paradise' then. I felt I was going and felt peaceful, then for some reason I returned to Earth and the life I still had to lead. I didn't ever tell a lot of people about that experience. But this time, when that unreal quality hit again—the floating—I thought, 'I've done this before; it's okay!' It was simple—not painful. I just felt like I was floating along and I didn't seem to be able to talk, but my mind was racing, man! I thought, 'I'm so thrilled to have known the people I knew.'

"I felt badly it didn't work with May" —actress May Britt, to whom he was married for several years— "and I knew that this was a strange thing to be thinking about, but I did it anyway. I thought about our children and wished the marriage had worked for them, mostly.

"Then I thought about Altovise"—his wife at the time of his passing—"and was so happy for that marriage. I knew all the years we were together that I'd needed her, but I realized we'd helped each other."

When there was silence, Valerie asked, "So while you were in this floating state, this limbo state, you're saying you had time to review your life and what you learned from it?"

"It didn't all happen at once," he continued. "I would float and think, then do what seemed like sleeping, where I felt or saw nothing. Then I would feel refreshed and would float and think again. I found myself, finally, in a very peaceful place, though I couldn't identify it exactly. Just a room—a quiet room—where I rested for a while."

Despite the warmth of the desert evening, a cool, almost cold, breeze entered the room and swirled around Valerie's feet. At the same time the blue mist returned, by the entrance to the suite.

"Oh no, I hope the spirit escorts haven't come to take him back so soon!" Valerie said out loud, and the light stopped abruptly, hovering in the corner. The breeze circled once more, leaving an icy cold in its wake then it moved in the direction of the mist, as though the two forces were watching from a safe distance.

"He's fine, everything's fine," Valerie said to the light. "Will you be able to continue?" she asked of Sammy Davis, Jr. "Can you tell us what you've learned now?"

There was a slight cough and then the voice continued, still soft but as strong as before.

"I was too much of a gambler," he said, "in every manner, shape and form. Should have taken better care of myself. I lived too fast, dissipated too much. Some of my friends probably never thought they'd hear me say it, but I've learned now. If I'd taken better care of myself, the body, the shell I was given by God, I may have still been 'alive.' I still had so much to do . . . I abused it . . . but I was abused, too, in return. Everyone wanted money, favors. Money came easily because I loved to work—had a love affair with my audience. But I couldn't do it all—I know that now.

"I've talked to Barbara Hutton here. I used to go to the Beverly Wilshire Hotel to visit people and I know she lived there. She's told me now that she paid people to stay with her in the latter part of her life. She bought people's attention. I did that, too, I think. Thought they'd like me more—respect me more—if I bought them 'things'. Fortunately here Barbara has found the peace and contentment she deserved and she shares that with her son Lance" —Reventlow, her son by her marriage to Count Court Reventlow.

"I'm sorry," Valerie said. "I hope you're not unhappy now."

"Not at all," the voice continued. "I just had to learn the lesson."

"Do you see other people now—are you with people?" Valerie wondered.

"I've seen Natalie Wood," he answered. "Because of the way she passed, she's not ready to talk just yet, but she will be . . . another time, another place. She sends love to her children and to R.J." —actor and her former husband Robert Wagner. "She doesn't think he was so wise to marry Jill St. John. It's not that he needed to 'do better,' just that Natalie says he needed a different type of person. But I'm not getting involved in that!

" 'The Man'—Martin Luther King, Jr. I've seen him. We've talked. He was a white man once, he said, who misused his slaves. When he finished that life and came to Paradise, he rested. Then when he was ready to reincarnate, he saw the life of Martin Luther King, Jr. on the 'screen' here—heard the speech 'I Have a Dream'—he said it echoed in his head, and when the question arose 'who would like this life—it will be a short life, but will help many people,' he said, 'I want the life!' And he came back in my lifetime—my last lifetime—to help his people—our people—all people."

"That's a beautiful story," Valerie said. "He answered his karma, didn't he?"

Then, changing the topic she asked, "Tell me, do you entertain at all now, or is your throat still too sore?"

"Not the throat, really," came the reply. "It doesn't hold me back. I just like to watch, not sing anymore. I'll tell you, when Barbara Sinatra gives charity affairs, though, I wonder how many people think they see me or feel me on stage? Because I'm there. I'm also with Liza Minnelli . . . I'm there, baby. Can people feel my essence? I'm there with them and once or twice I've even started tapping away in the background!

"I watch people here—they still get up and do what they love— Nelson Eddie, Caruso, Bill 'Bojangles' Robinson, Josephine Baker's here, Pearlie Mae (Pearl Bailey), Billie Holliday, Ethel Waters, Eddie Cantor— Man, what a bill! But I really and truly have no desire to join them. My heart's not in it.

"People are gonna think this is unbelievable, but I study religion— the Scriptures—the ways of rabbi's, ministers, priests. My heart belongs to that world now. I plan to come back as a religious leader one day. When I converted to Judaism, I had a love for it. It's an even greater love I feel now.

"I tell you, by the year 2008 there'll be a trend toward unity—of people and religions."

As these words were uttered the blue mist grew closer again, as though coming to usher Sammy Davis, Jr. away.

"Unity," the voice said, growing softer. "We're working for it here. There may only be one or two religions by 2008—people will be united . . . all faiths together . . . we're working toward it."

And then, in a hoarse whisper, as the mist totally engulfed Kenny/Sammy's body, "Help one another . . . love one another . . . peace . . . " and with this the mist grew brighter, swirled, and moved toward the door once again, leaving a trail of cold air in its place.

Kenny took one abrupt, deep breath, then sighed, stirring slightly on the sofa.

"Are you okay?" Valerie asked, rubbing his neck gently. "Kenny—are you back?"

"Water," Kenny mumbled, and as Valerie rushed off to get him a glass of water, our evening came to a conclusion.

CINEMA

JOAN CRAWFORD

★ ★ ★ ★ ★

THEN

I first met Joan Crawford through one of Hollywood's two "Queens of Gossip," columnist Hedda Hopper (the other "Queen" being Louella Parsons, of course). It was around 1950, I believe. I was still living full-time in San Francisco but had come down to Southern California for a visit and included a film premiere in my activities. It was there that Hedda introduced me to Miss Crawford. Our time together was brief—just a few words, actually, with her eyes brightening when she learned I was a psychic. I found her to be a very powerful, dynamic woman.

Sometime later, after I'd returned home to San Francisco, I heard that Miss Crawford was coming to the area to do some location filming for her next picture, *Sudden Fear.* The film company had rented a home on Pacific Heights—my neighborhood—and I felt it would be good to find out where she'd be staying in the city and call to wish her luck when she arrived. (Though she'd triumphed several years before with her Oscar-winning role in *Mildred Pierce,* her career was once again undergoing a slight slump and I knew this picture would be very important to her. Its success or failure could determine her future).

Psychically I was able to locate the hotel with one phone call and the reservations desk confirmed Miss Crawford would indeed arrive soon and stay two to three weeks during the filming.

Shortly after her arrival I called, telling the switchboard operator I'd met Miss Crawford through Hedda Hopper and was put through immediately. (Bear in mind that both Hedda and her rival Louella were among the biggest powers in Hollywood at the time, and any friend of Hedda's, as I was, would be a wise choice as at least an acquaintance). Miss Crawford thanked me for the moral support of my call and invited me to the set one day.

I followed through on the invitation and arrived on the set a day or two later. They were doing mostly exterior shots that day, as I recall, and I noticed Miss Crawford was very keenly aware of the combination of film lighting with the natural outdoor light. "This one needs to be stronger," she'd boom as she looked at one of the metal poles holding a light. "And that one over there—way too harsh."

Between takes we chatted briefly, and it was clear to me that her primary interest in inviting me to the set was to find out more about my psychic activities. "So you really give readings?" she asked. "And I hear you're good," she persisted, fixing me with a commanding look. I told her my clients said I was very good and she surprised me by saying, "If you don't live too far away, I would like to come over for a reading one day." I gave her my phone number and told her to call to arrange something, then as she was called back to film another scene I left.

Sure enough, two days later she called and we arranged an appointment time. When she arrived, my mom, Kaye and I were standing in our spacious living room. My mom was the first to notice what appeared to be a large, fairly fresh cut over her lip, more visible as she walked toward us. Following my introduction of Kaye to Miss Crawford, Kaye said sympathetically, "I hope that doesn't hurt too much."

"I'll be fine," Crawford said briskly. "It's a dog bite—it stings."

"Oh, how terrible . . . " Kaye began, but Crawford cut her off with a wave of her hand.

"It's my fault," she said. "I was stupid. I know better than to bend down quickly toward an animal who doesn't know me. I love animals very much and let me tell you, there are no stupid animals . . . only stupid people." This basically put an end to any formalities we would share before the reading, and Miss Crawford and I moved into the den.

The passage of time and of course a feeling of protectiveness towards my clients prevents me from recalling or revealing any intimate details of this, her only official reading with me. But I do remember portions of our conversation from that day, because her comments were so unique that I've repeated them several times over the years.

Just as I began the reading, I told her she shared something in common with another great actress I read—Ingrid Bergman. "You have the body of a woman but the mind of a man," I said, and explained that I meant this to be a compliment—I felt she was outwardly female but had a very strong will and determination on the inside. She knew what she wanted and how to achieve it.

"That's fine"—she nodded—"as long as you don't say I'm beautiful. I can't stand that. My features are too large for that—I'm a *handsome* woman," she said definitely, and I tended to agree with her.

I recall discussing career matters with her and telling her *Sudden Fear* would be a success (which it proved to be) and that her hard work on the film would pay off. "I always work hard," she said briskly. "Stardom is no mistake . . . it's a damned well-planned campaign," and I've quoted Miss Crawford's most profound line to would-be actors ever since.

I told her she might want to invite a spirit guide to come to her not only on the *Sudden Fear* set but any others in the future, to help her with her work, and she retorted, "Well, I guess it would be alright, if the spirit could survive the cold." I explained that spirits sometimes *make* an area cold when they come in—"that's one way their energy comes in, so your guide will be right at home in the cold," I continued.

"Well, then, that's fine." She smiled, and she proceeded to explain that she insisted on the temperature on her sets being kept cold because she felt she worked better in that environment. "It gives a person more energy," she insisted, and I suspect that's one reason why she ended her days in New York—in an effort to gain strength and energy from its cold weather.

When our reading concluded some time later, I couldn't resist asking about an item I'd read in Herb Caen's immensely popular San Francisco newspaper column. Caen mentioned something to the effect that "if you're wondering who the lady in the white turban is dining alone so often at Amelio's Restaurant, it is indeed Joan Crawford, here on location for her new picture."

Amelio's was a fine gourmet restaurant near Crawford's hotel, so I understood her choice of it for her near-nightly dining . . . but why alone? I wondered.

"I don't need to go with someone from the film company who'd bore me," she snorted. "I can bore myself if I want to, but I'm still my own best company."

As she left she thanked me for the reading and invited me to the set once again before she was due to leave the city. Not wanting to miss one more opportunity to see this dynamic actress at work, I happily accepted and returned to the home on Pacific Heights which was being used by the company, where I gave a few additional psychic messages to her between takes.

I had a friend at the time named Ronnie. He was a major Joan Crawford fan and had been ecstatic when he heard I'd given her a reading. He had desperately hoped he could return to the set with me, but, alas, he was working and could not get free.

Knowing Ronnie's devotion to Crawford, I asked if she'd do me a favor by giving my friend an autographed photo of herself. "I don't have any photos available," she said, "but tell me where to send, it and when I return home, I'll make sure he receives it," she promised. I gave her my mailing address and said I'd give the photo to Ronnie personally.

Two or three months went by and I felt certain the busy actress had forgotten about the photo or had made a promise she didn't intend to keep. But, true to her word, one day in my mail came an envelope with a return address on Bristol in Brentwood, and inside was a photo signed, "To Ronnie—My Very Best," and a most distinctive "Joan Crawford" signature (no one could make a "J" or "C" like Miss Crawford and I knew the autograph was authentic).

This incident perhaps more than any other proved to be the most memorable to me. She had determination, drive, and yet enough sensitivity and honesty to prevent her from letting down even one important fan. This, to me, was the real essence that makes a star a "Star." And that, in a word, was Joan Crawford.

> THOUGH SOME REPORTS LISTED IT AS CANCER, THE OFFICIAL WORD SEEMS TO BE THAT JOAN CRAW-FORD SUCCUMBED TO A HEART ATTACK IN A NEW YORK CITY HOSPITAL ON MAY 13, 1977.

NOW

One summer day, my co-author and I drove north, up the California coast, to an art show being held along the beach in Santa Barbara. Since

I am a lover of art, my plans were to enjoy the display (and hopefully purchase some art work to add to my collection), have dinner, and then begin the drive toward home, stopping just south of Santa Barbara at the tiny, fashionable suburb of Montecito. In Montecito, on the grounds of the beautiful Miramar Hotel, we would attempt to make contact with Joan Crawford, since she and I had occupied bungalows there, at the same time and separately, in the past.

While driving toward Montecito, I asked aloud of Miss Crawford's spirit, "We'd welcome you to come in to us with messages. We'll be at the Miramar shortly and invite you to join us there."

We pulled into the hotel's parking lot and left the car. It was by now about 9:30 P.M. and the night had become chilly, with fog rolling in off the ocean. It could have been the brisk night air, but I felt it was the sense of a strong spirit trying to come in which made me feel energetic. I also felt an uneasy tension making me restless, and I suggested that we take a walk across the grounds, past the tennis court and many of the individual cottages, until reaching the water's edge, which would perhaps work off that tension.

After we reached the sand, we walked for a few moments and then I asked quietly, "Are you ready to come in, Miss Crawford? We're ready for you—we welcome you." Strangely, the tension had continued to build during the walk and I felt it must be a sign of anxiousness on the behalf of Joan Crawford which I was picking up psychically—I was sensing her desire to begin the communication.

We left the sandy beach and walked back to a bench which was rather hidden from sight and a seemingly perfect place to work. No cottages were in the immediate area; thus no guests would hear us or question our activities on this foggy summer evening.

Arranging ourselves comfortably on the bench, we remained silent for a moment. There was a "tautness" in the air around us—it seemed "alive" and crackling with energy. This energy level filled our bodies, also, and we felt an urgency to begin—so much so that before we had a chance to even consider quietly singing a hymn or briefly meditating, we sensed that a spirit was about to enter.

Again, Valerie's notes take over, for reasons which will become apparent:

Kenny began mumbling and shifting position on the bench—head dropped forward slightly, eyes closed. He remained in this position briefly, then slumped backward against the bench, as though he were taking a brief nap or resting his eyes for a moment. "I feel her here with us," he said quietly. "I'm going to just keep my eyes closed, sit here, and allow her to talk through me if she will."

This was clearly a "semi-trance"—not so heavy that Kenny was totally "taken over" by Joan Crawford, yet strong enough to allow him to hear her voice and then allow it to come out *through* him, almost simultaneously. The voice would no doubt *sound* like Kenny Kingston, yet convey the *words* of Joan Crawford—common in a semi-trance.

"Whenever you're ready, Kenny, whenever you're ready, Miss Crawford," Valerie prompted, paper and pen in hand, primed for the note-taking which would hopefully follow.

Kenny swallowed repeatedly and his head nodded, but there was silence. "Kenny . . . Miss Crawford . . . anything you'd like to say?" Valerie asked.

"I couldn't have been any poorer-feeling when I was born. My formative years were full of tension and anxiety. I didn't have an ordinary childhood with ice cream cones and Saturday matinees. No shiny lunch bucket for me. I spent my days taking care of myself and everyone around me."

This was a strong voice, a voice filled with nervousness, reflecting the tension we'd felt earlier. It was also clear there'd be no formalities, not even a "Hello" first. Joan Crawford had been asked here to talk about herself, and talk she would, by launching right into a reflection on her younger days on Earth.

"Nobody ever singled me out and looked at me. No one gave a *damn* about me—so *I had to.* But somewhere, a core inside made me want to *be somebody* someday. I wanted to travel with people in better circles."

"You certainly succeeded in becoming an important person," Valerie replied. "You . . . "

"That's because I was a perfectionist!" came the interruption. "I was a perfectionist from the day I was born. I'm surprised I didn't direct the doctor at my own birth! I watched photographers, lighting men, everyone, until I became what I wanted to be—a movie star.

"Once I became a movie star, I wrote my own letters, signed my own name—no one could sign "JC" like I did. But I *had* to be perfect—I owed it to my public. After the housekeeper cleaned, I'd go onto the floor on my hands and knees—she *dared* to use a mop! No one could ever please me. People don't like perfectionists—they don't want to work hard enough to be equal to them. I didn't mind hard work—if I had it to do all over again, I would.

"After all, the hard work is what made me a star. I had what I wanted and it was done *my way*. Stardom was a mixed blessing, though, and sometimes it was pure Hell to maintain the image. I had clothing, homes—in fact, one of the most beautiful homes on Bristol, in Brentwood. But I couldn't actually afford it. I had to be a true "movie star," though, and stars lived in Bel Air, Brentwood or Beverly Hills. I *belonged* there.

"But I knew the moment I moved in it was wrong—ghastly. In trying to be the 'star' I bit off too much. I was a queen, but a queen who'd be damned. Of all the films I ever made, the title that fit me best was *The Damned Don't Cry*. And I *didn't* cry. I became an animal, fighting for survival. I was so unhappy it brought negative spirits in. I wanted to enjoy the house, desperately wanted that. Even after I finally left I thought-projected there. There were nice people in the home after me, but they were the *wrong* people—it was *my* house—*my* pool, *my* screening room. It was beautiful and it was *mine*."

"Former residents, and even your daughter Christina, told us the home was haunted or cursed," Valerie said.

"So they said it's been cursed, did they?" was her reply. "Well, it was a curse to me, too, in its own way. It was a love/hate home. It's time, though, for the curse to be lifted—enough people have been harmed. I hope it's over now.

"Christina—a lot of people have believed her, but don't believe *everything* she says. Her major problem was that she wished she'd been born Joan Crawford. When she *wasn't*, she tried to be even *more* popular. I feel sorry for her. I tried to give her love in my way. I gave too much to my children—a home, servants—they didn't appreciate it."

"You've described the unhappiness in your life," Valerie said. "But what about the *good* parts of your career; what about your friends? Could you tell us about what made you happy?"

A sigh escaped, then: "Oh I felt happy for a moment now and then, but I'd feel sad the next. There was no middle wedge for me. People never sympathized with me over it. *Now* you'd probably call that 'manic-depression,' but no one thought about that then.

"But about my career—my friends? I can't say I ever was content enough to trust anybody. Everybody was an enemy—it was constantly 'put your guard up.' When I was on Earthplane, I genuinely did not like people, that's all. I couldn't trust them—it was a dog-eat-dog world. I never felt *right* on Earth—I felt I should have had another head, more hands, *something*.

"Perhaps my relations with people weren't good, but I wouldn't give anyone a chance to hurt me. I was hurt enough as a child. So I used people like a ladder—step on the first rung, then the next rung. The big stepping-stone of my life was Doug (Fairbanks). He helped me fit into Hollywood society and royalty. My philosophy about my career? Be like a horse with blinders on—no looking right or left—always straight ahead."

"I'm sorry you're still bitter," Valerie attempted to console her.

"Maybe I *am* still bitter, but I'm just trying to tell you about my life," came the snappy answer. "Sometimes I still come across a little 'harsh' for people's tastes, I suppose. I just try to say things as I feel them, but then I tell myself, 'Zipper your mouth, Joan—watch what you say.' Now *that's* a change for me!"

"Wasn't there anything in your life you were happy about?" Valerie persisted.

"My career. Overall my career made me happy. And sex—I learned how to use it to make me happy. I became sexually active at a young age—lost my virginity at 12 or 13. Maybe that was too young, but I gained friends that way and most importantly I used it to get ahead. I knew what worked early on. People thought I was a little "weird," but I *was not* a lesbian. I was a strong, handsome woman who knew clothes, hair, makeup and carriage.

"I'll never ever divulge the truth of when I found out what I really was, but let's say, I discovered my own sexuality. I'm talking about what I *really was*."

"Can you give us a hint of what you mean?" Valerie encouraged her. There was silence.

"Tell us just a little more, won't you, Miss Crawford?" Valerie rephrased the question.

After the second request brought no response, it was obvious that no more information would be forthcoming. Changing the question slightly, Valerie asked, "Do you have anything else to say about your sex life, Miss Crawford?"

"I'll only say this—I was the way I was, and it worked for me. I knew what people wanted. I made a man out of Jackie Cooper, I'll tell you that. I tried with Rock Hudson, but I was either the wrong woman or the wrong sex!"

Before a comment could be made on that last statement, Crawford continued, "If you want to talk about my partners, I wonder if people really know that a world-famous actress had a daughter by one of the men in my life? *I* knew it, she *knew* I knew it—yet we were reigning queens together in Hollywood. Think about *that* awhile!"

A frown appeared on Kenny's face as he continued interpreting Crawford's remarks:

"People are always anxious to talk and gossip—that never changes. I remember going on a few talk shows after doing some drinking. Usually I was careful, and so at first I was sorry that I appeared that way. But then I thought, 'They'll do it anyway, so Hell, let's give them something to say. Let's give people something to talk about.' I could just hear them—'Was Joan Crawford drunk on TV last night? Did you see Joan Crawford?' Why not?"

Kenny's face relaxed into the first smile of the session. "Here we're equal. No one really talks badly about someone else. We don't worry about being stabbed in the back. This is the first time I've gotten to be myself— no barriers—people have x-ray eyes! But there is no need for barriers."

This was the first hint of happiness and contentment in the comments made by Joan Crawford, and Valerie seized the opportunity to point this out.

"Yes, I *am* happy," was the reply. "Or at least I'm getting there. I see little dogs and cats around. I love animals. There are animal spirits here, and people to take care of them until they see their former masters—

then how they run to them! In the meantime, any of us here can go pet them and love them. I like that.

"I have also seen some former Hollywood people here. Clark (Gable) is here. He's with Carole (Lombard), the true love of his life. I wish *I'd* been it, but he chose her, and I have to admit they were made for each other.

"Spencer (Tracy) is here and I've seen and talked to him. Now *he* was an actor's actor. He's waiting patiently for *his* true love—he'll be happy here in the future."

Kenny continued to smile. His voice, relaying Crawford's words, was relaxed and gentle as the conversation continued:

"Barbara Hutton—I've seen her here. You know, she was penniless when she passed away, but she doesn't care now. We don't *need* money here, isn't that something?"

"Who else have you seen, Miss Crawford?" Valerie asked when there was silence for a moment.

"Natalie Wood," came the answer. "I'll see more of her, too; I think she needs company. She would have liked to have talked to you, and I'm sure she'd have a lot to say, but she's still resting. She's still struggling a bit and grasping at straws. A traumatic passing can cause that."

"Have you seen Bette Davis?" Valerie asked cautiously, hesitating to bring up Crawford's former rival, yet curious to know the answer.

The smile vanished suddenly from Kenny's face. "Yes, I've seen her," was the rather curt reply. "And don't ask if we've made up. I have nothing to reconcile with Bette Davis. All the fights were done as a publicity campaign as far as I'm concerned. Everything was pre-meditated. She may have thought I was only a personality. Well, it's true, I *was* a personality but I think winning an Oscar should have been sufficient proof I was also an actress. But she fought hard to be a star—even harder than I did. If she had to kill, she killed."

Both the frown on Kenny's face and the tenseness in his voice returned and it was apparent that perhaps the rivalry was not yet over, contrary to Miss Crawford's insistence. But this was quite an accusation—Davis had *killed*?

"Could you explain your last comment?" Valerie asked.

No words followed.

"What did you mean, Miss Crawford?" she tried.

Again—silence. Clearly there would be no explanation and perhaps this was only an angry accusation.

"Should we just say you were *both* great actresses and move on, Miss Crawford?" Valerie tried tactfully.

"There were a lot of great actresses then—more so than there are today. Where are the Roz Russells, the Barbara Stanwycks, yes, even the Bette Davis's—though maybe one was enough. You won't find them like us today."

"Are there any current performers you enjoy watching from the other side?" Valerie asked.

"There are a few I suppose," came a reluctant answer. "Meryl Streep is excellent. Glenn Close is excellent. But certainly those people who want to bare it all are ridiculous. Madonna—she should *pay* to have her picture in the paper! No class; no dignity. Cher—she won an Oscar for that cute little thing she did, but she doesn't even *dress* like a star. She dresses like a burlesque queen! I'd like to have had her on *my* freezing sets!

"Even directors today are sloppy—Spielberg and that type. They may do a few films, but they don't look successful. Ascots—cashmere sweaters—now, *those* were directors. Oh, I've got to be careful—I'm trying to be a good person. I'm trying not to condemn. What else would you like to know?"

"Only one or two more questions." Valerie promised. "Actually, we wondered about your passing—was it difficult? Did you have pain?"

A long sigh escaped Kenny's lips. The previous look of agitation disappeared and a sad yet pensive look replaced it. "I had a struggle when I passed. Not because of illness or physical pain. I don't care how they listed my passing—cancer, heart—I simply couldn't fight anymore. I lost my desire. I simply wanted to go. It wasn't suicide; I just lost my desire at an important moment. The struggle came because, just near the end, I wanted the desire back again, but it was too late. I'd slipped too far and I couldn't recharge the old battery.

"One woman could have saved my life if I'd let her—Doris Lillie. She wanted to help me. But vanity and pride took over and I refused everyone. I wanted loved ones with me, but I wanted it all too late. That was the *real* struggle."

A sense of heaviness and sadness hung in the air. A moment of quiet seemed appropriate, then Valerie asked, "Do you feel you've learned from that lifetime, Miss Crawford?" and received a response in a sad, quiet voice.

"I've learned, and I'm putting it to use. I abused the bottle in my time, but I've learned. I'm teaching people here how to avoid being victims of the bottle so that when they're reborn, they won't have problems.

"But let me tell your readers something else I've learned. Closeness—the human touch—that's what I lacked, perhaps, and what I'm learning to develop now.

"Practice your penmanship! Write to your loved ones—say things on paper you might not say otherwise. 'I care for you;' 'I'm glad you're happy.' Send compliments—write thank you's. Write ... "

The last few words had grown faint, and suddenly Kenny's head dropped forward and he became limp, signalling the end of the contact. "Thank you, Miss Crawford," Valerie whispered, then, "Let me help you, Kenny," she said, rubbing his neck and shoulders to establish physical contact for him again with matters of the "real world."

We'd carried a bottle of water with us from the car, which we'd purchased in Santa Barbara, and Valerie lifted the soft drink-sized bottle to Kenny's lips. "Take a few sips, Kenny," she encouraged, and he slowly did so, choking slightly at first, then swallowing easier.

Kenny slowly opened his eyes, rubbed his face gently, and looked around as though awake from a sleep. "Welcome back," Valerie said, thus ending another spirit contact.

CHARLIE CHAPLIN

★ ★ ★ ★ ★

THEN

My two encounters with the world of Charlie Chaplin were brief and indirect. But oddly enough one story involves a person whom he loved very much and the other involves someone he no doubt despised for the way she altered his life completely.

I never had any particular urge to follow acting as a career, but many years ago my great friend, actor Edward Everett Horton, phoned me and said he'd like me to appear in a production with him at the prestigious training ground and theatre, the Pasadena Playhouse, just outside Los Angeles. "It would be wonderful to have you with me," he enthused. "But, Eddie, I'm no actor," I protested.

"Now, now, now," he said, "leave it to me. I'll call the woman who's directing the play and suggest that she let you read for the role."

He called me back to say he'd arranged an audition time. To pacify Eddie (and because I'd always found the theatre tremendously exciting, even as a patron), I read for the part. To my amazement, the director seemed delighted by my delivery. "You'll be fine!" she smiled.

"But I'm not ... " I began. "No, you'll be fine ... you've got the part!" she insisted, and I left in a daze.

I'd just begun to warm to the idea of appearing onstage with Eddie when I heard once again from the director. "I called to say I'm sorry," she began, "but the board feels we need someone of greater name value in the role. We're going with Charlie Chaplin, Jr." — one of Chaplin's two sons by actress Lita Grey—she explained.

Of course I couldn't deny the Chaplin name would draw at the box office. But partly because I was somewhat disappointed and partly because I psychically felt it to be true, I told her, "Oh, that's fine. But I predict the play will get bad reviews!"

Unfortunately for my friend Eddie it *did* get bad reviews, and sometime later he said, half seriously, "If it hadn't been for that damned Chaplin, who knows what could have happened!"

My earlier encounter regarding Chaplin was with a woman whose accusations had helped change the course of his life—for the worst.

About 1949, I invited a friend, actor Steve Cochran, to visit me in San Francisco to attend an Italian film festival and art show I was helping to organize, to be presented at the Casa Fugazi Hall in the Italian colony in San Francisco's North Beach area.

When he attended the festivities one night, he brought with him a woman I thought to be very strange. I disliked her aura from the moment I saw her enter with him—it was dark and troubled. When I could, I pulled Steve aside and said, "Forgive me, but *who* is that strange lady? I get *very* uncomfortable vibrations from her psychically."

"Oh," he said, "I meant to introduce you, but maybe you don't want to meet her after all, if you feel that way." "No, I'll meet her," I said, "if she's a friend of yours. But she's had some very dark, deep things going on in her mind," I persisted.

"I guess that's true," he said. "You see—she's Joan Barry."

The name didn't register with me immediately and he continued. "You remember—Joan Barry, the woman who filed the paternity suit against Charlie Chaplin a few years ago? Her charges have brought a lot of trouble his way since then, let me tell you," he admitted.

As I said, though I had no direct contact with the immortal "Little Tramp," for two brief moments my life was interwoven both with a son he loved dearly and the one person who perhaps brought him more pain than any other.

SIR CHARLES CHAPLIN (FOR HE HAD BEEN KNIGHTED BY THE QUEEN IN HIS LATTER YEARS) WAS 88 YEARS OLD WHEN HE PASSED AWAY ON CHRISTMAS DAY, 1977, AT HIS VILLA IN CORSIER-SUR-VEVEY, SWITZERLAND.

NOW

The waves were cresting several feet high, the sky was black, and the night air was warm and humid as Valerie and I sat on the deck of the *Stella Solaris*.

It was April 16, which would have been the 102nd birthday of Charlie Chaplin, and we felt the timing was perfect for making contact with him. We were about halfway through a three-week grand Caribbean cruise. This group of passengers seemed to be mostly early risers, which worked in our favor, since it was close to 11 P.M. when we first sat on the deck and many of the passengers had retired for the evening.

Perhaps one or two people momentarily strolled by as we positioned ourselves on the cushioned deck chairs, but even they disappeared as we sat quietly meditating and telepathically asking Chaplin to come in.

We chose this evening not only because it had been his birthdate, but because the atmosphere of being on a ship was so closely tied in to him, in a most traumatic way (Chaplin and family were aboard a ship bound for a vacation when he received word that his passport had been revoked—for "political and moral reasons"—and he was essentially "banned" from returning to America). Such an event was devastatingly memorable, to be sure, and therefore we felt his spirit might be enticed to return to the span of a great ocean to vent anger, frustration, or sorrow, and we wanted to encourage him to do just that.

We were lulled into relaxation by the repetitive sounds of the waves crashing and the ship's engines humming. Though the Caribbean weather had been particularly hot this spring, an even more intense warmth hit my face—a "flush," actually, and I suspected it was Chaplin, since spirits can make themselves felt by extreme cold or extreme heat. A moment later, Valerie said, "Oh—I'm so warm! Is it the air, or . . . ""It's him," I answered, "Welcome, Mr. Chaplin. Welcome, Charlie."

Valerie joined me in a second "Welcome, Charlie."

"I feel this warmth and an energy with it, but I'm very peaceful . . . this is a peaceful man now," I concluded.

"Yes, there's a peaceful, contented feeling," Valerie agreed. "Is he telling us he's at peace, then?"

"Can you speak *to* me, or *through* me, Charlie?" I asked. "Please feel free to come in to us," Valerie encouraged.

I recall a lightheadedness, then little else, and the following transcript describes what took place from then on:

Kenny's head dropped forward slightly and he mumbled, though the words were garbled.

"Can you speak clearly? Do you have something to say?" Valerie asked.

Again, the mumbling, then: "Question, please," in a voice which was much like Kenny's, though with a hint of a British accent.

"Oh, alright, I'll ask you a question," Valerie began. "I'd like to know how you're feeling now, and how did you feel when you first made the transition?"

Kenny/Charlie swallowed against a gurgling which had risen in his throat. Then, in a quiet voice, again tinged with British overtones, "Much better now, thank you . . . So tired at first. No pain when I entered this little piece of Paradise . . . just overwhelming tiredness. Of course, though I hated to think it, I was an old man, you know. The old body just gave way, I suppose."

"So you rested?" Valerie urged him on. "Did you see anyone you knew right away? Did anyone greet you?"

"Do you know, it was the strangest thing," he answered. "I recall thinking, 'What a curious place this is—very beautiful,' but I couldn't help saying to myself, 'So, then, there really is a Heaven—there really is such a place!' I was elated and full of questions, but so tired at the same time, as though a weight had been lifted which left me free to just close my eyes and let everything pass me by. And I know it was quite anti-social of me, but that's just what I did—closed my eyes to it all—didn't want to see a single soul at first."

"And then?" Valerie prodded. "When you finally did see people—who were they?"

Kenny/Charlie chuckled but said nothing.

"What—what's so funny?" Valerie asked.

Another chuckle, then: "What you'd probably like to ask is if I've been bombarded by all the women I knew in my time—were they waiting for me? Well, they weren't, first off. I may not have used good judgment or morals all the time, but many of those 'romances' were for publicity—not on my behalf, mind you—the young ladies knew my vulnerability and used it to their advantage. Did we love one another? Of course not."

Chaplin seemed to be warming to the subject, causing Kenny to sit up straighter on the deck chair. Squaring his shoulders, and in a stronger voice, he continued, the words coming easily and quickly. "The only women I ever loved were the first young lady I ever truly considered my girlfriend . . . "

"Who was that?" Valerie interrupted.

"It was a long time ago. Makes no difference now," he continued, crisply. "The other woman I loved was dear Oona." (Oona O'Neill Chaplin, daughter of playwright Eugene O'Neill and Chaplin's wife at the time of his passing).

"What about Paulette Goddard—you didn't love her?" Valerie asked.

"In my fashion." He sighed. "Yes, it was something close to love for Paulette." Then, smiling: "Many people say beautiful women often have no brains. Paulette should have dispelled this notion."

"Were you ever really married?" Valerie inquired. "Wasn't there some mystery about that?"

"Of course we were married," Kenny/Charlie snorted. "But the reason we said we weren't was because it gave us more publicity. Give the illusion that you're trying to hide a secret and the whole world will talk! Seriously, I was pleased to end my life close to Paulette in Switzerland." (Goddard lived a short distance from Chaplin's home in Vevey).

"Here's a tidbit for you," he continued. "How many people knew she also had one of the most fabulous jewel collections in the world? Didn't know that, did you?" he smiled.

"While we're talking about women, what does one do about sex on the other side?" Valerie asked. "That is, if you don't mind my asking?"

"There is no sex here," he answered. "And do I miss it? Oddly enough, no. At first, I thought, 'Wait now, what's this?' Because I felt young again . . . vibrant again. But the urge left me—simply left me after awhile."

"Does anything replace sex?" Valerie asked.

How can I describe it?" he answered. "There's a warmth, deep within. We touch and caress, but it's not sexual. Yet it's deeply satisfying—one's whole body vibrates with this warmth."

When the voice did not continue, Valerie waited in silence briefly, then said, "Anything else you'd like to say?"

It appeared the spirit contact might be growing weaker, because Kenny/Charlie leaned back against the deck chair and took a deep breath before speaking. "Question ... " was all that he said, indicating he had possibly run out of things to say spontaneously.

"Okay, I'll ask you something," Valerie cooperated. "I hope you're not too tired for this, but I do want to ask you ... Have you seen J. Edgar Hoover at all? And if so, what has happened between you?" (The former F.B.I. Chief Hoover was responsible for mounting an intense campaign and investigation against Chaplin, resulting in his "ouster" from the U.S.).

Silence followed. Valerie cringed. "Have I said the wrong thing? I'm sorry ... I just thought ... "

"No harm done," came a soft reply. "Just time to put the whole bloody mess behind us, that's all. As a matter of fact, I *have* seen the man—several times. There's no hatred there now. Don't misunderstand—I didn't run up and hug the man, but it's over. Things had to be the way they were. I'll say this—no one person should have had the power that was bestowed on Hoover. If ever the word 'vendetta' were properly used, it was used in association with him. But he had to live that life, as did Senator Joe McCarthy. They no doubt felt destined to do what they did, the way I felt destined to live my life as Charlie Chaplin. I knew making *The Great Dictator* was a risk, but I had to do it, regardless of the outcome. Enough said."

"Thank you," Valerie said cautiously. "I hope you're not upset. I just felt that was important. Have you seen anyone else that you've been *glad* to see?"

Again, the contact seemed to be growing faint, for Kenny/Charlie mumbled. In somewhat garbled speech, so quiet that it became necessary for Valerie to lean closer to hear, he continued, "My old partners (in forming United Artists film company) Douglas (Fairbanks, Sr.) and Mary (Pickford). Good to see them again . . . there's someone you should speak to sometime. Mary was very interested in the psychic world—

always felt she bought her home Pickfair using her ability."

Valerie waited for more, but Kenny/Charlie stirred in the deck chair and began breathing heavily. "Tired now . . . " he whispered. "I haven't done this much speaking before, though I've visited a few times . . . "

As the last sentence was spoken, the English accent had all but disappeared, indicating that the spirit was leaving and soon Kenny would once again be in full control.

"Kenny, are you back?" Valerie asked. "Thank you, Charlie . . . thank you, Mr. Chaplin, very much . . . Kenny, come back now."

Kenny sat quietly, then rubbed his eyes as though emerging from a sleep.

"Welcome back," Valerie greeted him. "How do you feel?"

"I'm fine . . . I'm okay," Kenny responded.

We sat in silence once again, listening to the waves until Kenny felt comfortable enough to return to a conversation once again.

We had thought this was the end of Charlie Chaplin, from our spiritual point of view, until seeing the movie *Chaplin* shortly after it opened. As we sat watching Robert Downey, Jr. portray The Little Tramp, we became mesmerized. As we emerged from the theater Kenny said, "He wants to come through again. There's more to say."

"I wonder what he thought of the film?" Valerie rushed on. "When or where can we get in touch with Chaplin again?"

And then, as we drove out of the theater parking lot, we remembered the Montecito Inn, near Santa Barbara, California, which had been our original choice as a place to contact Chaplin, since he and actor Fatty Arbuckle built the Inn in the mid-1920s and had used it as a hideaway for themselves and their Hollywood friends such as Marion Davies, Wallace Beery, Janet Gaynor, Carole Lombard, and Lon Chaney, Sr. until they sold it in the 1940s. It had seemed a perfect place to go and we would have done so until the cruise came along and we changed the locale to the ship, especially once we learned we'd be on board on what would have been Chaplin's birthday.

"Let's go there. Let's plan to go to the Inn," Kenny said. "I feel he'll come in to us again, perhaps stronger than before. There's more to be said."

Thus, this would become the only contact done in two parts and in two different locations. For while we were able to communicate with Chaplin on the first attempt, it was not a particularly strong or lengthy communication.

In addition to the strength we hoped he'd gained and the experience in making spirit contact, Kenny also hoped he'd built up more trust toward us. Before he may have wanted to talk in greater detail, yet felt hesitant to give us too much information at any one time. We felt it was possible the distrust went back to his having been banished from the United States in 1952. Though he said it was behind him, some small resentment may have remained.

Our hope as we drove up the California coast toward Montecito was that he'd feel comfortable in familiar surroundings, and would feel more at ease to open up to us.

We turned off the highway and proceeded toward the Inn, located on Olive Mill Road, in the midst of a quaint village atmosphere. We parked in front of one of the area's many tiny shops, across the street from the three-story black-and-white Inn.

Upon entering the lobby, it was clear there was an elegant formality to the Inn, and as we wandered around, the only levity came from several Chaplin posters scattered about.

"There's a coldness here," Kenny couldn't resist saying to Valerie, who, as usual, carried a tape recorder and note pad. "It's a coldness, but not from spirit. It's a formal, stuffy coldness instead. My first reaction is that I feel a financial setback for someone involved with the Inn. I believe it may have started with Chaplin, but it's continuing today and unfortunately may continue in the future. It's a financial problem for someone involved. But Chaplin would have been much happier if he's stayed here longer. He left behind a heaviness for some reason, but it could have been lifted if he'd stayed."

We had walked down a small flight of stairs to a sitting area, but now began our way back toward the front desk. "This hotel was originally built primarily as a convenience for Roscoe (Fatty) Arbuckle," Kenny announced.

"A convenience?" Valerie questioned. "Do you mean a getaway place or a meeting place?"

"A meeting place, but we won't discuss what kind of meetings," Kenny responded, obviously answering by way of information given him by a spirit, since he knew nothing about the hotel himself.

"I'll say this, too," Kenny continued. "I think we'll find that many details in the hotel—the glass doors, much of the decor, and even some of the walls—are not the originals. Much of this is not the same as when Chaplin built it. That may present a problem in bringing him in." (Extensive renovation changes the vibrations of a building; it becomes less familiar to a spirit, as the original fixtures and thereby their memories, have been removed).

We asked the desk clerk if she believed in spirits or if she or any of the other employees had ever felt anything unusual in the hotel.

"Oh, I believe," she responded. "And several of us feel very 'uncomfortable' when we go into one of the large suites upstairs. It's not an unhappy feeling exactly, but it's definitely a 'funny' feeling. When we show the suite, which is often used for meetings, or when we're in there preparing for a meeting, we've all said the same thing when we compare notes—'there's someone there. Definitely someone there.' It's strange."

To check on his psychic accuracy, Kenny asked the young woman how much, if any, of the hotel remained as it was in its original days. "Very little," she said. "In fact, the only thing I can think of right offhand is the elevator. It's the original, built in 1927."

Valerie and Kenny thanked her and walked the short distance to the relatively small elevator—actually more like an English "lift." It was here we felt a true sense of Chaplin's vibrations. It seemed the true heart and soul of the quaint hotel was in that elevator, and we simply stood inside it, allowing ourselves to be enveloped in its atmosphere.

"We welcome you, Mr. Chaplin," Valerie began quietly, for the elevator door was still open. (Then aside to Kenny: "It seems so formal here, I don't know whether to call him Charlie, Mr. Chaplin, or even Sir Charles"). "Anyway, we've come to your Inn to find you and we certainly would love to communicate with you," Valerie continued, this time pushing a button to close the door. "Let's just ride up and down in this a couple of times," she suggested.

"I feel a certain warmth and contentment here," Kenny said, eyes closed and leaning against one wall as we began our elevator ride. "And truthfully, I don't feel much contentment in other parts of the hotel. This is all that remains to strongly attract Chaplin here."

"I wonder if he's been back here in spirit before?" Valerie asked.

Kenny silently listened, then nodded. "Yes, he's whispering in my ear. He's been back, as have several of his friends. And he'll continue to come back sporadically. But he's not found his 'niche' here." Kenny turned his head sideways, listening again.

"There's still a certain amount of discontent that he occasionally feels on the other side as well, but he tells me it's better there than it was here towards the last," Kenny continued.

"Well, why . . . " Valerie began, but was interrupted when Kenny listened intently to the spirit voice again and said (to the voice) "Wait . . . slow down . . . what are you telling me?" Then, to Valerie, "He says he's not going to try speaking through me. 'Too tedious,' he says. He'll speak *to* me and I'll tell you what he says as we go along."

"He says, 'Very few, if any, people know about the hideaways here— the tunnels that I put underneath the hotel.' He's also telling me that he and Douglas Fairbanks, Sr. used to take advantage of secret tunnels built around the Garden Court Apartments in Hollywood. 'Got rather used to those little passageways,' he's smiling."

"Secret hideaways here? Where?" Valerie prodded. "Ask him if they still exist!"

"He's just smiling," Kenny answered. "He won't tell, but he says, 'they served their purpose.'"

The elevator had returned to the first floor again and this time we walked out once more into the lobby.

"Let's go to that area down there," Kenny said, pointing to a small sitting area off of a larger parlor section. This area contained only one or two small tables and a few chairs and was just outside a bar/cafe whose most charming adornments were frosted glass doors carved with a likeness of Chaplin.

"I'm going to ask him to continue now," Kenny said, closing his eyes and appearing to listen and concentrate. He nodded then, as though he'd connected with Chaplin once more, and said, "Go ahead with your questions, please. He's ready."

"Well, first," Valerie began, "tell him we enjoyed the film version of his life. But what did *he* think of it—can he tell us?"

Kenny smiled and spoke, a minute pause in between phrases while he listened and then repeated: "No question about it . . . he enjoyed it immensely. He was on the set many times . . . If anyone were to ask Robert Downey, Jr. if he felt a presence with him, he'd have to say yes. 'I went home with him,' Chaplin says. And during scenes in Switzerland" —Chaplin's actual home in Vevey was used for part of the film—"I was there on the veranda. I was there!' he says."

"Then you were pleased with his portrayal of you?" Valerie persisted.

A loud crack, like a thunderbolt, hit the wall next to us, followed by tiny knocks which seemed to ricochet off other parts of the wall. This was indeed confirmation from Chaplin, we were certain.

Kenny listened, then said, "He says, 'There—you have your answer!' He says Robert Downey, Jr. would have been *his* choice to play him on screen. He feels 'the young man,' as he calls him, has a brilliant career ahead but must . . . what? I can't hear you" (an aside to Chaplin). "He must guard his health and curb his social problems. He and he alone can and must be responsible for his actions and he must let nothing stand in the way of his career right now."

Again Kenny seemed intent on listening. "Oh, you know who he's talking about?" he continued. "Our friend, Anthony Newley (the actor/singer and co-creator of such memorable songs as "What Kind of Fool Am I?," "The Candy Man" and "Who Can I Turn To?").

"Because he did Chaplin's life on stage?" Valerie asked. (Newley did a tour de force performance of Chaplin's life in musical form several years ago).

"Yes," Kenny answered. "Chaplin feels he was most capable, and he says, 'I was onstage with *him* as well.' He says, 'He had the great pathos to play me, as did Downey, Jr. Our lives all ran parallel in many ways. But the timing was off with Mr. Newley . . . wrong timing and the production needed stronger direction.' He's sighing."

"He feels badly about that?" Valerie asked.

"Badly, yes," Kenny responded. "Oh, this is interesting," he smiled, "he says he tried to work with Newley to compose songs after that. This was to more or less 'pay him back' for what Newley may have felt was a disappointment. Chaplin's composing music on the other side, he says, and writing sonnets and plays for his friends, so was happy to try to work through Newley. 'Such a talented man,' he says."

"So he's working again now?" Valerie asked. "In our other contact he seemed so peaceful, as though he were just relaxing and spending time with people."

" 'Can't seem to forget about work,' he tells me," Kenny said. "He says, 'We see a film of sorts here before we're reborn—to choose our life and choose our parents. When I saw the film last time, I fell in love with the idea of the film itself! It happened right then—that fascination.' "

"What does he think of films today, other than *Chaplin*?" Valerie asked.

"He doesn't look too pleased," Kenny said. "I can see him—he's standing right behind you now, and he's shaking his head."

"I'm so cold all of a sudden!" Valerie cried softly.

"It's no wonder," Kenny explained, "because he's right behind you. He says he'll still speak to me, but this way I can see him, too. He's shaking his head and says films today leave *him* cold. 'Not much feeling or warmth, and so much nudity,' he says. 'It should be saved for one's private life, not necessarily for celluloid.' "

"No other films he's particularly enjoyed?" Valerie urged.

"Again, he shakes his head sadly," Kenny said, looking over Valerie's shoulder. "He says there's not enough creativity. Directors and producers hand over more control to the audience than to the actors. He says Hollywood doesn't need more actors or actresses. It needs great personalities . . . quick thinkers."

"People who could improvise the way he did?" Valerie suggested.

"Exactly," he's saying, and nodding his head. "What's that?" (looking at Chaplin). "Oh, he says the person closest to his form of quick thinking and improvisation is Robin Williams. 'Like that chap,' he smiles."

"If Chaplin's composing and writing again, has he more or less forgotten his family—the ones who are on the other side and the ones still on Earthplane?" Valerie wondered.

"He looks shocked," Kenny said. "He says, 'Never!' A long sigh escapes his lips, follows by a satisfied smile. He says he's found his Oona again, now that she's on the other side (Oona O'Neill Chaplin passed in

1991).'I'd rested sufficiently to greet her when she arrived,' he's telling me.'And I've spent considerable time with her, though *she's* resting now. It's as though no time elapsed since we had last been together. It's absolutely 'delicious' spending time with her,' he continues.

"He also says he visits his son Sydney in Palm Springs, California from time to time, but he looks sad now and says he should take better care of himself. He says he's greatly happy, too, spending some time with a son he somehow never knew too well—Charlie Chaplin, Jr." (Charlie Chaplin, Jr. passed away many years ago at a relatively young age).

"And, he reminds us, he still spends time with his old friends Mary Pickford and Douglas Fairbanks, Sr. He says 'She and Doug are friends here now, and they return to the home—Pickfair, I mean—quite often. They're not really possessive or mean, they just don't want anyone else in 'their' home!' he's telling me."

Valerie wondered aloud whether the current residents felt the presence of these spirits.

"Don't know that," was the reply. "But the previous owner—sports executive Jerry Buss—did, he says. He says Mary Pickford told him she and Doug made Buss, or someone close to him, quite uncomfortable!"

Kenny smiled and watched over Valerie's right shoulder. "Oh, this is very unusual," he began. "He's going back to talk about the *Chaplin* film again and says not only was he often on the set, but he was particularly there when Geraldine was around as well." She played her grandmother in the film. "Listen to this—he says he *actually inhabited* Robert Downey, Jr.'s body for a split second during one scene. This scene supposedly took place on a movie lot, when Geraldine's character hugged Downey as Chaplin. 'I inhabited his body for that brief moment and what a joy!' he smiles. 'Actually hugging her!' he says warmly."

"That's incredible," Valerie said softly. "It's so sad, but so sweet."

"He's just smiling happily now," Kenny said. "Do you have other questions for him?"

"Just this," Valerie concluded. "Does he plan to come back to Earth— I mean to reincarnate?"

"He says 'I have every intention of returning to the place called Earth for a new beginning.' He's telling me that he feels he has to come back. 'To be truthful,' he says, 'I don't particularly want to, but I need to learn lessons. I feel I need to learn the art of getting along with people—being a bit less driven and more aware of relationships. People called me a genius in my own craft . . . I appreciate that. Perhaps they'll consider me a double genius next time, for I plan to come back as a twin,' he smiles. He says he's seen a film of that life already and it 'quite appeals' to him."

"Can he tell us where it will be?" Valerie asked enthusiastically.

"I see an American flag directly over your head," Kenny said, "which is ironic considering his being removed from America . . . but he tells me that's the very reason for it. He'll return as an American and have no problems with citizenship. He holds no grudge—he enjoys this country. He says—what? He says he gave to America as Chaplin but feels America also gave to him for many years. He wants to return with a peace of mind and sense of belonging he always lacked before."

"What city—does he know yet?" Valerie persisted.

"Ah, one of my favorites," Kenny smiled. "He's going to return and live a life in San Francisco . . . says the climate is more like England and Switzerland. He says he's leaving now . . . no more to say except this . . . he'll wait until Oona is ready to return with him. They'll find one another and marry all over again."

On this romantic note, our second communication with one of the film world's greatest legends came to a close, and after resting a bit, Kenny suggested we leave the Montecito Inn and begin our drive home.

GRETA GARBO

THEN

I cannot recall the exact date when I met "The Magnificent Garbo," as she sincerely liked to be called—it was sometime in the late 1950s. But more detailed memories of the circumstances surrounding the meeting, the location, and of course Garbo herself are forever etched in my mind.

I was living in San Francisco at the time, in a large home on Pacific Heights. My phone rang one day and the caller was a dear friend, world-famous nutritionist Gayelord Hauser. I had known Gayelord, one of the true founders of the health food movement, for quite some time, having been introduced to him by my great friend Clifton Webb. Gayelord had spoken to me often before of his friendship with Greta Garbo, or "Miss G" as he fondly referred to her, but I'd never had the pleasure of being introduced to her.

During this particular call Gayelord told me that Miss G, Gayelord, and Gayelord's longtime friend Frey Brown would be journeying to San Francisco from Gayelord's home in Beverly Hills, arriving in about a fortnight.

"I think it's time you met Miss G," he said determinedly. "And I think she'd like to get a little psychic reading from you," he continued. "So why don't we plan a luncheon and reading at your house?"

Pretending to be indignant, I said, "Oh, really now, Gayelord, you're inviting not only yourself but two other people to lunch!" He laughed and said, "No, Kenny—you know how fussy I am about food. I'll bring everything myself and I will prepare the luncheon, too."

This sounded too good to miss—Gayelord Hauser in my kitchen and Greta Garbo in my library, all at the same time! I encouraged Gayelord to set a date and offered the services of my houseboy, Modesto, as "chef's assistant" for the day. I'm normally not a morning person but I knew Gayelord was. I also knew he'd want to get an early start in preparing the meal, so we agreed on an arrival time of 10 A.M. for the day of the luncheon.

At precisely 10 A.M. on the appointed day, the chimes rang. Three happy people greeted me as I opened the door—Gayelord, sporting a blazer, sport shirt, and an ascot and carrying a bag of food, entered first, followed by Frey Brown, also carrying assorted items, and close behind him stood "the immortal one." Their jovial mood was contagious and I immediately felt comfortable having all three in my home.

Gayelord proceeded immediately into the kitchen to begin preparing a luncheon he promised would be fit for a (very healthy) king. After all the bags of food were deposited in the kitchen, Miss G and Frey joined me in the library, where I lit a fire to combat the foggy San Francisco morning.

As we sat talking I was of course struck by Garbo's beauty. But she had a poise and a natural grace as well, and it seemed to me she could just have easily passed for a San Francisco socialite rather than a world-famous, though reclusive, movie star. Chatting as we did about films, friends we shared on the East and West Coasts, and then moving on to a discussion of the psychic world, I came to realize almost immediately that Greta Garbo was surprisingly fun-loving, direct, and easy to talk to, and that we would no doubt become friends.

Time passed quickly, and before we knew it, Gayelord was summoning us to his exquisite luncheon. Following the meal I gave Garbo what would be the first of many brief psychic readings.

Only once during that first reading do I recall a sadness about her, and it showed briefly in her eyes. It was when she asked a question about her career and if she'd made the right decision in leaving Hollywood behind, for I feel she'd truly wanted to go on acting and secretly regretted her decision to quit. I put my index finger under her chin, looked into her eyes and said, "A wise man once said 'the past is the past and the charm of the past is that it *is* the past.' " I found myself doing this several times throughout our association whenever her eyes clouded, and as far as I remember, it worked every time and the light returned to her face.

This first reading set the pace for the next thirty-five years as I sporadically gave readings to the screen's greatest *Camille* in a changing variety of locales from San Francisco to Beverly Hills, Palm Springs to New York City. In most cases Gayelord set up the appointments and was present before and after the readings, where we then changed to a more social mood and the psychic world took a friendly back seat to show business, politics, nutrition and other topics.

We shared many other meals together as well, from one end of the dining spectrum to the other, representing Garbo's change in tastes. Sometimes it would be amidst the elegance of Chasen's or Trader Vic's in Beverly Hills. But she was equally happy at Dupar's, a family coffee shop in Southern California's San Fernando Valley.

For the most part Garbo disliked going out into crowds, though. I feel this was partly a fear of being recognized but most importantly of having someone rush over for an autograph. She felt uneasy with the idea of strangers crowding in on her. Again, as with my client and friend Marilyn Monroe, I feel agoraphobia played at least a small role in Garbo's need to be indoors, at home, and therefore "safe" at times. Part of her reclusive nature was not simply to turn her back on Hollywood, but to turn away from people in general, purely out of fear. Fortunately these fear attacks were infrequent, but when she did have plans to go out socially and felt panic coming on, she'd carefully dress in designer clothes and was easily able to pass for a glamorous society matron, not the "eccentric Greta Garbo" the public was looking for.

Yet on braver occasions she had great fun with the "Garbo look." Oddly enough, during these times, she didn't mind being recognized and seemed to actually welcome it as an ingenue who'd just appeared in her first film might. "Look, I wear my hat and dark glasses today," she whispered with a hint of a smile as she, Gayelord and I approached our usual booth at the back of Dupar's. And sure enough, dressed in her hat, glasses, and a simple jogging suit, she'd cause whispers and stares as she passed by and sat down.

The waitresses at the coffee shop were protective of Garbo, though, and once again she felt "safe." She had the luxury of being recognized, but the security of knowing people would be prevented from running over to her. I teased her that she was her own best public relations person—she knew how to get attention and be worshipped from afar, simply by changing her manner of dress and creating the character of "Garbo."

My fondest memories are the lighter, even comical times with the Magnificent Garbo. Once, Gayelord and I were talking on the phone and he said, "Oh, I have to go now, Kenny. Miss G is getting anxious— she says it's time to watch La Belle on *Hollywood Squares*."

"Who is La Belle?" I asked.

"Oh, it's that funny man, Paul Lynde," he answered. "Miss G loves him and that's her nickname for him. I must go turn on the TV and watch with her. I'll talk to you later, Kenny."

Garbo was so fond of Lynde's sense of humor and performance in the center square on the game show that she wrote him a fan letter. To my knowledge, it's the only one she ever wrote!

Her fans would never have suspected it, but the following comical instance happened on several occasions. I'd receive a phone call from Gayelord, telling me Miss G was visiting him at his Beverly Hills hilltop home. He'd say, "She's been telling me all day, 'I need flowers,' so we're going out tonight. Do you want to go?," and I'd know exactly what he meant.

We'd set a time, usually around midnight, and I'd drive to his home, picking up Gayelord and Garbo. She'd be carrying a pair of large scissors and we'd actually drive through the neighborhood, passing row after row of large estates, many with lush gardens or flowering bushes. Miss Garbo would say, "Here—stop, please!" and she'd silently open the car door, run onto the lawn, cut a few beautiful flowers, then hurry back to the car, childishly giggling along the way! This proceeded until she had a collection to rival any florist's shop in town!

Gayelord had told me early in our friendship about Garbo's love of flowers, and how a flower figured prominently in his first meeting with her. He'd moved to Beverly Hills and was living on Angelo Drive—a wealthy area, needless to say, although Gayelord was not as wealthy at the time as people might have thought. Once a week, on Wednesdays, as I recall, he would hold a luncheon at noon. He'd moved to the area on a shoestring, but wanted to be included in the mainstream of Beverly Hills society, and felt the luncheons were a way for him to introduce himself and his nutrition beliefs to the elite ladies of the area. Word spread quickly, and on any given week eleven fashionable women, plus Gayelord, would gather—names like Gloria Swanson, Lady Elsie Mendl, Constance and Joan Bennett, Lady Peel (Beatrice Lillie) were commonplace at the gatherings.

One week, the butler said, "Mr. Hauser, a lady called and said she'd like to make a reservation for next week—for Greta Garbo." Gayelord didn't really believe the message and thought someone was having fun with him—Garbo would indeed be the biggest name he'd ever drawn to the function. But he played along, saying, "Alright, fine, we'll keep a place for Miss Garbo for next week, then, won't we?"

He didn't allow himself to spend time thinking about the possibility of Garbo attending, until the following Wednesday afternoon. He'd instructed the butler to keep a place setting open. As noon approached and the other ladies gathered, Hauser became more convinced the phone call had been a hoax. But at one minute before noon, the doorbell chimed. He went to the door himself and opened it to find the legendary Garbo herself standing there. "Our eyes met instantly," he told me, "and she offered me a flower—a poppy, I believe—and it was love, Kenny," he sighed.

Garbo stayed for lunch—and far beyond that. She dismissed her chauffeur and car and basically "moved in" with Gayelord that very day—staying for six weeks, during which time they, as he told me, "made love, talked, ate properly, and fell in love. She gave me fame from that moment on, and to think it all began when she handed me that flower."

This love of flowers carried through to the colorful decor in Garbo's New York apartment as well, where I remember arrangements of cut flowers and beautiful paintings of flowers everywhere.

It was in that apartment that I met with Garbo after our dear Gayelord passed, this time to hold a seance and attempt to make contact with him in spirit. I'd told her that Valerie and I would be in New York for a few days following a working cruise in Spain, Portugal, and Morocco. "You must come see me!" she insisted. It was very important for her to know that Gayelord was doing well. She wanted to know if he was peaceful and happy, and I do feel we were able to get those answers for her. We were also, happily, able to make contact with dress designer Valentina's husband George Schlee in the spirit world; he was a very important person in Garbo's life also.

As usual, however, though the New York visit had a serious purpose, we managed to find something amusing during our time together.

During a "brave" period, she agreed to go to lunch with us at the Russian Tea Room. We called for her in a taxi in front of her Upper East Side apartment and saw that she was quite elegantly dressed; only a truly astute Garbo-watcher would recognize her that day.

We settled into our red leather booth in the smoking section, since at the time both Garbo and I shared a cigarette habit. Following our delicious luncheon, Garbo and I "lit up." Unfortunately, the *non-smoking* section apparently began at the very next booth, which Garbo was closest to. As we were each midway through a second cigarette, the young man (obviously a strong anti-smoker) seated next to us stood up and prepared to leave. He fixed an angry look at us and said, "I can't take it any more—just who do you think you are, puffing smoke in my face like that?" As he stormed away, Garbo, pleased her "society matron" disguise had worked, chuckled and whispered, "Ja, who do I think I am!"

My last encounter with the "Magnificent One" was ironically in Hollywood, the town she'd turned her back on long ago. Garbo admired Henry Mancini's music and I arranged for her to join Valerie and me in our box at the Hollywood Bowl. She was not in the best of health by then, but looked forward to the evening nonetheless. It was a quiet time and an enjoyable concert, marred only by what happened at one point.

Throughout my association with Garbo I'd managed to keep our meetings a secret. Yet ironically, after all those years, it was at our final meeting that a reporter from one of the tabloids apparently recognized the casually dressed Garbo and chose to report her Bowl attendance in a column a week or two later. The silence had been broken. I assured Garbo it hadn't come from me, and of course she knew that.

Truthfully, at that point, we wondered why we'd bothered to keep things so quiet. She'd begun by being reluctant to have it known she was seeing a psychic, but as time went on, we'd become friends as well, and the psychic world became much more accepted and even quite "fashionable." We agreed it wasn't quite as scandalous as we'd thought it would be, having our association mentioned briefly in a tabloid. At this point, since our silence had been broken, I promised her, and she knew, that if I were ever approached by a reporter again, I'd never say anything unkind, and perhaps that was finally all that mattered.

When Garbo passed away, *People* magazine called and asked me to talk briefly about her for inclusion in a tribute they were doing. I agreed, knowing finally that Garbo wouldn't mind. Of course, following that article there were requests from other magazines and from TV talk shows to discuss her sex life and other private aspects, but I'd made a vow and stuck with it—only *good* would I say about Miss Garbo.

To this day, all I've said or *will* say about The Magnificent Garbo is that she was truly a phenomenon. She was a legend, and I'm honored to have known her. When asked, "But how did she look—didn't she age badly?" I answer, "If you'd seen the Garbo I saw—the sparkle in her eyes, the glow of her skin, and the sense of humor about her life—you'd agree that she had indeed stayed, in the important ways, eternally beautiful."

GRETA GARBO PASSED AWAY FROM HEART AND KID-
NEY FAILURE ON APRIL 15 (EASTER SUNDAY—ONE
OF HER FAVORITE DAYS), 1990, IN MANHATTAN'S
NEW YORK HOSPITAL.

NOW

I received a phone call one day in early 1991 from Tina Smith, Entertainment Director for Sun Line Cruises. She offered me the opportunity to lecture and do my one-man night club performance aboard the largest of Sun Line's three ships, the *Stella Solaris*, during a three-week Caribbean cruise scheduled for April.

The offer sounded delightful, and after coming to terms with Tina businesswise, I readily accepted. I adore being on the high seas, and since I was formulating plans for two books, including this one, I felt it would be a wonderful chance to relax, take time off from telephones and private clients, and begin writing.

Tina sent me a copy of the ship's itinerary, and when it arrived, I glanced down the list of various ports we'd be visiting. Immediately two dates caught my eye—April 14 and 15.

April 14 was meaningful because we'd be calling at Barbados. I'd long wanted to visit the island. Former *Peter Pan* and *South Pacific* star Mary Martin and I had spoken often at dinner parties, where I'd given her psychic messages. We'd also discussed her New York neighbor and my client and friend Greta Garbo, and it was at one of those social gatherings that Miss Martin lovingly told me about her home on Barbados. This was my first exposure to the topic of the island and it intrigued me. She also told me that another distinguished actress, Claudette Colbert, owned property and still spent time there. By the end of the conversation, she made me feel that Barbados was indeed a much talked-about and sought-after location.

Returning from my reminiscence to concentrate on the ship's itinerary again, I saw that we would sail away from Barbados during the evening and see the dawning of April 15 at sea. This was also a significant date, of course, since it was the first anniversary of Garbo's passing. I recalled conversations Garbo and I had where we found we shared a love of the high seas. She'd also told me about a visit she'd made to Barbados in a search for, in her words, "Paradise." She'd spoken of including a neighboring island, Grenada, in her search as well.

The *Stella Solaris's* destination for April 15 just happened to be— Grenada!

It seemed to me these were very strong omens urging me to attempt to make a spirit contact with Miss G during this time. I was certain the combination of ocean travel, Barbados, and Grenada would provide a most conducive atmosphere.

The cruise aboard the luxurious *Stella Solaris* proved to be delightful in every way. When April 14 arrived, my "ghostwriter" Valerie and I were extremely enthusiastic. We decided to hire a limousine to show us around Barbados and found our driver, Ralph, to be most accommodating and very proud of his homeland. We rode awhile, admiring the beautiful greenery, aqua-blue water, and the many sights, including a scaled-down version of England's Trafalgar Square, with a statue in honor of Lord Nelson. As we rode on, I said, "Tell me, Ralph, would you drive us by the homes of the American actresses Mary Martin and Claudette Colbert?" (I asked this for two reasons—one, out of curiosity to see the homes of these ladies, of course, but most importantly because I felt that seeing their homes would continue the omens we'd been building up, and pave the way for our spirit contact with Greta Garbo, which we planned for later that evening).

Ralph, who'd been very talkative beforehand, suddenly became very protective. "Very sorry, sir, but we're awfully private here," he said in his Caribbean but distinctly British accent.

"But you do know Miss Martin used to come here often?" I asked.

"Yes, I do, sir. I've heard she used to live here. But I can't take you to the spot. And about Miss Colbert—her home's too far for us to reach in the time we'll be together. Besides, when she's here in Barbados, she keeps the gates open and you can see the home, but when she's not in residence, the gates are closed and you can't see a thing sir," he concluded.

We were slightly disappointed, but I could tell Ralph either was unable to, or chose *not* to, help us locate the homes, and we still wanted to enjoy the tour of the beautiful island. Our car continued up a hillside, allowing us a magnificent view of the area. We stopped at a posh hotel and wandered around its sprawling grounds before pausing for a cool and refreshing tropical drink while gazing at the ocean.

All too soon, we decided it was time to begin our drive back to the ship. As we rode, Valerie and I again discussed the fact that we were sorry not to have found the two homes, Mary Martin's in particular. Since she was a New York neighbor of Garbo's, we'd hoped seeing the home would be an omen that we had indeed made a good choice in deciding to do a spirit contact with Garbo later.

As we approached the ship, the sky seemed to "open" and release a torrent of rain. It was a tremendous downpour and after thanking the very congenial Ralph we decided to wait under a covered souvenir area until the rain eased and we could continue walking the several hundred yards to the ship. As we browsed through the souvenirs, a taxi arrived and a couple departed. They waved to us (though we didn't know them, we'd passed one another on the ship) and came over to join us. We commented on the rain, whose drops now seemed to be the size of silver dollars, and then the woman said, "We attended your first lecture aboard ship and I wanted to tell you we really enjoyed it. We look forward to your next one." I thanked her and she continued, "Oh, let us introduce ourselves. I'm *Mary* and my husband is *Martin*. So that you don't forget us, when you see us, just think of *Mary Martin!*"

Here was the next omen we'd been waiting for! I told her that all day long, all we'd been *doing* was thinking of Mary Martin! I briefly explained why, and told Mary and her husband of our plans to contact Garbo. They seemed intrigued and wished us well. "I know it will go well," I smiled, "because you were sent to us by spirit as a promise that Garbo would be available to us. Thank you," I grinned. The rain eased as quickly as it had begun, and we parted company from our newfound friends, wondering if our delay at the souvenir stand hadn't been *forced*, by way of rain, so that we could meet Mary and Martin and receive our omen.

We set sail about 9:00 P.M., and later that evening, in fact just before midnight, Valerie and I meditated in the stateroom with a red candle we'd brought with us. We had decided to wait until midnight to begin in earnest—that way we'd have the "best of both worlds"—the end of our Barbados adventure and the beginning of April 15, the anniversary.

We'd extinguished the lights and were sitting in the darkened cabin asking Miss Garbo's spirit to come in. Since it was only her first anniversary of passing into the spirit world, we were prepared for there not to be a lengthy contact and we were also aware that the contact might not be as strong as it would be in the case of a spirit who's been gone a long time and has thus gained strength on the other side. These spirits are better able to make themselves seen and heard because they've rested longer and are more accustomed, perhaps, to returning to Earthplane for a visit. We wanted "Miss G" to know we would be patient and open to any type of contact. Thus I said, "We welcome you, Miss Garbo. You're welcome to come through to us any way you can. We'd love to hear from you or feel your presence."

We waited in silence. "Please come in when you can, Miss Garbo," Valerie coaxed. "Just know that we're here waiting for you."

Again we sat in silence. Suddenly, against one wall of the cabin's living room, we heard a faint knock. "Is that you?" I asked. "If so, you're certainly welcome."

The cabin began growing ice-cold, an unusual feat since it was impossible to open its double picture windows, and the only door led to a hallway. We were essentially "sealed" into the spacious cabin. The cold air felt refreshing because the Caribbean heat had been oppressive since our voyage began. We'd run the air conditioner several times, but naturally turned it off as we began the evening's work. Actually, this type of cold was not typical of an air conditioner—it was stricly the cool, breezy feeling of a spirit's energy coming in, and we were now convinced Greta Garbo was joining us. "We feel your presence," Valerie said, "and you're very welcome."

"Tired," Kenny said faintly. "I'm hearing a sigh and a voice saying, 'Tired'—a whisper in my ear," he continued.

"Is Garbo trying to tell us she's too tired to do this?" Valerie asked.

"No, she's here and she wants to come through," Kenny insisted. "But again she whispers 'Tired.' She says she was very tired when she made the transition to spirit. I'm being shown an image of a grandfather clock, with all the parts worn out, and she says, 'That was me.' She's still tired now—still resting and trying to gain strength."

"Does she seem sad to have passed away?" Valerie asked.

"No, I don't feel a sadness with her," Kenny responded, "I feel that no one in particular was holding her here on Earth. All her friends—Cecil Beaton, Gayelord Hauser, Aristotle Onassis, Noel Coward—were gone before her. Now I hear her say, 'It was time to bid adieu to life'."

"She's enjoying the rest she's getting?" Valerie asked.

"She's resting, yes," Kenny answered, "but she's also showing me a vision of herself out walking among trees and flowers. She says, 'I walk more now.' Now she chuckles and says, 'And no one can stop me from picking flowers here!' "

"Can you find out whether she's with anyone on the other side?" Valerie inquired. "Has she seen any of her friends or does she spend time with any of them regularly?"

"I feel like I want to smile," Kenny said, "and the smile is coming from Garbo. She tells me she's with Gayelord Hauser now. She says 'He's helping me. I was always safe with him, as I was with George Schlee.'"

As Kenny paused for a moment, another cold breeze swirled through the room, causing the candle to flicker and the flame to grow taller. We heard a distinct ping on the glass candleholder, as though someone had struck it with a finger or fingernail.

"She's growing a bit stronger," Kenny said. "I feel she's enjoying this contact and has more to say. Let's ask about George Schlee." (Schlee was the husband of clothing designer Valentina. They were neighbors of Garbo's in New York and Garbo had an affair with George and was in fact with him at the Crillon Hotel in Paris when he passed away, yet she escaped the suite just after he passed, before anyone found them together and before anyone knew he was gone. Valentina refused to speak to Garbo when she learned of the affair, and this continued following her husband's passing. I knew Garbo felt guilty over the entire incident and I held a seance once in her apartment where we were able to bring Schlee back in spirit and ask him to forgive her. But I wondered how they felt *now*—had there been a confrontation in the spirit world?)

"Okay, Miss G," Valerie began. "Can you tell us if you've seen George or Valentina, and are there still hard feelings?"

Kenny cleared his throat and turned his head sideways, as though listening intently. "She says 'Should have known ... '" he asserted.

"What does that mean?" Valerie pursued. "*Who* should have known? Or *what* should they have known?"

Kenny continued, "She says 'I should have known it would end tragically—an involvement with a married man ... unfaithful to his wife ... he could have gone on to be unfaithful to me.' "

Again, Kenny appeared to be listening carefully, then he continued, "She says it was her karma to fall in love with someone she couldn't have. She deeply regrets, even today, leaving him in the hotel, but I hear 'Panicked!' She says Valentina was right in not talking to her, and then she sighs heavily."

"But now—have they resolved their problem?" Valerie persisted.

Kenny smiled. " 'All's forgiven,' she says. She also says the seance in her apartment broke the ice and made it easier to face him in the spirit world."

Kenny reminisced for a moment, recalling another seance he'd held with Garbo, where they attempted to contact Charles Boyer, a Garbo co-star whose supposed suicide had upset Garbo. He said they were unable to contact Boyer, but were able to receive messages through his beloved wife, who had passed from cancer. She'd told Kenny that Boyer had been very distraught and lonely—deeply lonely, since losing her and their son Michael, who'd lost his life by gunshot, playing Russian roulette. Mrs. Boyer told Kenny that her husband overdosed on barbituates because he temporarily lost his mind, but it couldn't be called a classic suicide.

He continued by remembering that this had pacified Garbo slightly, but she still worried about Boyer's spirit, and it seemed appropriate to ask her if she'd located him yet, or been told anything about him, in Paradise.

" 'No talking yet' she tells me," Kenny began. "She shows me him lying down, resting. He's just barely able to wake up now and then. It's like a very deep, deep sleep. She's gone to see him and has sat by his side once or twice, but there's no response yet."

Valerie asked if this was normal after so much time (Boyer passed in 1978). "It certainly can be," Kenny answered. "There's no time in the spirit world, so the year someone passed is relatively unimportant. It's an individual process of waking up and progressing. But overdoses, whether suicidal or not, usually take a very long time to adjust. After all, it was not that person's time to go—they tampered with nature and the Master's will and plan for them. Their presence in the spirit world is unplanned—like trying to get into a posh restaurant without a reservation. So the spirit is in limbo, or deep rest, until the timing is right."

"Back to Miss G now," Valerie said. "Is she still with us?" As if in response, a rap was heard near the television set.

"I take it she's still here!" Valerie said. "Any significance to the television set?"

Kenny smiled. "She's reminding me about 'La Belle' Paul Lynde, and how she loved watching *Hollywood Squares*." She says she saw Joan Rivers sitting in Lynde's square on the show after Lynde passed, and she learned to enjoy Joan."

Kenny smiled again and Valerie asked why. "I just hear the word 'gossip,'" he said. "Whenever I saw Miss G on Earthplane, she wanted to know the latest gossip about everyone in show business and now she says 'Joan Rivers . . . good gossip . . . I love it!' I feel Garbo will be paying a visit to Joan Rivers now and then when she's a bit more rested. Joan might watch out for her, because Garbo will be around!"

Valerie swallowed somewhat nervously and said, "I know this might be difficult for her to talk about yet, but can Garbo tell us why she left Hollywood, or if she regrets doing it? And why did she become so distant from so many people?"

Kenny continued the questioning, acting as an interpreter in a sense. "Can you tell us, Miss G—are you sorry you were such a recluse?" He then paused and listened, then shook his head. "She says, 'No'—she doesn't regret that she left films. She says, 'Remember what you told me . . . I had to get away.' "

"Do you know what she means?" Valerie questioned.

"Do you mean the illnesses?" Kenny asked of Garbo.

In answer, the wall cracked twice. "Ah! That's a definite yes," Kenny said. "I'd discussed this with her many times, and though we tried to work on it she constantly battled it," he began explaining. "In fact," he continued, "she's showing me an airplane and her sitting in it, with a vacant seat next to her, and she reminds me that she often chose to travel that way. She felt she *had* to."

"What? What are you talking about?" Valerie sounded puzzled.

"You know how fearful of crowds she was at times," Kenny said, and Valerie agreed she'd seen this on a couple of occasions—a look of terror could cross Garbo's face if a person approached too closely.

"Greta Garbo suffered from claustrophobia *and* agoraphobia," Kenny revealed. "It took me a long time to convince her of this, but she'd sometimes feel totally claustrophobic indoors, as though the walls were closing in on her, and she'd *have* to get out and walk. Yet at other times, when she *did* get out, she was terrified—she panicked and literally froze at the sight of people. It wasn't that she didn't *want* to talk—she simply couldn't."

"So was that the main reason she left show business—to avoid having to deal with people?" Valerie asked.

"She couldn't deal with people, and particularly with the idea of having to report to a film studio on a particular day, whether she felt capable of it or not," Kenny responded.

"But she said she's walking now and seeing people. Is she coming out of these problems at last?" Valerie asked hopefully.

"She is," was Kenny's answer. He smiled and said, "She also tells me she doesn't have to wear 'those kooky clothes' now. She says she looks back and laughs at how she dressed—dark glasses, floppy hat, baggy clothes. 'They thought I was trying to hide when I did that,' she laughs. 'But secretly I wanted people to whisper, 'That's Garbo! There goes Garbo!' They sought me out more when I left films—I became a bigger star! I wanted them to see me, but just not get close to me.' "

The candle flame seemed to get smaller, nearly flickering out, and the room temperature rose considerably. We sensed that perhaps Garbo was growing weary from this, her first spirit contact.

"I know you're getting tired, Miss G," Kenny said, "and we don't want to overtax you. Do you have any last words to say to us?"

Kenny put his hand to his forehead and eyes and said, "She's showing me the hospital where she passed. I feel gratitude on her behalf. She's showing me a newspaper now, which quoted the hospital as saying, 'It is with deep regret that we announce the passing of Greta Garbo.' I see that sentence before me, and Garbo says, 'How nice . . . nice compliment. Not 'fallen star' or 'recluse,' but they 'regretted' . . . nice.' That touched her," Kenny continued.

Again he held his hand to his forehead and said, "Now she's showing me a stack of newspapers and magazines, from many different years, and she says, 'Thank you . . . to the press.' "

"Thank you for what?" Valerie asked.

"She says 'for keeping my memory alive . . . then and now. Thank you . . . thank you.' "

Then there was silence.

"She's leaving us," Kenny stated definitely. "Thank you, Miss G," he called out.

"Thank you—come again," Valerie joined in.

Kenny and Valerie together blew out the red candle, got the smoke in the palms of their hands, and Kenny said quietly, "Rest well now, Miss G."

BETTE DAVIS

THEN

I never had the pleasure of meeting Bette Davis, but was near her on what were, for me, two memorable occasions.

While living in San Francisco, I became friends with many celebrated stage and screen stars through our mutual appearances on radio and television. A good number of them later became my clients, as well, and we also met at dinner and cocktail parties.

One of my favorite people at the time was the fine actor Hugh Marlowe. We had talked at a party one night, and Hugh told me he was working on a new film called *All About Eve*, which was shooting on location in San Francisco. He told me the film starred Bette Davis, Anne Baxter, Gary Merrill and Celeste Holm and that he was very pleased to be a part of it.

"Say, I'm not on call tomorrow," he said, "but how would you like to have lunch and then go over to the Curran Theater"—which was posing, for purposes of the film, as a theater on New York's Broadway—"to watch Bette Davis work?" He'd heard me say before that I'd admired Miss Davis's work since I'd been a child, and as I'm sure he suspected I would, I quickly said "yes" to the opportunity of watching her at work.

Following our lunch the next day, we arrived at the Curran and sat in the tenth row of the theater, which was empty except for cast and crew.

Soon Miss Davis walked out onstage, followed by Gary Merrill. During a final few moments of their rehearsal of their lines, I gathered that, in the scene to be filmed, Merrill's character of Bill Sampson would tell Davis's character of Margo Channing to, in essence, "pull herself together," to be strong and not let anything bother her or interfere with her career goals.

The director, Joseph Manciewicz, was seated in the front row. He yelled "Action!" and filming of the scene began. Manciewicz soon yelled "Cut!," however, because he had seen the sound man shaking his head and waving his hand—the classic pantomime for "No!" Manciewicz asked what was wrong and was told that the sound man had picked up the street cars clanging by outside on Geary Street. This was a normal and expected sound for San Francisco, but highly unlikely in New York, where, after all, the scene was supposedly taking place.

Several more takes, in fact about two to three hour's worth, were interrupted for much the same reason—sound or technical problems. The sound man would shake his head and wave his hands, indicating that yet again he'd picked up noise—sometimes at the beginning of the scene, sometimes not until the end.

Finally, the scene was completed and seemed wonderful, at least to *my* eyes and ears. Miss Davis was accustomed by now to glancing at the sound man when she *did* finish the scene, to check on the status of the situation. At last, he nodded and gave the "OK" sign with his hand. With a sigh of relief, Davis started to leave the stage. Mr. Manciewicz asked, "Where are you going?" She said she intended to smoke a cigarette in the box seat area on one side of the theater, where at this point, a woman, whom I understood to be her mother Ruthie, was seated.

"Excuse me, but we'll do the scene again," Manciewicz told her. "Why?" she asked, to which he replied, "Because I have never seen a worse performance by an actress!"

Davis, who'd been standing with her weight shifted to one foot and the other foot dangling, lifted that foot, jerked it, and sent the shoe flying across the stage. "An actress is only as good as her director, Mr. Manciewicz," she haughtily replied. There was an icy silence for a moment, then Manciewicz turned his attention to the technical people, asking them to reposition their cameras, props, etc. for another take. Davis stalked to the box seat, picked up a pack of cigarettes and lit one, furiously smoking and puffing in silence.

There was tension in the air, yet surprisingly, when the director concluded the technical adjustments and announced "Places," calling Davis and Merrill back to the stage, Davis returned without a word, to resume working.

The next take of the scene was breathtaking. This time, after checking with the technical people, Mr. Manciewicz said, as though no previous harsh words had been exchanged, "Bette—that was just marvelous!" to which she replied, "Why, thank you, Darling!"

Shooting was called to a halt for the day, and thus ended my first and, as it turned out, only chance to see this magnificent actress at work in the flesh.

Several years later, on a visit to Las Vegas in the late 1950s, I entered one of the more elegant hotel/casinos and took a brief stroll through the lobby and into the gaming area.

As I stood watching the flurry of activity, I came across comedian Ben Blue, who was also "drinking in" the energy-charged atmosphere. I'd never met him, but walked over to introduce myself. We spoke a few moments and then we were both drawn to the sight of a blonde woman seated at a gaming table. She was wearing enormous dark glasses, yet the glasses did not hide the fragile skin or strong features of her face. She was feverishly puffing on a cigarette. Ben and I looked at each other and said, almost simultaneously, "That *has* to be Bette Davis!" I'd only seen her previously in San Francisco, but of course her screen image was etched in my mind.

Ben and I walked closer to the table and saw that a casino guard was keeping people at a distance. I stepped up to the guard and said, "Excuse me, but is that ... " "NO, it isn't!" he snapped, cutting me off.

I wasn't convinced and said to Ben, who was watching from a few feet behind, "*You* go ask him!" He stepped up next and said to the guard, "Sir, I just wanted to know, isn't that woman ... " "NO!" the guard again interrupted.

Apparently two "no's" convinced Ben, because he seemed ready to concede we'd made a mistake. I, however, became more sure than ever; there was no mistaking the presence of Bette Davis. "It *is* Bette Davis!" I said, "There's no one else quite like her!" "Alright," he said, "I'll bet you breakfast tomorrow that you're wrong. But here's what you can do to find out for sure. Let's go back to the lobby. Then you'll get a brochure and envelope from the hotel desk clerk. You'll put the brochure into the envelope so that it appears full.

"Now, then, you wouldn't want to write 'Bette Davis' on the envelope because they might think it was from a fan and try to protect her. So you'll mark the envelope 'Personal—to Mrs. Gary Merrill'." The romance which began on the *All About Eve* set had progressed and by now she was married to Merrill. "If the hotel clerk doesn't recognize the name or says there's no one registered like that, then you're wrong, my friend."

After I did as he suggested, we went back to the desk and I gave the envelope to the clerk. She looked at the envelope, smiled, then said, "Thank you—I'll see that she gets it," and put it in the mail and message slot for one of the guest rooms!

Ben shook my hand and said, "You've got yourself a breakfast." However, I told him it was unnecessary. Breakfast seemed anticlimactic to the *real* prize—I'd once again come face-to- face with the great legend and magnetism of Bette Davis.

From that point on, I had to be content, as the rest of the world was, with seeing her on the silver screen; but my two encounters will be etched in my memory forever.

> BETTE DAVIS SUCCUMBED TO CANCER ON OCTOBER 6, 1989, IN THE AMERICAN HOSPITAL IN PARIS, AFTER BEING HONORED IN SPAIN AT THE SAN SEBASTIAN FILM FESTIVAL.

NOW

My co-author Valerie and I drove down the Southern California coast one day to Laguna Beach, a little over an hour's drive from Los Angeles. Our intention was to attend their renowned art festival, but as we reached the area, I felt surrounded by the spirit presence of Bette Davis, whom I knew had been a longtime resident of the area. I sensed this would be an excellent opportunity and location to make contact with her.

I saw a real estate office just ahead and felt an overwhelming desire to go inside. Since I try, at all times, to follow these psychic instincts, I drove up a hill to the side of the building, where I saw their parking lot. I pulled into a parking space and walked back down the hill to the office—located in a very quaint and cozy villagelike section of town. There were art galleries, coffee houses, and tiny craft shops everywhere and the feeling of energy and creativity seemed to further convince me somehow that I would soon be in communication with the spirit of Bette Davis—a very creative and energetic lady.

We walked into the office and were approached by a blonde female who introduced herself as a broker and asked if she could be of help. "Yes," I said, and then, surprising even myself, I asked, "Is the former Bette Davis property for sale?"

She drew in a quick breath and stared wide-eyed for a moment. "Well ... yes, it *is* for sale," she said slowly, "but it *just* came on the market— we just received word on it today. How did *you* know about it?" she asked.

I suggested we go to a more private place in the office and then explained my psychic impression of the actress's presence. The broker told me she understood very well about the psychic world and now remembered having seen me on several talk shows. "The home is on the market for $6.9 million plus." She smiled, "are you interested in seeing it?"

Of course I *was* interested in seeing the home, though I had my own special reasons for wanting to do so—I knew a visit to her former home would bring me even closer to Bette Davis's spirit, which had already begun making itself known to me as I entered the town she once loved.

The broker said she would set up an appointment and excused herself to make a phone call. She returned smiling, saying she'd made an appointment within the next hour.

I asked to drive by one or two other properties in the meantime, since I did feel a strong "pull" toward Laguna Beach and felt that perhaps I would truly enjoy making a move to the area at some point in time—although at considerably less than $6.9 million!

We left the office and drove by several properties. We then entered the famed Woods Cove area, which is very reminiscent of the New England states—quiet, peaceful, tree-lined, and filled with cottagelike homes of all sizes.

The broker said, "There is a smaller home in this area which was also associated with Bette Davis; in fact, I believe her mother lived there. It's not for sale, but would you like to drive by it?" My answer, naturally, was yes, and we drove to the home, a typical New England cottage in design, with lovely wooden shingles with white trim, a thatched roof, and a tremendous amount of greenery.

I left the car and walked up a brick pathway onto the property. I sensed Miss Davis slightly, but also felt the presence of another female even stronger.

An encounter with a spirit occasionally leads me to a spot where perhaps the average person might not go, and I found myself walking up the brick stairway onto the front porch, admiring some straight-back white wooden chairs placed near a window. As I gazed up, looking *out* of the window was a sandy-haired man in his late thirties or early forties, staring at me! He moved to the door, opened it, and stepped outside. "May I help you?" he asked, a very gentle question considering I was standing on what was apparently *his* property!

I quickly explained the situation and hoped that he was interested in the psychic world and open to what I was saying, as I explained that I was pursuing the spirits of Bette Davis and her mother.

To my delight, he smiled and said, "That's fascinating! I've admired Bette Davis for years and yes, this was her mother Ruthie's home."

I walked back to touch one of the chairs again, attempting to pick up a psychic impressions from it, yet I didn't sense any connection to the legendary actress while touching the chair.

"No," he said, "those belonged to Cecil B. DeMille"—famed director of such films as *The Ten Commandments* and *The Greatest Show on Earth*. He continued, "I used to live near the DeMille mansion in Los Angeles, and I acquired the chairs while living there."

"Then you must have known Lily Tomlin," I said, as we strolled into the country-lane gardens behind the home. "Lily has lived near the DeMille estate for many years," I told him. He smiled broadly and said, "Oh, I know! She was my neighbor and is still a dear friend."

I explained how I had first met Lily when she invited me backstage in New York after seeing her tour de force, one-woman show in *The Search for Signs of Intelligent Life in the Universe.* I brought in several spirits to her that evening, including the petite Russian character actress Madame Maria Ouspenskaya, who told Lily she would win the Tony Award (which of course she subsequently did).

The talk about our mutual friend Lily and our combined interest in the psychic world completely broke the ice and he graciously invited the three of us—the broker, my co-author, and myself—in to see his home.

The tie to Bette Davis was definitely present as we toured the cozy cottage with its wood interior accents, but not as strong as I'd hoped, perhaps because the home had not been hers but her mother's. Her mother Ruthie, as I understood it, had been such a strong woman in her own right that even though her daughter Bette had spent time in the home, it was only natural Ruthie's spirit would be stronger in her own former home.

I was anxious to view the larger residence the screen great *did* call home, and after hearing that he'd long been a Davis admirer, I invited my newfound friend to join us, to his apparent delight.

We got into the car and drove the brief distance to the oceanfront Bette Davis home, still located in Woods Cove. There was a large white adobe wall and massive wooden door in front of the mammoth estate, yet many exterior touches were reminiscent of the small home we'd just left—a brick pathway, thatched roofing, and greenery, still giving the hint of a New England or Cape Cod style of architecture.

I stood for a moment and touched the door, feeling enveloped by a warmth and love. I knew many happy hours had been spent by Miss Davis in this home. I made a silent request of her that she make herself known to us, so that I could convey her thoughts and feelings to her fans.

Since I was eager to pick up Bette Davis's spirit in the home and knew a quiet atmosphere would be best for this, I suggested to my co-author that we attempt to stray from the others in the party as often as possible while walking through the residence.

We all stood together now at the door and rang the bell. The listing broker greeted us and led us into a lush open courtyard with a fish pond.

We then entered the home, passing from the parlor into the living room. The interior of the home continued the white adobe look of the outside wall, with the addition of beautifully-textured dark wood paneling and woodwork.

The living room had an almost British feeling, due in part, I'm sure, to the furnishings belonging to the current occupants—dark-colored fabrics and chairs and tables in dark wood.

Approaching the center of the living room, I began to feel a cool breeze. It was very slight at first, as though someone had walked quickly by, though I turned and noticed everyone behind me standing in place.

As the others moved on to another room and I was left with Valerie, I once again felt a cold sensation—stronger this time and more like a gust of wind.

I felt an excitement, as though someone wanted to "show off" this magnificent mansion, and I knew that someone was Bette Davis.

The other members of the group talked in the kitchen while Valerie and I remained in the living room. We quietly—*very* quietly—spoke aloud, asking Miss Davis to guide us through her home and give us any messages she desired.

I touched one of the windowpanes, then the woodwork, and then stood still. Within seconds I felt a faint touch on my arm and felt a slight weakness throughout my body. It occurred to me that since she had not passed too terribly long before (just under a year earlier at this point) and since she had been so ill prior to passing, Miss Davis might very likely be unable to make full contact by way of materialization to me (where I could fully see her before me and hear her speaking). It was also possible that she might find it difficult to communicate at first if she were fairly new at working with a psychic or medium. These things do take practice, and a spirit gets better as the communication progresses.

I spoke quietly again and suggested that she speak when she was able and send thought vibrations to me when that was comfortable. (Spirits adapt to thought transference rather quickly on the other side and are often able to carry on entire "conversations" with one another without ever opening their mouths—they just "sense" the thoughts being sent, if they choose to do so telepathically).

On this plane, we might be inclined to call it "mind reading," but that is more of a magic act. In the spirit world it is a natural and mutual method of communication, not merely a way of "guessing" a driver's license or birthdate, as is done here by mentalists or magicians.

I hoped that the actress's spirit was adjusted enough to the other side that she could respond to me either by this method of sending thoughts, or by actually speaking to me, and was rewarded after quietly asking my first question: "Are you with us, Miss Davis? Am I correct that you're still a bit weak?"

Immediately I heard a very faint, "Yes . . . here . . . weak . . . " in my left ear, followed by another featherlight touch on my arm. Valerie and I welcomed her spirit and said we were enjoying her home immensely.

My new broker called us into the kitchen just then and we walked to our left and found our way into that area. The kitchen again contained much wood and a built-in wooden eating area with benches and cushions.

Our new friend, who lives in Ruthie's house, came over to me and said excitedly, "You felt her in the living room, didn't you?"

I told him I *had* and he said, "I knew it! I think I felt something too— almost a familiar feeling. Maybe she's been in my home in spirit, too, and I'm a little accustomed to her!"

He then joined the two brokers again as they walked on toward a few stairs leading back to the entry hall. Valerie and I again felt the presence in the kitchen, and I asked Bette: "Tell us about when you passed. Who greeted you when you entered the spirit world?"

She again spoke in my ear, barely a whisper at first, "When I was asked to go to Spain . . . I felt I wouldn't return here . . . didn't even want to tell dear Kathryn (her loyal assistant and friend). Suspected something . . . less energy . . . 'hunch' told me I would not come back home. Now I wish I'd . . . written it down . . . they'd be saying 'Bette Davis must have been psychic!' "

This was the first spark of energy and humor I'd sensed in her, and I hoped it meant she was finding it easier to communicate with me now. "Ruthie . . . " I heard. "She greeted me . . . It was so, so good to see her again!" she said, choking with happiness. "We live together now . . . like it was in the early days."

Valerie was curious. "Ask what type of home they live in," she prompted. I did so, and heard a gentle laugh. "Tell the curious one it looks more like a hut," she said. An image flashed before my eyes and I realized she was placing the vision there. I saw an adobe-style building, yet the material it was made of seemed to be a light-colored silk or rayon, like a parachute material. There was an opening like a door, only again it was made of a lightweight fabric.

I had been told much earlier by my spirit guides who communicate with me regularly that residences in the spirit world are not as we think of them here. The fabric covering had been mentioned by my guides, as well, and they'd told me it was mainly to give the bare necessity of privacy—voices are not quite so detectable and spirits may do as they please without anyone viewing them. The need for privacy still exists in the spirit world, yet it is not privacy as protection against a curiosity about viewing the human flesh, sexual activity, or bodily functions. There is no existence of these elements in Paradise. This privacy merely allows spirits to speak, study, or sit quietly without any outside distractions. It is a carryover of a need from Earthplane.

My beautiful vision was interrupted by Miss Davis's voice once again—stronger and more distinct this time: "One other thing we carry over is any craving we had on Earth!"

I asked what she meant and she spat out, "Cigarettes! How I loved smoking! Thought it made me more sophisticated when I first began, then I couldn't seem to stop. But it's UTTER HELL losing the craving now! No one does anything in excess here—it takes some getting used to!"

I heard a hearty laugh and she continued, "Tallulah Bankhead and I had our differences when we had our careers in force. She always thought I purposely did roles she'd already done. The first thing I had to do when I spoke to Miss Tallulah Bankhead here was to establish that *All About Eve* was *not* her life story. I know she always felt *I* had done *her* life story. How ridiculous! The film was based on the life of that marvelous stage actress named Irene Worth. Once I set that matter straight with her, I think she finally accepted me as an actress—aren't I lucky?

"But we have finally reconciled, and believe it or not, she's actually helping me! She smoked one hundred and ten cigarettes a day in her time—she's certainly learned enough about losing the urge to smoke to teach me!"

I wondered silently how the two were accomplishing this goal, and the thought entered my mind, "We sit quietly and reflect—you might call it meditating. We also take long walks together and she drills me over and over again that smoking isn't part of me anymore."

I realized we were now thought-communicating, which would be very helpful in eliminating any curiosity from the others as we then joined them and moved on to other rooms in the multi-leveled home.

We climbed stairs to one of the large bedrooms. It was most unusual, having been built with one section actually open and overlooking the living room below. I wondered at the lack of privacy in a room in a mansion such as this.

I then noticed another oddity—the current owners had hung paintings literally from floor to ceiling, and I drew the attention of the others to this attractive but highly unusual decorating touch. In a moment a thought struck me, in the form of a female voice; "Yes, I liked paintings, too, but this is a little 'much,' isn't it? And in one of my bedrooms at that!"

The five of us, and of course Miss Davis's spirit, stayed in the bedroom talking for a moment before moving on. I heard her voice tell me, "I'll be back when you get downstairs. Go to the game room." Without realizing what I was doing, I asked the listing broker to show me the game room downstairs. He looked strangely at me, totally unaware that a spirit was guiding me and wondering how I knew so much about the home's floor plan, having never been there before. "Yes, there *is* a game room downstairs," he said. "Follow me."

We arrived at the downstairs level and I felt the strongest sense of Bette Davis so far. "Tell them there's an original toilet seat which was placed down here, in a storage area near the wine cellar," she whispered in my ear. Again, since I was feeling increasingly directed by spirit, I spoke without censoring my words, mentioning the toilet seat. I received curious looks all around.

"I'm not aware of a toilet seat, but there is a wine cellar," the broker answered. I heard a hearty laugh echo in my ears and knew the actress was enjoying herself while revealing these "secrets."

The others wandered onto the deck overlooking the breathtakingly blue Pacific Ocean, and again Valerie and I lagged behind, this time still in the game room.

As we stood near the pool table, the area became icy cold. The cold permeated every bone—swirling around us from head to toe. At the same time, I heard a buzzing in my right ear. The buzzing grew stronger and then became the sound of a loud female sigh. I sensed the talented actress had more to say.

Soon she spoke into my ear. "Do you know who else I've seen? Absolutely my favorite actor and co-star, Mr. Claude Rains. Isn't it wonderful that we can see our dear friends again? He'd been here long enough before me that he was well adjusted, and once, soon after I arrived here, I was sitting with my eyes closed, resting. When I opened my eyes, he was standing next to me holding my hand! Such a dear man and such a comfort!

"We didn't speak much that time, because I was so tired. But we've had a chance to speak since and I told him I think we should do a scene from *Mr. Skeffington* for an audience over here. Wouldn't it be marvelous? I'm sure neither of us have lost our touch, and there's still great interest in entertainment here, not only by the show business community but by many others as well.

"Do you know," the voice continued, "there's one man today who's capable of the magnetism of Claude Rains, and that's Burt Reynolds. He's terribly underrated and such a talent. He's also got the sex appeal of Clark Gable. He may not be as 'pretty' anymore, but he's wearing well with age, like fine wine. And the older he gets, the better he'll become, if those in power at the studios will just realize it. This man reeks of the leading man qualities and would also do *so* well onstage.

The icy chill left the area where I stood and it appeared to me that the great legend had temporarily stopped the contact.

I walked onto the large deck and gazed at the wide expanse of the ocean. As I reached the deck's railing, I felt an urge to look upward and back. There, atop the chimney, was a huge *D* in black script.

As I looked at the *D*, a faint whisper in my ear said, "Tired now ... come back tonight ... outside. There's more ... oh, indeed, there's more."

Knowing the contact was ended for now, I suggested to my broker that we could leave any time. We soon did so, passing a stained glass door along the way. The design was in rich Earth tones of yellow, brown, orange, and red, with a large crest of another *D*, this time with a crown atop it. I was told by the broker that this had been a fond reminder of Davis's film *Elizabeth and Essex* in which she played the Queen.

Valerie and I returned after dark to the tree-lined street, and parked near the wall surrounding the actress's former home. While in the car, we briefly meditated, asking Miss Davis's spirit to return and continue our contact. We then left the car and walked over to the wall.

We waited quietly, watching and listening for any sight or sound which could mean the strong-willed legend had come back again. The night was still and for a moment there was no sound at all.

"Please come in, Miss Davis," we called in a whisper, "you're welcome to come in."

Again there was silence. Gradually I sensed a buzzing in my right ear. It became more pronounced, and began sounding like the roar of an ocean. In the midst of this sound I detected a faint whisper. "Yes, here we are again." I welcomed the familiar voice of Bette Davis and said, "Do you have anything else you'd particularly like to share with us? Perhaps something about your daughter B.D.? How do you feel about her now?" (I wondered if she had forgiven her daughter for the accusations made in B.D.'s book, *My Mother's Keeper*).

Suddenly the weakness in her voice was gone and she boomed strongly, "I discussed it all before, when the questions came up. I can't forgive and I can't forget," she cried in my ear. And then, putting an end to the discussion, she added, "True friends won't bring it up anymore, so please, I don't wish to discuss it."

"What, or whom, *would* you like to discuss?" I asked.

I heard a happy sigh and then, "Someone *worth* discussing," she said, "Miss Greta Garbo. I never had a chance to meet her in Hollywood or New York, but I always wanted to—she fascinated me. Now that she's here, I'll go pay her a visit one day. She may still be resting and not able to talk, but at least I'll *see* her, and then wait until we're both more rested before we have a lengthy talk. I'm determined to finally know that woman!" she told me excitedly.

I couldn't resist asking if Bette had seen her former co-star and one-time assumed arch rival, Joan Crawford. "Ha!" was the haughty response I heard, followed by "That one! It's still uneasy between us. She's embarrassed by the advances she made toward me on the *Baby Jane* set, because she's dropped those tendencies now. She always had a rather absurd approach to lovemaking. She told me she wrote in appointments for it the same way she did her doctor's appointments or hairstyling appointments!

"Let's say it's 'uncomfortable' between us. Of *course*, there was rivalry. She used to call herself a 'handsome personality.' Now that may well be true. But if you want to count Oscars, you know which of us was the real actress."

I asked her what, besides hard work, was the secret to her success. One word rang out in my ear: "Support!" she said. "What does that mean?" I asked. "Dear Ruthie," she continued. "She gave me such loving support and helped promote me. I've been forever grateful for that.

"Having a family stand behind you can make all the difference. One young man I've been watching who has that today is Ron Howard. When he directed me in a television picture years ago (*Skyward*) I couldn't believe such a young man could be capable of it, but he carried it off and has improved ever since. His parents have been in full support of him all along, like my Ruthie was.

"He could never have directed the likes of me so early on in his career, or later on Don Ameche and Hume Cronyn, in *Cocoon*, if he weren't capable. Of course, he was never a child, was he? He was always a little old man, serious and earnest, even when he was chronologically a young boy."

Valerie asked me to ask Miss Davis if there were other stars she'd like to discuss. I heard a laugh, and then her words; "There are so few stars to talk about, in my opinion. It's a dreadful crime that the entertainment world doesn't produce stars anymore. There are good actors, but they're overshadowed by directors, the material—the actors get lost and get lazy."

"Any examples?" I asked.

"Kathleen Turner" was the answer. "She should have done much better on Broadway with *Cat on a Hot Tin Roof*. Why, she could have won the Tony Award! The role was certainly meaty enough, but I feel Miss Turner was lazy after having done films. She didn't have enough technique to carry the role onstage. She didn't *command* the stage. To be a star, one has to work damned hard and never take anything for granted. That's what I did, and I wasn't surprised when I became a star.

"Real stars are enduring. The dilettantes disappear soon enough," she laughed. "You know, there's one particular actress I was unfortunate enough to work with whose career and personal life are shaky. The world would be absolutely shocked to learn that she takes—can you believe it—cocaine suppositories? You'd never suspect her—what a waste. Not so much of talent or professionalism, which I always found negligible in her, but it's a waste of a human life, which is very precious."

For the next few moments, I called out names of various celebrities she'd known or worked with, and asked Miss Davis if she had comments about them. The following were her responses:

James Woods: "I'm so grateful to him for the photo he shot of me, which was later used on the cover of my book *This 'n' That*. Since he's an actor by trade, some may call him an amateur photographer—but what an amateur!"

Dorian Harewood: "Such a hard worker and underrated as an actor. I recognized this young man's talent when he was a young boy working with me in *Miss Moffat* on Broadway. He'll reach great heights—if he does not become impatient."

Robert Wagner: "Dear Natalie Wood will talk to you herself someday. She's such a lovely person—such a delight. She was a young child when I first met and worked with her. I became so fond of R.J. (Wagner), too.

"I've heard of his marriage to Jill St. John. Natalie has, too, and she's very upset. I feel Miss St. John is very wrong for R.J. I don't see him spending the rest of his life with her—he's got too much class."

Kathryn Sermak (her loyal assistant and friend, who was with her at her passing): "God sent Kathryn to me at the exact moment when I needed her. Some people felt Kathryn took advantage of me in some way—NOT TRUE! She gave me the strength to go on. I'm sure she was tired at times, yet she gave me energy just being around me.

"I'd like to see my life story done, and they couldn't find a better or more honest person to assist with the script and the filming than Kathryn. I leave it to her to see that they properly cast my role. Kathryn, dear—consider Carol Kane. She's unusual enough to play me and it would skyrocket her to movie stardom forever."

The last few words were most confusing and seemed to be coming from a tunnel: "I'm waiting for Frank," she whispered. "He'll be here before long." Before I could ask for an explanation, I sensed Miss Davis's spirit was drifting farther away.

I listened for a moment, for any additional words or sounds, but the air seemed still and empty. On this rather mysterious note, our time with Bette Davis drew to a close.

THE POLITICAL WORLD

★ ★ ★ ★ ★

PRESIDENT HARRY S. TRUMAN

THEN

Though people are always intrigued to hear stories about my many celebrity clients past and present, they are perhaps most impressed by one particular client's name: Harry S. Truman.

Invariably, when I guest on radio or television, no matter how much time is spent talking about Marilyn Monroe, Mae West, or Greta Garbo, the interviewer always gets around to asking, "But you've read for two U.S. Presidents, too, haven't you—Eisenhower and Truman?," they'll say reverently.

And certainly, when I give thought to it, I am equally impressed at having given these two great men psychic readings. Yet, in both cases, and in Mr. Truman's especially, the men were so likeable, and the situations happened so quickly and easily, that it *is* only in looking back that it dawns on me what experiences I've really had.

In the case of Truman, my first meeting with him came when I was a very young man, living in San Francisco. My friend, drama coach Reginald Travers, and I had separate but fascinating career goals, and shared office space while pursuing these goals. Through the courtesy of Ben Swig, onetime head of San Francisco's posh Fairmont Hotel, Reggie and I were given space in the hotel and called it the Player's Club. Reggie produced plays on the area's stage, while I used the space, at alternate times, as a gathering place for spiritualists, giving readings and holding seances there.

One afternoon while in our small office I heard that then-President Truman was going to be briefly staying at the Fairmont while campaigning for election (he'd been first elected Vice President, then became President when F.D.R. passed in 1945, thus this was his first run for the presidency) and a motorcade, going through the heart of the city along Grant Avenue, was planned for that very day.

Suddenly it seemed very important and exciting to me to go and see the President along the motorcade route, and I left my office immediately.

Naturally, a huge throng of people had had a similar idea and the crowds were enormous, but I found a spot that wasn't too heavily populated, quickly jostled for a place and waited. Before long, several cars, including the President's, proceeded along Grant Avenue, passing my section of the crowd. I was able to glimpse Truman waving as he progressed in his open car. About a block past me, the motorcade came to a halt and I watched with interest. A figure I assumed was Truman got out and went into the crowd to shake hands with someone. (That night on the news, it was revealed that President Truman indeed had a habit of doing this, much to the dismay of the Secret Service. This particular day the motorcade had passed an Oriental restaurant Truman had frequented before and Truman recognized the owner, who was standing outside. Truman went over to shake the man's hand—and make reservations for dinner that evening!)

After watching Truman leave the restaurant owner and get back into his car, I heard a voice tell me, "You've got an omen that he'll definitely be elected—turn around." I turned to look behind me and saw that through all my jostling amongst people, I had ended up in front of a department store aptly named the White House!

Following its glimpse of the campaigning President, the crowd disbursed and I returned to my office. It was assumed that Truman also returned to Nob Hill, to his quarters at the Fairmont, to await further engagements later in the day.

About two hours later, the telephone in my office rang and one of the many performers or technical people who frequently spent time at our space at the club answered the phone and called out to me, "Kenny, it's Ben Swig." I immediately went to the phone and Swig asked me how long I'd be in my office. "Oh, quite some time today," I told him. "Good," he said. "I just wanted to make sure." Curious, I asked why. "Oh, someone's going to call you," he said evasively, "and they particularly want to call you themselves, but I wanted to be certain they'd be able to reach you." With this, he hung up.

No more than fifteen to twenty minutes later, someone again called me to the phone, but in a most unusual tone of voice. "Kenny," they said disbelievingly, "*this* person says he's the President of the United States." Thinking someone was indeed trying to have some fun with me, I went to the phone on a lark and said hello.

I heard, "Harry Truman here. I want to talk to the spirits."

"Sure you do," I thought to myself, wondering which of my friends was doing what seemed to be a very good impersonation, but I simply said okay into the receiver. "So how does one go about that? When could we make it?" the voice continued.

Marveling at the person's persistence and their ability to keep from laughing, I said, "Well, immediately, if you want." In this split second it seemed a thousand thoughts crossed my mind—Truman *was* staying at the hotel, and Ben Swig *had* said to expect a phone call. *Had* Swig spoken to the President—had they somehow, incredibly, mentioned the spirit world and then gotten around to briefly discussing *my* activities at the hotel? Could this be happening?

When I'd concluded, fighting my way through this haze of thoughts, I realized the voice on the phone was saying, very seriously, "Right away would be fine ... I'll send someone down to escort you up to my suite."

The next sound I heard was the person hanging up their phone. "This must be legitimate!" I suddenly realized, and before I had time to do or think much of anything else, two men appeared at my door wearing earphones and quickly surveyed my office. "We're ready to go to the President," one of them said, and the next thing I knew I was being propelled into the hallway and inside the elevator.

When we arrived at the designated floor, the elevator doors opened and I saw more men in the hallway, all looking somewhat the same—same type of suit, same earphones. They briefly scrutinized me as the two who'd come for me brought me toward a suite and knocked on the door.

"I'm in a whirlwind," I thought, "this isn't happening," and before I could continue, the door opened and Harry Truman himself stood directly before me.

The men seemed to vanish and I was left alone with the President. "How are we going to do this?" he asked in his unmistakably no-nonsense manner, and as he did so he took off his suit coat and draped it over a chair, revealing his white shirt and suspenders.

"He's so ordinary . . . he's so little," I thought incredulously, and somehow I couldn't be intimidated, even knowing he was our nation's leader.

"I'll need a piece of jewelry—a ring or a watch," I told him as we sat facing one another in chairs across a conference table.

"Fine," he said briskly, and removed a pinkie ring. He matter-of-factly tossed the ring onto the round table and looked directly at me.

As I picked up his ring, I asked him to call out his first name three times so that I could pick up vibrations from the sound of his voice. With a slight twinkle in his eyes (for how often these days did he establish himself on a first name basis with someone he'd just met?) he called out strongly, "Harry, Harry, Harry."

Not knowing how long I'd be spending with him, I never completely allowed myself to go into a trance, in case it would be too time-consuming. Thus, I remember some of the details of that reading (the rest has evaporated with time, or is too personal to reveal).

I do recall that I brought a woman into him from the spirit world and he seemed greatly pleased and genuinely touched. He smiled and told me the woman was his mother, who'd passed away the previous year. He also told me how she'd come to him in spirit just after her passing: Truman was on a plane, dozing off, when her face came before him. Soon afterwards, his doctor, who was on board the plane also, woke the President to tell him he'd just received word that Truman's mother had passed. "I knew she was gone," he said, "when I saw her in the dream." He felt she was saying good-bye to him, in spirit, by way of the dream.

Toward the conclusion of the reading (approximately twenty minutes at that point, I would guess) Truman frowned slightly and said, "My real question is—will you ask the spirits if I'm going to be elected?"

I thought of my omen from earlier that day (the White House store) and also listened to another spirit voice that moment, and said, "Oh, yes—definitely!" He smiled and said, "Fine . . . that's fine."

Then, as abruptly as it had begun, I sensed my time with Mr. President was up. He was that kind of man—conduct your business, then move on to the next order of business. Before he had a chance to "dismiss" me, I quickly said, "May I ask *you* a question, sir?"

"Sure," he said casually.

I asked him how he managed to always appear calm. "How do you handle it when you begin to get nervous or excited, sir? How do you settle down and maintain your calm? You always seem so at ease."

"Well, first, let me tell you I'm *not* always calm," he confessed. "I have to work at it, because I don't like to let my temper get the best of me, either. But I try to find humor in the situation, to conquer my nerves and anger," he continued, and proceeded to give me an example. He revealed that he was, in his words, "one of the world's worst drivers," yet when he was a junior senator and still driving himself around, he was often honked at for running a red light or otherwise driving recklessly.

"To hide my embarrassment and control my anger— as well as the other person's"—he chuckled, "I'd honk back when they honked at me, then I'd wave to the person and mouth hello to them as our cars crossed paths." Truman said this totally disarmed the person who'd honked in anger—did they know him? Surely this must be a friend who was recognizing them and waving hello—and nine times out of ten they'd quickly wave and smile back. "It never failed to ease the tension and make me laugh," he said, and this was a clever example of finding humor in an otherwise irritating situation.

We smiled at one another, then he shook my hand, thanked me and excused himself. As if by magic, the same two Secret Service men escorted me back to exactly the same spot in my office where they'd originally picked me up. We walked through my doorway, to the exact location in the room, they said thank you, and vanished.

Since then I've tried to remember—"was I searched, and if so, at what point?"—but it all happened *so fast*. It was truly not until I was back in my office that I thought, "Something awesome just happened to me—I just gave a psychic reading to the President of the United States, *and* I called him Harry!"

The full impact of my meeting with Harry Truman struck me when, along with the rest of the nation, I listened to radio reports on Election Night 1948. I kept thinking, "I'm rooting for the man to win the election, as are many others, but I actually know him!"

I stood in the kitchen in the home I shared with my mom Kaye, making myself a late-night snack of a chicken sandwich and listening to the election stories. Ironically a reporter from Missouri announced that

Truman had, around six that evening, prepared himself a chicken sandwich, drank a glass of milk and retired early, declaring that he was prepared to accept defeat if need be, but he was not going to worry. The image struck me as amusing and I recalled his telling me, "Find something amusing in the situation and it will help you maintain your calm." Perhaps having a sandwich and going to bed struck even the President as an odd and therefore funny idea, and helped ease the tension of waiting for the election results. Whether that was the case or not I don't know, but I do remember reading that he fell asleep and had to be awakened by the Secret Service in the wee morning hours to celebrate his victory.

I was to meet him one more time during his presidency. This was about three years after the reading in San Francisco. This time we were both in New York. Mr. Truman was staying at the Waldorf-Astoria Hotel and I was staying somewhere nearby, having come to New York to see a series of plays and friends, including my former neighbor, dear Katharine Cornell, in *The Constant Wife*.

A New York friend of mine who was involved in politics and public relations called to say he'd spent time at a social function with Truman, where the conversation had turned to "unusual people." My name came up and Truman asked if my friend knew where to find me. He said, "Well, he wrote to tell me he'd be in New York—I've been meaning to call him anyway—I have his hotel phone number." Through this mutual friend another appointment was made with Mr. Truman, this time for about five in the afternoon.

I remember fewer details of the psychic information I dispensed this time; in fact, the only thing I remember is that he requested, and I succeeded in bringing in, his mother again in spirit. I remember, however, more of our casual conversation following the reading. I've told the details of this conversation on various television programs for years and often wondered whether hosts fully believed my stories, because of the intense interest in the spirit world it revealed about the President.

Finally, several years ago, I was vindicated when Margaret Truman, in the book she wrote about her mother, Bess Truman, related the same stories which I'll share and paraphrase again here:

Mr. President leaned in to me conspiratorially as we talked in his New York hotel suite and said, "You know, I listen to the 'ghosts' walk around the hallways in the White House. But they don't frighten me," he boasted. "In fact, even when they rattle the windows or move the drapes back and forth, I just smile and invite them right on in."

I told him I admired him for his honesty and he claimed he felt he could use all the help he could get, so if they wanted to come back in spirit to guide him, so much the better! "They may still want to dabble in their work a little!" he smiled.

"And you know," he winked, "I've asked to be buried on the grounds of the Truman Library I hope to build one day soon, back in Independence. I kind of like the idea because I just might want to get up now and then and stroll in my office there!"

This was indeed a most unique, candid and charming man—a President who was also proud to be a spiritualist!

Though this meeting lasted longer than the first it, too, was over all too soon. We were not to meet again, but needless to say I've never forgotten this feisty, strong-willed man and I've been eternally grateful to have seen the other side of him—a very human and indeed highly spiritual side.

To this day I'm proud to include him as one of the spirit world's staunchest supporters.

> EIGHTY-EIGHT YEAR OLD HARRY S. TRUMAN WAS IN A COMA FOLLOWING HEART AND LUNG PROBLEMS AND PASSED AWAY ON DECEMBER 26, 1972, IN KANSAS CITY'S RESEARCH HOSPITAL. AS HE REQUESTED, HE WAS BURIED IN THE COURTYARD OF THE TRUMAN LIBRARY IN INDEPENDENCE, MIS-SOURI.

NOW

With no special plans to contact him that evening, I said to Valerie one night, "Truman wants to come through. He wants to talk tonight." I just felt him around me—felt his presence and an urgency, as though he had much to say.

We completed the project we were working on (material for an upcoming lecture I was set to give) and prepared for a "sitting."

We turned out all major household lights but one which was in a back wing of the apartment. Valerie assumed her regular position at the desk, note pad and pen before her and a red candle glowing brightly. I stretched out comfortably on an orange loveseat, and together we waited.

After a moment's silence I led us in singing "In the Garden." The hymn seemed to give us both strength, yet there was still no indication that a spirit—particularly Harry Truman—would enter. For a brief moment Valerie thought out loud, "Perhaps Truman can't come in, or chooses not to come in this evening, after all?"

But shortly the air seemed to crackle with energy. I clearly saw a vision before me and shared it with Valerie: "I see the sky ... the moon ... stars twinkling brightly. Now that scene disappears and I see a blue sky and pink clouds ... pink clouds! The pink is slowly fading to white now, and a man emerges from those clouds. He's dressed in white. He's coming closer and taking a long, white handkerchief out of his pocket, taking off a pair of glasses and cleaning them with the handkerchief. He doesn't need the glasses on the other side, but he's showing us them for identification purposes."

Valerie interrupted to say, "Do we know who it is? Do we know who the man is for sure?"

"Why, yes—it's absolutely Harry S. Truman!" I told her.

The glass patio door shook and cracked so loudly that Valerie cried out, "Oh, dear! Is it going to break?"

I smiled, "No—he's just making himself known. He's beginning to talk now. He says, 'There was a lot of joking about the S in my name standing for 'Solomon'—but I was not Jewish, for what it's worth. The Roosevelt name wasn't changed, either, from a Jewish name. Don't know why people thought to joke about all that,' he's telling me. He also says, 'No, no, no—Roosevelt wasn't President even in February or March of '45, when everyone thought he was. Look at the wire photos—it was a double they used. Roosevelt had had a double for a while anyway, due to fear of assassination attempts. And they lost a double or two, I believe, who were assassinated. The gunmen thought they got the President. You never heard those stories before, did you?' he says to me.

He's continuing now, 'I was briefed for five to six months before I took office because Roosevelt was basically incapacitated. I think it's time people knew he wasn't in office when the newspapers said he was. He passed away months before and a double was used while I prepared to officially take office.'"

"My God!" Valerie said. "That's incredible!"

"He's walking right in front of me now," I told her, and then I felt very light. I was not necessarily lightheaded, just feeling light, as though I were floating. This is the last I remember for quite some time and Valerie's notes therefore take over:

Kenny, in essence, "disappeared" and a very strong, brisk-talking, and feisty voice came through him. The inflections, the sense of humor and the no-nonsense candor were unmistakably Harry S. Truman's. This was not to be our usual give-and-take spirit contact—there was no chance for me to ask questions. Harry Truman, in spirit, presented what amounted to a speech, or "Spirit State of the Union Address," if you will.

It was at times a bit rambling or repetitive, but it is presented verbatim so as not to disrupt Truman's intention. I feel it proper to say, "Ladies and Gentlemen—the President of the United States, Harry S. Truman":

"The young people today . . . I feel sorry for them. They can't seem to find true love like I had with Bess. She was my soul mate, long before I even realized it. My body and soul belonged to her. She was my companion, my friend, my sounding board. I made no mistake when I married her—no, no.

"Somehow, from the moment I entered politics I had a dream—'I'll live in the White House one day,' and Mama Truman said, 'Me, too.' And sure enough it happened.

"I think a President used to be elected because the people found confidence in his leadership. Now I don't give a damn—excuse me—I don't care what people say, the American people began going wrong with the Nixon/Kennedy election. They were reading an aura when they didn't elect Nixon the first time. They were reading the man correctly. The analysts said, 'Oh, he didn't have proper make-up during the debates—he wasn't a matinee idol like Kennedy'. Truth is, the people just didn't *like* the man. But they didn't do much better to choose Kennedy. Nixon lacked charisma and Kennedy had it, but that doesn't make a President. Then later Bobby Kennedy ran—he wouldn't have ever gotten as far as he did without the Kennedy name. Bobby looked like a waif, poor thing.

"Roosevelt told me a story about Winston Churchill one time. He'd invited Churchill to stay at the White House during meetings, and one night while Roosevelt was in the bathtub, Churchill knocked on the door, then came in—just came in—to talk! He carried a brandy snifter and a cigar and just sat on the tub in his nightshirt and I'll be damned if they didn't talk! (He'd had a little too much brandy, I assume). He'd flick his cigar ashes onto the side of the tub, then brush them right into the water with his nightshirt! Felt pretty comfortable, I guess!

"I feel comfortable *here*, too. I'm where I belong now—with Bess, my mother. I'm perfectly content and I may not go back to Earthplane.

"But while I'm speaking of that, I'm sorry to say there may not *be* a United States of America much longer if things don't straighten out. The United States people made a mistake voting for Clinton, that's my opinion, plain and simple. That marriage would have been over if he hadn't been running for President. If he'd stayed governor, there'd have been a divorce.

"I was around Earthplane one night when a TV host—that Rush Limbaugh fella—showed a film clip (not distributed to the rest of the media) where Hillary said she was contacting Eleanor Roosevelt for advice. Well, what's wrong with that? So what if Hillary talks to Eleanor Roosevelt? I talked to all the 'ghosts'. I'd pass their paintings, look at them, and have a little talk.

"Back to Nixon again—Kissinger said Nixon was rumored to be having mental trouble because he was talking to people who weren't there. They thought he was having a nervous breakdown, or to use a popular term of your day which I hate—he was 'stressed out'. He was okay—he needed help—we know that—so he talked to spirits. He was a shifty-eyed individual, but I can't fault him for talking to the spirits.

"The Clinton regime will be a Kennedy story all over again. By the way, I see Joe Kennedy here. I bid him the time of day, that's all—can't be a hypocrite. I see John, too—they're just not my kind of people, that's all. Money spoke where they were concerned. Joe bought his son the highest office in the land—that's no secret. John was a good enough man, just not ready to be President.

"Do I have any regrets? Very few. I had a good time in my life. I remain united today behind everything I did and stood for. I took blame when it was mine, and took compliments when they were mine during my Presidency.

"Now Perot—Ross Perot—he had a system the people wanted. He had the money (his own money) but he also had the right opinions to be a figurehead, and kept up the campaign even after he "lost." He's a family man like me. He stuck up for his family like I did for Bess and Margaret.

"What's wrong today that families aren't stronger? Psychiatrists—that's one reason. And women's lib—that was the worst thing that ever happened to the country. Equality is fine. Now people want superiority.

"You've got to have your own personal strength from within—not strength you get from a psychiatrist. I wouldn't have waited like Bush did in Iraq. Do I regret the A-bomb? Absolutely not. I'm still glad I dropped it. I'd have dropped it on that man Hussein. Absolutely. He'll poison the water, the food—he'll kill anyone to 'win.'

"Bush and Reagan came out of the White House looking like the did when they went in. It was Nancy and Barbara who aged—*they* were strong! This ticket (Clinton) isn't even really in power now. But give the ticket *next* time around a chance. Eventually General Colin Powell will be in power. I didn't care for military men before, but we need them now; we've got to know where the country stands.

"The administration talks about budget cuts? We'd have to cut by trillions of dollars to make it work!

"Homosexuals in the Army? If they're men, they're in the Army—enough said.

"Speaking of the Army—I see MacArthur. I have no regrets—I see him, I pass the time of day—that's it. As I said to Dean Acheson the other day (the best Secretary of State the country ever had), and by the way he still calls me Mr. President, though some here call me Harry, anyway I said, 'I have no regrets. MacArthur riled me up sufficiently. He defied the commander in chief.' Maybe I didn't fire him 'properly,' but he had to go and he went.

"He *staged* that walking out of the water onto the beach for that famous photo, you know. Now when Lauren Bacall bounced up on the piano when I was playing, as Vice President, *that* was one of the most remembered photos, and we didn't have to do it nine times!

"I didn't mention it to MacArthur here, but what playwright wrote his speech, 'Old soliders never die'? Now *my* speech, 'The buck stops here'—*everyone* remembers that. Psychiatrists ought to try that—'the buck stops here' instead of blaming everyone else for a person's trouble. The media talks too much about psychiatrists, too.

"I used my office as I used my intuitive abilities. I listened for help, then acted. You'll notice before I even came here to the other side people were already saying, 'Harry S. Truman has been vindicated'—history has proven me right.

"I felt I was right about Nixon, about MacArthur, about the A-bomb. I have a clear conscience, as it should be. Why should I come back to Earth to live again? I've answered my karma.

"There's not enough hope or dreams today for young people. We need to give them dreams. If they had them, there wouldn't be so much promiscuity. You didn't find Harry Truman flirting, Now people even talk about promiscuity with Presidents! I'm sure some of them haven't been loyal to their women, but now unfaithfulness is being glamorized.

"If a President tends to business, he has enough to do to fill an eighteen-hour day—no time left over for womanizing. I'm just plain against it. Other heads of state are respected. If people in foreign countries took the reputations of their leaders they'd be hung or shot. The American people talk and laugh about it now.

"If there's one word I hope I'm remembered by, it's *loyal*. I tried to be a great friend, I tried to give a hundred percent. People in marriages today are told to make it a fifty-fifty proposition. Where's the other fifty percent? It's a hundred percent for each person!

"How can we feed every nation in the world and have homeless people in the United States? Does that make sense? Of course not.

"We shouldn't be giving so much money for foreign aid, under any circumstances. This isn't fair trade taking place today. We can't sell our products overseas, but *they* can sell *here*. I'm not going to explain it to you—think it over."

"I believe every young person should give two years to the military now—man or woman. I'm more pro-military because we need a stronger country on land, sea and in the air. We need total protection for the United States of America.

"The best seamstresses, mechanics, and workers are here. Why do we concentrate on imports so much and not exports? The budget can't be balanced that way.

"Yes, Ross Perot would have been the man. This may be conceited, but I think he woulda gotten the votes if he'd stayed in all long, because people thought of *me* when they voted. We know there couldn't be another Harry S. Truman, but the comparisons were there.

"You know, they used to talk about my 'daily constitutionals'—I didn't *run* around the White House—not good for you. I got up before the Secret Service to take my constitutionals—they had to do almost a two-step to keep up with me. Healthy for a body to walk.

"About health—I believe people have the right to smoke if they want. Separate places for smokers might be fine, but banning it entirely—for what? People work at a company, run out on a break to smoke—it costs the company more than if they'd let people sit at their desk and smoke. Don't make a mountain out of a molehill!"

For the first time, there was a moment of silence, and Valerie wondered if the contact was over.

"Is there anything else you'd like to say?" she asked. Obviously this was only a brief chance for Truman to catch his breath, however, because he replied, "What is this—a press conference—'any questions?' I have more to say. Tell the media not to print everything about the President—his agenda and whatever. Not necessary at all.

"You want to deal with gang violence? Use the 'eye for an eye, tooth for a tooth' approach and it would be stopped. The news media glorifies it. More severe penalties are needed. Second offenders are given third and fourth chances. Millions are spent on criminals and when they come out they repeat the same act. 'Eye for an eye'—remember it.

"They'll see me again at the White House, but not while Clinton's in.

"I told Bess the other day—what's wrong with the United States now? The President's guarded by the highest amount of security possible, and that's fine, but four blocks from the White House there are bars on people's windows, they're so afraid. Every man, woman and child should be able to walk the streets without fear of robbery, murder, or attack.

"Balance the budget—put the American people first. Buy American, sell American. No person should be homeless or hungry.

"I love this country. Good night and God Bless America."

To which Valerie could only reply, "Goodnight, Mr. President, and thank you."

As a footnote, the above contact lasted about forty-five minutes and was a complete spirit take over. As a result, Kenny required water afterwards to help "center" him on Earthplane again. It was only with considerable coaxing and talking that Valerie was able to call him back again. It's apparent Harry Truman was, and still is, a strong man, for his spirit easily took control, to our delight.

ADOLF HITLER

THEN

I was a teenager in 1945 when I heard, as the world did, that Adolf Hitler had passed away in his bunker in Germany along with his long-time mistress (and new wife) Eva Braun. My first impression—a psychic impression—was, "Of course that's not true!" I never said the word "dead," even in those days, but I heard a spirit voice say loudly in my ear, "They're not dead!"

I had read little about Hitler, but was fascinated by "der Führer," mostly because what little I did know of him convinced me he was a genius who, needless to say, badly misused his gift.

A couple of years later I entered the Army as an older teenager and became, as luck would have it, an Army instructor for the 88th Infantry Lido Study Center, on the Lido off Venice, Italy. It was there that I developed a similar feeling about the misuse of another dictator's talents—those of Hitler admirer Benito Mussolini.

The Italians spoke about their former leader, saying Mussolini was indeed a great man who built wonderfully modern buildings and train stations for the Italian people. He helped them progress, but then met the "former paper hanger" (Hitler) and changed his personality and his entire lifestyle.

During my stay in Europe I remained convinced that Hitler was indeed still alive, and somehow being in the midst of the Italian discussions of the two dictators only heightened the belief.

On a brief vacation to Milan during my military days, I attended the reopening of the La Scala Opera House, where Toscanini was guest conductor.

While in Milan I also went to the site where Mussolini and his mistress Claretta Petacci had been hanged in public a year or two prior.

While standing there, I heard what I felt was the spirit voice of *Il Dulce* say to me "Hitler is not here" (meaning on the other side, with Mussolini) and then "No Eva Braun here, either," the spirit continued.

Later, when I returned to Venice, I received further confirmation while out socially one evening at one of the most famous rendezvous spots in the world, Harry's Bar. My friend, actor/singer/dancer and then *Lieutenant* Dan Dailey and I met in the Special Services Division while arranging entertainment for the servicemen, and we had come out this evening for a drink at the world-famous restaurant and night spot. I looked over toward two women seated several tables away from us and saw Mussolini in spirit behind one of them. I told Dan I felt compelled to go tell the woman about this phenomenon.

I hurried off toward the woman, hearing Dan following quickly behind me. As I approached her, I said to the woman, in the best Italian I had learned thus far, that Mussolini's spirit was behind her.

She dropped her martini, the olive plopping onto the table in the midst of the crash. The maitre d', seeing the glass fall, hurried over as the woman shouted at me angrily, "Who are you? How dare you say such a thing to me? You must know who I am, to say Mussolini is with me!"

Of course I did not know who she was; I merely wanted, out of curiosity, to find out why Mussolini was with her. The maitre d' pulled me aside quietly and asked what I'd said to the woman.

"I told her I saw the image of Mussolini behind her," I began explaining "Sir! You just told that to the *sister* of Claretta Petacci!" he said abruptly.

Needless to say, I spoke no further to the woman and told no one, even Dan, what Mussolini's spirit had said when it was standing behind the woman, but indeed Mussolini had stared straight at me and said, "He's alive!" and I knew he'd once again been referring to Hitler.

Following my Army years, I appeared on radio and television, expanding on these earlier psychic impressions by saying I felt Hitler had escaped the bunker and was living in Austria, working as an accountant.

I felt Eva Braun had fled the bunker with Hitler and by mutual agreement, divided her time afterwards between Paris and Argentina. I continued to say this until 1970, when I was told psychically that Hitler, whose approximate age would have been 81 at that time, finally passed away in Austria, after living the rest of his life in obscurity. I thus added this new development when relaying the story from then on.

In 1978 I was taping the first of my television series, *Kenny Kingston: A Psychic Experience*, for Metromedia in Los Angeles. Prior to another week's taping I was having my hair styled one day at a salon near my home. The stylist said, "I certainly enjoy your show and I have a fascinating story I'll bet you'd like to use sometime." (People always tend to approach those of us in show business with their "fantastic idea for a show," or a "great script" they want to present to us, and I find it's always best to listen politely, for every now and then the person's enthusiasm is well-founded).

That was an understatement on this particular day. The man told me the following, in his light German accent:

"As a young boy, I was in Hitler's army. On occasion we were inspected by der Führer himself, and the few times I saw him, I thought, 'I'll never forget those eyes.' They were piercing, calculating, hypnotic— unlike any others I'd ever seen or would see again.

"Many years later, sometime in the 1960s, I journeyed to visit my uncle, who was working as an accountant in Austria. I'd planned to have lunch with him one day and arrived at the accounting firm to meet him. He greeted me, then asked me to wait while he washed his hands prior to our leaving.

"As I waited I glanced around. Though there were several desks in the office, it seemed most of the other workers had already left for lunch. One worker remained, however—an old man, hunched over his desk writing.

"I looked at the man and he must have felt me looking, because he glanced up. I froze, mesmerized, and thought, 'Oh my God— those eyes! Hitler's eyes!' A chill ran through me and I thought, 'I've got to talk to him. I have to know for sure!'"

The stylist began attempting small talk with the old man by saying he currently lived in the United States but was visiting Austria. The man only stared. "I love America," the stylist continued, "it's such a free country."

The old man stood up, put his pen in his pocket and looked as though he would walk away. "I've got to taunt him. I've got to test him and *make* him reveal himself," the stylist thought.

"America certainly has a great president," he said as he walked closer, "but there was never any leader as great as der Führer." He paused and was amazed to see the old man straighten and begin pacing, as though infused with new strength.

"Yes, a great man. A great man!" he said boldly. Then he abruptly stopped his pacing and fixed the stylist with one last icy stare. To his utter surprise, though the man's eyes were as steely cold as ever, the stylist saw huge tears threatening to spill out of them. "The old man stalked away," he recalled, "and I never saw him again. But I *know* it was him!"

I quickly asked him to guest on my show, to confirm once and for all the psychic impression I'd held for years, and he agreed to do so. "For fear that people would think I was insane, I've kept the secret all these years," he told me. "You're the only person other than my wife that I'd trust to understand this."

However, a few days later, when my talent coordinator, Barbara Burgess, called to confirm a taping date, he was more hesitant. "My wife says there could be trouble from this," he hedged. "I'm not so sure it's a good idea." Barbara did some quick thinking and said, "What if we camouflage you, or shoot you in silhouette? No one needs to recognize you," she assured him, and finally he agreed.

We taped the show, using the camouflage. This was to be the last show of the season and it turned out beautifully.

However, the Hitler mystery prevailed. For some reason, whether due to spirit intervention or a political influence I was unaware of, Metromedia *never aired* the program, choosing, instead, to repeat an earlier broadcast!

To my knowledge, the tape still exists in a vault somewhere at Metromedia in Hollywood, California.

Three years later, in 1981, the *Los Angeles Herald-Examiner* newspaper ran a story from London. It revealed a research team's conclusion that the dental records previously used to "prove" Eva Braun had 'died' in the bunker were *not* those of Braun. One possible theory, according to Reider F. Sognnaes, head of the team: "It is possible Eva Braun escaped."

Perhaps the Hitler mystery will never be solved scientifically or historically, but I trust my spirits and need no further proof to convince myself they've told the truth all these years.

ADOLF HITLER SUPPOSEDLY COMMITTED SUICIDE IN HIS BERLIN BUNKER ON APRIL 30, 1945, WITH HIS NEW WIFE EVA BRAUN AT HIS SIDE. BUT AS NOTED ABOVE, MY THEORY DIFFERS WITH THIS VERSION, AND I MAINTAIN PSYCHICALLY THAT HE PASSED AWAY SOMETIME IN 1970, AT THE AGE OF 80, HAVING LIVED OUT THE REMAINDER OF HIS LIFE IN RELATIVE OBSCURITY IN AUSTRIA.

NOW

"This is one contact we must do outside," I told Valerie when we began making plans regarding Adolf Hitler. "After all, this is a man considered to be one of history's most evil personalities," I decided, "and I wouldn't want his vibrations in my home. I also wouldn't risk inviting his spirit into a hotel or other public building, either."

Thus the idea of contacting him in an open space came about. After mulling over the idea of a park or bit of vacant land, we chose the beach instead, because it seemed the most comfortable spot for us to sit while attempting the contact; we also hoped the sea might have a calming influence, should the spirit vibration be negative, as I suspected it might.

We asked several people to join us for this contact; all were people I'd had present at other seances in the past, thus they were accustomed to spirit contact. One or two declined when asked because it was Hitler we were hoping to reach, but finally five agreed. They were nervous yet curious about such an undertaking and thought it would be a most unusual event. They each requested, however, that their names not be used. "I'm curious about it and I want to do it, but I don't want anyone to *know* I did it," was the typical response.

Thus these "anonymous" people—three men and two women—gathered with us on the beach near Ventura, California, at 7:00 P.M. one summer evening.

It had been an unusually hot day for the area and the setting of the sun brought welcome relief. The weather alone seemed like an omen to me—not only had it been a hot day in a location which was normally only pleasantly warm, but even the night air stayed still, where usually cool breezes set in. "Something strange is happening already," I told the group as we settled on plaid blankets on the soft white sand.

The beachgoers had cleared out for the day, and only a few people mulled around a quaint shopping area across the street from us. Other than these few people, who were at a distance, we were totally alone.

The older of our two female guests, a woman in her late forties, said, "I'm a little nervous about this; I hope it's not going to be too frightening."

"Let's begin by placing the white light of protection around us right now, to ward off any problems," I suggested, and we visualized this white glow of soothing light surrounding our bodies.

Valerie and I brought a red glass-encased candle with us and Valerie placed it in the sand and lit it, not knowing whether it would stay lit during the session or not, due to our being outdoors. For the moment, though, since the air was still, the flame glowed strongly.

"I want everyone to know that I am not, under any circumstances, going to allow myself to go into trance tonight," I informed the group. "I will interpret what spirit tells me, but I will remain in control at all times. Adolf Hitler will have no chance of taking me over, even assuming his spirit is capable of it," I assured them.

"Good—oh, I'm glad!" the other woman said, and her young gentleman friend agreed. "We were hoping you'd say that," he said.

"Let us just relax, then, and we'll begin by asking that we receive information regarding the spirit of Adolf Hitler or that his spirit itself is able to relay information to us," I said. "I'm going to go partly onto the other side and allow myself to see, hear, and feel what is occurring there, and we shall see what happens."

We sat in silence, a tense energy passing among us. I did not go into a deep trance and was not taken over by spirit, therefore I remember much of what took place, but I again rely upon Valerie's notes to supply the minute details of our evening:

The silence we felt was unusual; whereas often there is a peacefulness about a spirit contact, or a happy eagerness, this silence felt charged with excitement yet fear, anticipation yet anxiety.

Breathing deeply, Kenny said, "I'm in a total state of relaxation now—going partially onto the other side. I feel I'm coming close to his spirit now . . . I'm getting closer . . . he's coming closer."

With these last words, an eerie dark cloud seemed to settle down over the group. True, the night sky made our surroundings dark anyway, but this was a heavy black cloudlike mist, which hung close above our heads.

"I feel I could suffocate!" the older woman said. "I don't like this feeling!" she cried out. "It will be okay," Valerie tried to pacify her. "Just remember the white light of protection and we won't let anything happen to anyone."

The woman fidgeted, then said, "No—I can't! I can't breathe! I'm sorry—I can't stay, I'm too nervous!" and with this she quickly stood up, said "Goodnight" and left our group.

A friend of hers, a stocky man in his fifties, said, "I came with her, I'll have to leave, too, then. Plus, I want to make sure she's all right. And to tell you the truth, I'm a little shook up, too."

And so, our already small group dwindled to five.

"Okay, let's band together and send each other strength," Kenny said, attempting to calm our remaining group members. "I'm not in full trance, so I know that they left, but we'll be fine. We must just be careful. There is a sense of negativity with Hitler, even after all these years—negativity and uneasiness."

"I just don't want to see his face!" said the youngest male in our group.

"We'll work against that," Kenny said. Then, he inhaled sharply. "I see him right before me, as I draw closer to the other side. Believe me, people don't want to see his face! They'd panic if they saw his face now—they'd faint. There would be mass hysteria! He looks dreadful!"

"What do you mean? Disfigured? Angry?" Valerie asked tentatively.

"You don't want to know," Kenny replied. "Dear God—he hasn't answered any of his karma to speak of. He hasn't even begun to answer it!"

Kenny's voice was slightly agitated and Valerie said, "Maybe you should back away from him for a moment, okay? How about just asking one of your guides or some other spirit to talk about him?"

"Yes," Kenny agreed. "I'm calling on a higher force. This force is coming toward Hitler and ushering him away for the time being. He's being led away like a common criminal. Another spirit force, who keeps records of progress being made and who knows the entire lifetime someone spent, is here with me. This is a wise spirit, a male, and he's telling me, 'I'll help you because you truly want to be enlightened; you hope to aid people and inform them.' He says 'Hitler knew the type of life he'd lead when he entered the world last time and began his life. He'd lived other lives, individually hurting people. He carried that over to his life as Adolf Hitler. He knew the wrongdoings he did.' In his early life he used drugs, I'm told, but he used them to keep from going insane.

"In fact—this is strange—I'm being shown that his famous mustache came about quite by accident, after he'd had a siege with a bad combination of pills. He was shaving—I can see this!—and his hand was shaking. He tried to take some from the left side, to trim it, and he cut too much. He tried to even it by cutting the right side, and he cut too much. He was left with his trademark 'clump.' But he looked in the mirror and thought, 'this makes me look different than anyone else.' He was a born actor—a born performer. He basked in attention.

"Under this powerful medication he took, he was often brilliant—a master—but he misused it so dreadfully. He began with two or three people, but soon he mesmerized the masses, I'm told."

"I understand he wanted to study art when he was younger, but he was rejected from art school," Valerie said. "Do you suppose . . . is it possible if he'd been accepted and became an artist that things would have been different?"

"No! He was an insecure person who turned that insecurity into rage," Kenny insisted. "He would have led a perverted life even as an artist. He'd have abused and mistreated on a one-to-one level no matter what."

The candle, which had been steadily burning, began flickering wildly, though there was barely a hint of a breeze.

"Looks like we're losing the candle," said one of our men. "No, I think it's just spirit coming in again," Valerie said.

"Yes, look," said the only other woman who'd remained. "No matter how it dances around, and I don't know what's making it do that, the flame doesn't go out! But I'm cold," she said. "Is there a cold breeze starting up, or is that spirit energy?"

"It's spirit, I think," her boyfriend announced.

"You're right," Valerie agreed; "it's icy cold right here in our circle, but it's not a natural cold. It's definitely spirit."

Just then Kenny spoke again, confirming what we had been speculating. "He's being brought closer again. He's going to be allowed to communicate with us, to answer a small part of his karma. He's only allowed to do this because this higher, guiding force is staying with him. Normally, he passes among others in the spirit world and is totally shunned. He has no place reserved for him yet. If anyone were ever in a state of limbo, it's Adolf Hitler. No one has accepted him yet. His aura—his very essence—still gives him away.

"He's totally disgusted people in spirit because he's accosted women once or twice in spirit, asking for very bizarre sexual favors—distasteful sexual favors from spirits who are so much elevated beyond that."

"What do you mean?" one of the men asked.

"Excuse me," Kenny apologized, "remember that I'm just telling what I'm being shown. I'm seeing that he's asked women to stand over him and urinate, which was one of his perverted sexual pleasures in life."

"Oh, my God! Oh, please!" Valerie shrieked.

Kenny's contact with the "watchdog" or "spirit warden," if you will, continued. "I'm being told that no one talks to Hitler—they avoid him ... "

"No wonder, after what you just said," the other woman interrupted.

"No, it's much more than that," Kenny insisted, "as we can all imagine. He has philosophy, some small seeds of brilliance which he could share, but no one wants to hear it yet, especially from Hitler."

"What about those who worked with him? The men who were part of his regime? Doesn't he even spend time with them?" one of our males asked.

"No, he's alone," Kenny said with certainty. "His lieutenants, his officers have 'smartened up.' They realize their wrongs and are mortified by them. They, too, have karma to answer for, but they have admitted this and are trying to redeem themselves. One step is to abandon Hitler, they feel."

He continued, "This is interesting; I'm being shown a scene, from soon after Hitler arrived in Paradise, which as I've said was much later than people believed. When he arrived, some of his former comrades wandered nearby, to peer at him as he 'came to'; yet when he called out to them, they said, 'A dictatorship was wrong—you were wrong—we were wrong.' He said, 'What? What did I do? The world needed a leader and I became one. I became der Führer! I loved uniforms. My army became my family; you were my family!' he called out to them, but they turned and walked away."

"I have goosebumps!" the young woman in attendance said anxiously.

"Yes, it is an uncomfortable feeling," Valerie agreed. "I feel like I must keep watching over my shoulder."

"Shh—listen—did you hear that?" one of the men said in a sudden, hushed voice. "Like a scream?"

We sat in silence, waiting.

"Yes!" Valerie cried out. "Oh—the screams—the shouts—it's terrible! It's like the sound is coming from an echo chamber!"

"That's the sound I heard!" the young man confirmed.

"It's Hitler's anguish you're sensing," Kenny said. "He often shouts in anguish and frustration on the other side. But you're also hearing the echoes of those he harmed over the years."

"It's awful!" our man said. "Let's work on releasing it; let's put the white light around us again," he suggested, and we did.

"We may not be ready for it, but they're going to allow him to speak now," Kenny said. "He's coming—he's here."

"Let's let him get close, but not *too* close," Valerie suggested.

"Absolutely," Kenny said, "because as I feel his spirit more deeply, I must say he still does not have good intentions. He knows he has to answer for what he did, but he hasn't begun to pay the penalty—hasn't chosen to. He's told the higher forces that he wants to come back—to choose another life to answer his karma, but no one believes him. They can't trust him. What if he reincarnated into another life of evil?"

The ocean roared, the waves crashing against the sand. It seemed even the sea was not at peace this evening.

"He's trying to take me!" Kenny said anxiously, as his head fell forward and he seemed to be entering into a trance.

"Don't let him!" Valerie said firmly.

"I can't let him take me over—evil!" Kenny nervously insisted, the candle flame illuminating the concern on his face.

"Don't give in to it!" Valerie insisted. Then, to the unseen negativity which was Hitler, "Keep your distance—you can't have access to him!"

Kenny breathed deeply and then appeared to relax slightly. "He's backing away; it's all right," he sighed. "He's talking about the bunker, about a tunnel under the bunker. He says he and Eva Braun escaped and two others were actually found in their place. He says Eva went to Rio, then Buenos Aires. 'We escaped!' he says proudly."

"Did they meet again?" Valerie asked. "Did they plan a rendezvous somewhere?"

"He says it's unimportant," Kenny answered. "He says, 'I did not really love her anyway—she was not my true love.'"

"Then who was?" the youngest male in our group asked.

"He speaks of his half niece. It's Jilly . . . no, G- Geli," Kenny said. "I feel an obsessive quality about that relationship, a heaviness. Not many even knew of the relationship, but he became a 'madman' over her."

"Yes, there was something about that," said our oldest male group member. "But I don't remember quite what it was I heard once."

"I think she was killed or something, wasn't she?" our female interrupted. "Or am I wrong?"

"He says he accepts responsibility for Geli's life," Kenny said. "He says, 'I destroyed her as I destroyed thousands of others.'"

"He destroyed—you mean he killed her?" Valerie wondered.

The cold air swirled menacingly around us again, as though in answer.

" 'I was responsible,' is all he'll say," Kenny answered. "He says 'it was a sampling—a prelude—of things to come.'"

"How terrible," Valerie said.

Kenny continued, "He started with girls before Geli, I'm told. He abused them—harmed them—destroyed them by obsessively wanting to keep them captive."

"Such a shame, with such young people," Valerie observed disgustedly.

"I feel young people today must be cautious," Kenny warned. "He's trying to send negative influences to them, to cause riots and gang warfare. We must put the white light around the youth of today. They must become stronger, more positive."

"Yes, we must work on that," we all agreed.

"He says 'Many people still try to mock me—imitate me. Your cult leaders imitate me. If I was so wrong, why do people follow those leaders?' "

"That's a point," our young man agreed. "I guess you could say the religious cult leaders are like dictators, aren't they?"

"But he sneers and says, 'they'll never touch my power. There was only one Führer!'" Kenny said.

"He still doesn't understand, does he?" Valerie said bitterly. "I can't begin to sympathize with him because he still hasn't changed."

"He hasn't truly repented," Kenny agreed.

"When he does, will the spirit world open up to him more—will they help him pay back his sins?" Valerie asked.

"Yes, of course," Kenny said. "But it will be a long time in coming. He seems to feel somewhat sorry, yet he hasn't lost his menacing ways. They were too engrained in him from too many other lifetimes. He's still mesmerized by his own power, though he knows it harmed thousands of people."

"Oh, please! I'm so cold!" said our female guest. "Is he close by? He's not behind me, is he?" she feared.

Kenny reassured her, "No, he's not behind you. He's still being kept at a distance. He's talking, though. He says, 'I knew the countries I invaded weren't ready—not prepared for me'. Now, let me ask you—he says he has advice. Do you want to hear it?"

"I'm not sure we do," Valerie interrupted.

"I'm afraid he's going to continue anyway," Kenny said. "He says, 'If people of any country are smart—if they have any sense at all, which I doubt—they'll require their youth to serve in the military. Two years of military. In return, give them two years of schooling afterward. Military—schooling—does youth good!' I'm just passing along what he says. He says 'the war was only won because the stupid Allies misinterpreted messages. They won because of a mistake!' "

"How dare he!" Valerie said. Then, "What does he mean?"

Kenny told her, "He says 'the Allies relayed instructions and information back and forth—we intercepted it and began to follow. But the Allied troops couldn't follow simple orders. They fouled up and went the wrong direction or at the wrong time.' "

"I don't want to hear this!" protested one of the men. "Let's ask him to leave!"

"I hear the echo chamber again," Valerie said in panic. "The screams are back—many more this time!"

Then, just as the tension seemed to reach a peak, total silence took over. But it was an eerie silence—was it 'the calm before the storm'?

Kenny soothed our fears, saying, "Oh—it's over! He vanished! It's over as quickly as it began! He's gone!"

Collectively we sighed with relief. The oppressive heaviness had been lifted from us; no more cold air, no more screams, no more Adolf Hitler.

"Thank God," Valerie said. "I didn't know how much more tension we could have taken."

"For once," Kenny said, "in fact for the only time I can remember, I can say I'm glad to see a spirit go."

And the rest of us shakily agreed.

ROYALS

★ ★ ★ ★ ★

THE DUCHESS OF WINDSOR

★ ★ ★ ★ ★

THEN

While other young children were interested in cowboys or clowns, I was fascinated instead by the British Royal Family—King Edward VIII in particular. Needless to say, none of my tiny friends shared my interest, but as my mother later told me, I spotted photos of His Royal Highness in newspapers or on magazine covers and would entertain myself, sitting alone, alternately smiling and quietly studying his face in the photos.

The world watched and listened as the story of Edward VIII's abdication unfolded, followed by his marriage to American divorcee Wallis Warfield Simpson. Together, following his abdication of the throne, they became the Duke and Duchess of Windsor. My mother explained the details to me in terms she felt I could understand. She said that for days afterwards I ran around the house, and then into the streets near our home, declaring, "He gave up the throne for the woman he loved!," paraphrasing the speech Edward VIII had given upon stepping down as King. Naturally, when I ran to tell my playmates, they were unimpressed. But I apparently sensed that it was a very important matter indeed.

Some time later, my parents and I were driving from our New York home into Canada to spend time at our summer beach home. We crossed over a bridge near the border and as we did we heard sirens and saw a motorcade passing the border and going in the opposite direction from us. When we got to the border, my father asked the border inspector who was in the motorcade and he was told, "Oh, that was the Duke and Duchess of Windsor, on their way to the airport." I remember sitting in the back seat in awe, thinking, "I got *that* close to them!"

Little did I know, at that moment, the encounter was but a taste of the future for me, though our next contact would be years away.

In my late teens, I entered the Army and spent time in Italy as an Army instructor, and later in Special Services as an announcer for various performers, including Metropolitan Opera stars Grace Moore and Lawrence Tibbitt. While in Italy, I was fortunate enough to be introduced to many well-known people, including the world's most famous partygiver, Elsa Maxwell, who introduced me to many of her illustrious friends.

Elsa told me of the thriving "business" she conducted through her party giving, and through the bookings she did for the Duke and Duchess of Windsor. She would arrange for the couple to appear at a party, asking a fee of, say, $25,000 for the appearance (though she'd settle for $10,000 or $15,000). Elsa would request a cashier's check or money order in advance so that it could be cashed *prior* to the party. The Duke and Duchess then received the cash from Elsa—minus her standard fee of ten or fifteen per cent for arranging the engagement!

One day, after I'd given her a psychic reading, Elsa said, "I think I know someone you'd like to meet. The Duke and Duchess of Windsor are coming to Italy soon and I think Wally would love to have a reading."

Shortly thereafter they arrived where I was staying in Venice. Much to my delight, Elsa introduced me to the couple at a friend's villa on the Lido de Venezia, facing the Adriatic Sea. I gave them their first reading there, followed shortly afterwards by another reading in Venice, at their hotel (the Danielli, I believe).

Indeed, as Elsa predicted, Wallis Simpson was enthralled with the psychic world. The Duke appeared distracted, and would wander in and out of the room. The only time he appeared truly interested was at the beginning of the reading when I asked both of them to call out their given names three times. (Spirits generally respond better to someone's given name, as opposed to a title or even a nickname). Thus they called out, "Wallis, Wallis, Wallis" and "David, David, David" (for although his first name was Edward, David was part of his name, and the former King felt it was the most appropriate one to use, since he'd become known by that part of his given name by all those close to him). I continued calling them those names to encourage the spirits to remain and give messages. David got a twinkle in his eye, thinking, I suppose, "Imagine this person, whom I do not know well, calling me, a former King, David!" He would then listen attentively to a few brief messages.

Wally also got a "kick" out of my calling the Duke "David," and Elsa later told me she said, "I like Kenny's spunk—he could be the *male* Duchess of Windsor!"

Though she also believed in numerology and astrology, Wally was more intent upon bringing back relatives in spirit. I recall very few specifics, except that I brought back an "Aunt Bessie" to her on one occasion, and she seemed most pleased and touched. She told Elsa afterwards "He has an 86% accuracy and an 86% sense of humor to go with it," to which Elsa told me she countered "*I* think it's more like 92% myself."

My memories of the Duke are of him attired mostly in pin-striped suits, while the Duchess was either in a suit or a long-flowing hostess gown. What drew my attention, always, were the jewels she'd hand me during the reading (I always ask for jewelry or another personal object to hold—something which has been worn close to the person for at least two hours and thus has their vibrations strongly on it; this is the art of psychometry). There I was, holding her pearl choker, or a gorgeous ring with huge stones, never realizing that later there would be such a flurry of activity over the auctioning of those very pieces.

The Duchess was indeed a fashion trendsetter, and often on the "Ten Best Dressed" list. Some of the leading couturiers of the day considered it an honor to have her wear their designs, at no cost to her.

There were exceptions, however. When Elsa and I were visiting the Duchess at the couple's hotel suite at the Waldorf Towers in New York once, Wallis's secretary knocked on the inner suite door. "Excuse me, Your Royal Highness," she interrupted, "but that designer is on the phone again, and he says he'll send the sheriff and have you arrested if you don't take his call." Wally sighed, "Excuse me a moment—this will be the last call from him!" and she reluctantly went to the phone. She listened to the caller for a moment. "Just a minute!" she shouted angrily into the phone. "This is the Duchess of Windsor speaking! You should be honored to have me *wearing* your clothing! Consider your bill paid in full!"

She slammed down the receiver and returned to us. "Imagine!" she huffed. "He wanted me to *pay*!" To which Elsa laughed her infectious laugh and replied, "Oh Wally—was that another *Mr. Dunning* calling you?"

It's worth noting here that though her officially-ranked title was less than his ("Her Highness"), the Duke instructed staff members and friends to always refer to Wallis as "Her Royal Highness" or "Your Royal Highness." Anyone *not* showing this respect which he felt she deserved was heavily chastised if not banished from their lives forever.

The above incident actually reflects two things. One was certainly Wallis's temper, which I'd seen flare on a couple of occasions, and which I understood from Elsa helped contribute to many a good argument between Wallis and David.

But the secretary's use of "Your Royal Highness," and the Duke's command to use the title, also reflected his love for her. I knew without a shadow of a doubt that they were soul mates. Their love was very strong, and they were able to communicate without words—just a look or a touch could say it all.

As is the case with soul mates, I felt strongly they had known each other in a previous life. Thus there was a continuing bond, and they would feel "at home" with one another, as though they belonged. The soul mate connection is perhaps difficult to fully explain, but it's something the two people involved can feel, if they're sensitive people, and of course as a psychic I can immediately sense it as well. Theirs was almost an indescribable love and very rare indeed.

Another friend of mine, Broadway and film star Clifton Webb, was a dear friend of the couple. Clifton first rose to fame as a musical comedy star and dancer on Broadway, and he taught the Duke and Duchess various dance steps which they "premiered" at parties.

Clifton told me of an incident which occurred once when the Duke's health failed. He received a phone call from Wallis from the Duke's hospital room in Texas. The famed surgeon Dr. Michael DeBakey was scheduled to perform heart surgery on him the next morning, but the Duke was getting cold feet.

Clifton said he asked to speak to the Duke and cursed him when he came on the line. "You son of a bitch," he yelled, "you gave up the throne for her—now have the surgery and *stay* with her. If you're half the man I think you are," he continued scolding, "you'll have the surgery just as soon as possible." He said he hung up the phone and prayed his harsh words had done their job. And indeed they did—the Duke had the surgery and of course it no doubt lengthened his life considerably.

Perhaps my most vividly remembered encounter with the couple was my last. I had given them a brief reading at their bungalow at the Beverly Hills Hotel on their only joint trip to California. Following the reading, I asked the Duke where he truly considered home to be—New York—Paris—Palm Beach, Florida? Unhesitatingly, and with a warm and intimate smile, the Duke replied, "Kenny, *home* is where my Duchess is."

Of Wally, I asked, "What advice would you give to women the world over?" She smiled and said, "I'd tell them, 'Don't complain and you'll never have to explain.'"

I've repeated these bits of philosophy often during my lecture appearances through the years. The smiles and sometimes tears they evoke from audiences tell me what I have known all along—there was and always will be a glamour, a regality, a fascination, and certainly an unmistakable love which belonged to the Duke and Duchess of Windsor alone.

WALLIS WARFIELD SIMPSON—THE DUCHESS OF WINDSOR—PASSED AWAY IN PARIS, FRANCE ON APRIL 24, 1986, AT THE AGE OF 90. SHE WAS BURIED BESIDE HER HUSBAND, THE DUKE OF WINDSOR, AS HE HAD REQUESTED, IN THE ROYAL CEMETERY AT FROGMORE (NEAR WINDSOR CASTLE).

NOW

In 1934 the Prince of Wales traveled to Glasgow, Scotland to attend the unveiling of the luxury liner, the *Queen Mary*, named in honor of his mother, the reigning monarch.

During the mammoth ship's long years in operation the great and the near great sailed aboard it, and these passengers included the (by then) Duke and Duchess of Windsor, following his abdication of the throne.

In 1967 the ocean liner made its last voyage, from Southampton, England to its final resting place in Long Beach Harbor, California, where it has remained, open ever since for public tours.

Because of its tie-in to the royal family and most importantly since she and David were passengers on at least two and possibly more occasions, I felt the ship would be an excellent place to attempt to reach the Duchess's spirit.

Thus, one Sunday, following a lecture appearance I made at a hotel in Anaheim across from Disneyland, Valerie and I meditated in a private section of the hotel, asking Wallis to come in to us when we boarded the ship. We then set off on the freeway toward Long Beach and the harbor where the *Queen Mary* was docked.

Upon arriving, we walked aboard ship with a keen sense of deja vu. I had entertained aboard the ship, doing my one-man psychic show for private events following its docking in the harbor, and this made it seem familiar to me. But also, though we had never sailed aboard the *Queen Mary*, we've both cruised extensively on other ships, and the atmosphere aboard the *Queen Mary* still gave the illusion of the grand seafaring days it once represented. It was easy to forget that we were not actually sailing on the high seas at the very moment we boarded the ship.

Valerie and I took a preliminary stroll around the ship's Promenade Deck, past huge poster-sized photos of former passengers, taken on board the ship. We passed Gloria Swanson, Clark Gable, Buster Keaton and Sir Winston Churchill before coming to a rather secluded area leading toward an elegant dining room, which was closed for the day.

Though the ship was somewhat updated to accommodate modern-day tourists, the old world ambience was left very much intact—rich wood paneling on the walls, elegant soft lighting, deep burgundy-toned carpeting. The dining areas and cafes which were once used strictly for passengers are now still in operation, changed only slightly for today's usage. Along the walls leading into this particular dining room we saw glass display cases housing 8x10 photos of additional celebrated former passengers. A few tourists found this area and browsed past the photos as we stood there.

When they left, Valerie and I were alone, and I said softly, "We're ready for you, Wallis, if you're with us."

"Have you come aboard ship with us?" Valerie asked quietly, turning on a small tape recorder to record the following events:

We waited—content in the peaceful silence and the relative darkness of this corridor. Kenny closed his eyes and nodded. "I feel her with us," he smiled. "Welcome!"

"Oh! She's welcome!" Valerie responded. "I hope she'll tour the ship with us and tell us how she's doing and what she's feeling."

"She's here," Kenny repeated. "And do you know what I'm hearing? The tune that became her 'theme song'—'Mr. Sandman.' And she's telling me—turning his head sideways and listening—'When I made an entrance into any dining room, anywhere, the trio or orchestra would swing into 'Mr. Sandman' in honor of me. And for David, they'd play 'I Would Climb the Highest Mountain.' We made an exquisite entrance anywhere we went! We were an exciting couple and it wasn't just that he was a former King!'

"Oh, you know who I'm thinking of?" Kenny grinned. "Elsa—Elsa Maxwell! And it's because Wallis is thinking of her, too. She says, 'When Elsa gave her grand galas, for hundreds of people, they still seemed intimate somehow. They were attended by people of culture and breeding—no lewdness, drugs, or excessive drinking.' She says she has only good memories of those days and I know what she means—Elsa gave wonderful parties," Kenny recalled.

"Does the Duchess feel comfortable on board this ship? Does it bring back happy memories of voyages with the Duke?" Valerie wondered.

"She says the memories are pleasant enough because some of the most civilized people in the world traveled on the *Queen Mary*," Kenny answered in a somewhat haughty voice, "but she doesn't need memories of times with David." Then, in a gentler voice he continued, "She says 'I'm with him constantly. When I joined him in Paradise, it was as though no time had elapsed since I'd last seen him. I held him, you know, when he passed away. But it was so different with me. I was really so alone when my time came. There was no one I loved to hold me.' Now, this is interesting—she says, 'The angels held me, though, and the moment I passed, I felt their warmth engulfing me. Immediately there was no more sense of being alone. Soon afterward I was reunited with David, and we haven't parted since. It's glorious!' she tells me."

We had stayed in this corridor or anteroom leading to the dining room for a few moments, and another small group of tourists could be seen approaching. "Shall we move on?" Valerie asked. "Will she come with us if we stroll other areas of the ship's deck?"

"Yes, that will be fine," Kenny responded, and we walked off toward the open spaces of the ship. We paused to look at a large photo of Marlene Dietrich and Kenny chuckled.

"What?" Valerie asked. "Is the Duchess talking to you again?"

"Oh yes!" Kenny replied. "She's with us—glancing at this photo. I feel her over my shoulder and she's saying, 'Marlene Dietrich came here (to the other side) not long ago. She had her eye on David on Earthplane, and I knew it. She thought she could protect him—care for him. But no one could protect him or mother him like I did. I've seen her here, and the next time I run across her I'm simply going to say, 'Marlene, dear—there is no jealousy on my behalf. I won David—the man and the heart—and he's *still* mine, even today.' "

"So she and the Duke are still soul mates even in Paradise," Valerie mused. "That's sweet."

"She says she'd like to share something with you and with women the world over," Kenny said in definite terms. "She says 'you get the scent of a man—even across a crowded room— and you know he's for you. You see his smile; your eyes meet. I felt like that about His Royal Highness. That's what it means to be soul mates,' she says."

"I understand," Valerie smiled. "Thank her for sharing that."

"No, she's not quite done yet," Kenny interrupted. "She says, 'it may have taken me several marriages to find my soul mate, but I did it. Women should be more selective in marrying.' She also says if it were more difficult to get married in the first place and less difficult to get divorced, it would probably be better."

"That may be true," Valerie smiled. "Does she mind if we move on now?"

When there was no response, we simply began walking on past a bakery, an ice cream stand and assorted shipboard shops, at the same time enjoying the view of the water and coastline to our left as we walked. The sun was gloriously bright and pelicans and seagulls soared above.

We came across another poster-sized photo, this time of Fred Astaire, and we stopped to admire it.

"Oh, this has her attention!" Kenny exclaimed. "She says, 'he may have been a fine man, but he copied the fashions of the Duke.' Ah! She's

quite urgent to tell me more—I feel her touching me on the shoulder—
she's impatient to talk . . . Okay, go ahead, Wallis," he said, listening once
more. "Not so fast," Kenny asked. "Alright—she says she helped David set
fashion trends and she herself was deserving of being on the "Ten Best
Dressed" list each time she was on it. She's a little feisty now—she says
'Why should I have paid for my clothing? Any designers should have
been honored to have the Duchess of Windsor wearing his creations!"

"Ah, I see!" Valerie chuckled.

"She's reminding me of a story I may have told you before," Kenny
continued. "She is recalling a time she and David were enroute to
England. When they arrived, they discovered the luggage containing
David's dinner shirts had gone astray, and they were due to attend a dinner party—a black tie affair—that evening. She told him, 'David Dear,
you have a beautiful white cashmere turtleneck. Wear that under your
tuxedo. And, oh David, just replace your maroon boutonniere with a
white carnation.' The Duke said, 'Wallis, please—one just doesn't do
that. It's not good manners.'

"She's laughing now, and telling me she said, 'Since when do you
have to worry about manners? You set the styles for men all over the
world! And you have the Duchess of Windsor telling you to wear it!'

"He wore the turtleneck and apparently, when Prince Philip (a guest
at the party) told the Queen of the outfit the next day, he said, 'I must
get a white turtleneck. If the Duke of Windsor is wearing one, it must
be in fashion!' She loves that story!"

"What does she think of fashions today?" Valerie asked, as we continued our stroll.

"She says, 'It's too bad personalities of the world aren't better
groomed,'" Kenny answered quickly. "She says, 'It must be most distasteful
to the public who idolize them to see them in jeans. I always felt I owed
something to my public to always look regal,' and she's not too pleased as
she's speaking to me. I feel impatience around her, as though she's not
very tolerant of the people who dress sloppily," Kenny observed.

We walked a bit more and saw a sign pointing to our right. It read
The Queen's Salon. And as we approached the entrance we saw a pleasant and touching surprise—a photo, perhaps three to four feet tall—of
the Duke and Duchess, taken as they walked the ship's deck once upon

a time. He bore a jaunty smile; she wore a special grin, as though she held a great secret, which perhaps she did.

"Oh! This is perfect!" Valerie exclaimed. "They're right at the entrance to the Queen's Salon! Let's see what's inside and then come back out here to the photo."

As we started through the door Kenny said, "*This* is where I've done my performances before. I remember the room now, only I entered from another direction," and indeed once we stepped fully into the spacious room, its fireplaces, wooden pillars and flooring, theatrical stage and indirect lighting were very familiar to him. The room felt like an English drawing room, magnified times ten—very dramatic yet intimate. This was no doubt where entertainers performed during the *Queen Mary's* voyages, and as Kenny could attest to, programs have been presented in the room ever since.

We returned to the photo outside the salon. Once again waiting while an occasional tourist or two meandered by, we then gazed fondly at the Duke and Duchess.

"This is a riot," Kenny chuckled. "She says 'I must admit as I see this it doesn't do me justice, but I suppose I was never the most beautiful woman. But fascinating I was—alluring I was, nonetheless.' Don't you love it?"

"She looks so happy in this photo," Valerie observed. "So happy, in fact, that she looks quite attractive."

Just then we heard a loud *ping* against the protective glass covering the photo.

"Ah! She's a little upset over that!" Kenny laughed. I feel very warm right now—very warm. I think she's 'hot under the collar.' She says she knows she was attractive, in her own way—she worked at it. 'I knew I'd be important one day,' she says, 'so I looked in the mirror and carried myself proudly. I watched my posture, my carriage. I thought, 'I'm doing this for me,' but later I was also doing it because I was the Duchess of Windsor.' She's very pleased this photo is here. She says it's very appropriate and they certainly presided at many a grand ball similar to those which could be held here," Kenny continued.

"Besides her posture and carriage, what were her fashion secrets?" Valerie wondered. "Can she tell us now?"

Without a moment's delay, Kenny nodded then responded: "She says women—and men, for that matter—should find a fashion that's becoming to them and stay with it. 'That's what I did,' she says. 'High fashion doesn't go out of style,' she's telling me."

"Anything else?" Valerie encouraged.

"She says, 'Yes, it's an amusing thing. When applying make-up, a woman with gorgeous eyes and an unattractive mouth will spend a half hour trying to re-do the mouth and only a couple of minutes on the eyes, when it should be the reverse. Play up your best feature! People seem to have forgotten Helena Rubenstein's advice!' She says, 'What happened to compacts? They seem to have disappeared totally—and they can be of such help!' Does that make sense?"

"Sure it does," Valerie answered. "I use one, but a lot of women I know don't wear powder or carry compacts these days, I guess."

Kenny nodded briskly. "'Tell them to reconsider,' she says."

Kenny tilted his head sideways, listening. "Okay—Okay, I'll say it," he spoke toward his left shoulder, where apparently the Duchess was standing. "She's feeling a little feisty again, making me feel anxious because she wants to talk. She's so grateful to have a chance to speak. She says, 'I personally feel some women have ruined their chances . . . they've lost their place in society as ladies by refusing to have doors opened for them or refusing to have their cigarettes lit.' She's not a very big fan of this type of independent activity, she says. 'It's independence when it's uncalled for,' she snaps at me. Okay—I told her I'd say it!" Kenny sighed.

We continued standing near the photo, partly because we were somewhat mesmerized by the love which seemed to pour forth from it and partly because it provided a good source of energy. More messages came while we were at this spot than at any other.

"This may not be something she'll want to answer," Valerie began hesitantly, "but does she have any comments about the current royals?"

Kenny was silent a moment, then began, "She says, first she wants to establish that while she and David entertained John F. Kennedy and found him one Kennedy they enjoyed, the people were, in her words, 'foolish' for calling the Kennedys 'The American Royal Family.' She says 'there was only Royal Family as far as I'm concerned, and that was David and myself. We set our style—we set our own pace.'"

"But about today's royals?" Valerie urged.

In a haughty manner unlike his own, Kenny responded. "She says 'Princess Diana turned out to be fashionable after a 'Pygmalionish' start—a true sense of fashion regarding her clothes and her carriage. But when did it become fashionable to do what she did to Charles? Or to display one's body on the beach the way she and that Duchess (Fergie) did? And let's not even discuss the royals of Monaco! When they lost Princess Grace they lost all their charm. It's too plebeian and far too petty bourgeois to even discuss!'"

"Uh ... I think we should quit while we're ahead," Kenny said quickly. "I feel she's quite worked up over this, unfortunately I'm also losing contact with her. More tourists are on board now and it's getting noisier."

Indeed, when we had boarded earlier in the day, the ship had seemed relatively quiet, but as time had gone on more people were walking the decks and with these people came the buzz of talking and laughter, no doubt making it more difficult for Kenny to maintain the link with spirit. There was too much interference.

"I understand," Valerie said. "Does she have any last words to say before we lose her?"

"Wait—I'm trying to hear," Kenny said, intent upon listening. "Ah, yes. She says 'Now I realize I was right when I said 'The Heart Has Its Reasons.' I've had time to evaluate my life as the Duchess of Windsor and I know that my reason for living that lifetime was to be with David. In doing so, I feel I fulfilled a commitment I had made—to God and man. What more could I have asked for?' she says."

It was silent. "I think she's leaving us," Kenny stated. He closed his eyes briefly and concluded, "Yes, she's going. Let's thank her for coming."

"Thank you, Your Highness," Valerie whispered.

"She likes that," Kenny smiled. "Yes, thank you indeed, Your Highness. Come again."

DIANA, PRINCESS OF WALES

THEN

On July 29, 1981, I watched, with the same curiosity as the rest of the world, the televised wedding of Lady Diana Spencer to His Royal Highness the Prince of Wales.

Even then, as I witnessed the pretty blonde becoming the Princess of Wales, I didn't see the marriage as a lasting one. And while the world began a 'love affair' with Diana, I was clearly in the minority. My fascination will always be, instead, with the Duke and Duchess of Windsor.

I've been in London many times and have even attended performances at a West End theatre or the Royal Albert Hall when the Prince and Princess of Wales were in attendance. While others were trying to catch a glimpse of the couple, I preferred the company of my own theatre companions instead.

This is not to say, by any means, that I disliked Diana. I felt she was predestined to become a royal princess and did a tremendous amount of good during her brief life.

My overall lack of fascination for her certainly didn't influence my psychic opinions of the Princess of Wales. I have never allowed that to happen. On the other hand, I've never been a psychic who would tell things in a private reading or in public unless I believed them to be true.

Thus, soon after the marriage—in fact when the world still thought of them as newlyweds—I began making dramatic predictions about them during my lectures and nightclub appearances. I recall, for example, appearing at a country club in Santa Barbara and saying, "An indiscretion in the marriage of Prince Charles and Princess Diana will mean *she* will never be Queen and *he* may never be King."

While my entire performance as a whole was very well received and the audience had responded most favorably to my other predictions, the "boos" for this particular prediction were deafening!

The following year, when young Prince William was born, I expanded the prediction by saying *he*, instead of his father, could become Britain's next monarch. When William was still a toddler, the United Kingdom's popular talk show host, Jonathan Ross, was taping several episodes of his show in the United States. My forecast about William shocked this talented host and his audience, judging by the gasps all around!

Many years later, after Prince Harry was born, I made some additional predictions which turned out to be *chillingly* accurate. In the spring of 1991, the *Daily Star*, one of London's leading tabloid newspapers, made arrangements with me to do a two-day feature on the topic of auras. The articles appeared in June.

One day's installment focused primarily on my career and my philosophy about colors of auras. But most importantly, my aura reading of Princess Diana was featured. The true accuracy of the reading was not known at the time of publication. In fact, the elements unfolded over time, with the final point unfortunately involving her passing.

I said, for example: "A daring action, just for a moment's pleasure, could cause Diana enough *regrets* to last a lifetime." This was written before the Andrew Morton book was published, which more or less brought the tragic or scandalous aspects of Diana's royal life into the open for the first time. But it's since become public knowledge that precisely during the summer of 1991, when my articles appeared, Diana gave her family and friends permission to cooperate with Morton in writing the book—a move she was later quoted as saying she deeply *regretted*.

And furthermore, her aura prompted me to comment: "The weakest point of her body is her *digestive* system . . . and she must be careful not to become depressed." Again, unbeknownst to the public at the time but *certainly* common knowledge later, Diana went through several bouts of depression. And her *digestive* system was weakened from the ravages of bulimia, the binge/purge eating disorder she suffered from which was later revealed.

I mentioned some facts of lesser impact (but nonetheless true): Diana was "too sensitive" and "had her own psychic gifts," which I believe to be the true sense of healing she brought to many patients she visited over the years. But one passage will stay eerily etched in my memory. I'd forgotten about it entirely until my secretary came across the *Daily Star* clippings while sorting out my press material one day.

In the passage, I warned that Diana's danger period was from *July through November*. I also cautioned her to beware of *fast-moving cars*. As I read the clipping, the August 31 auto accident which claimed her life unfortunately rang all too true.

Diana, we know, consulted psychics for guidance in coping with her fishbowl royal life. But she also sought guidance from astrology on a number of occasions, and I appeared in New York on a talk show, *Sally Jessy Raphael*, with her astrologer, Penny Thornton.

Penny and I established a bond while discussing the royals backstage prior to the taping of the show. As we compared notes—hers from an astrological standpoint and mine from a psychic one—we found many similarities in our theories, which we later discussed on the air.

I told Penny I felt Charles would be another Duke of Windsor in the sense that he didn't truly *want* to be King. I suggested that he might well let his personal life act as the catalyst to his bypassing the throne. Penny wholeheartedly agreed, saying this very tendency was indicated in Charles' chart.

I also told her of my previous forecasts regarding the indiscretion . . . the fact that I felt Diana would never become Queen. Interestingly, not only did Penny agree from her astrological point of view, she revealed that Diana herself had expressed that same feeling to her.

We also agreed on another issue. I said I felt William might well become the next monarch (or at least be the best choice as monarch). She told me his chart indicated that very thing.

We remained in contact sporadically after that appearance, and when Penny sent me a copy of her book, *With Love from Diana*, I was pleased to see that many of the theories we'd discussed were now in print.

It fascinates me that while we arrived at our conclusions by completely different methods (astrology vs. the psychic or spirit world), the end results bore much of the same information, and it did not necessarily bode well for the royal family, and Charles and Diana in particular.

★ ★ ★

It occurred to me on a couple of occasions regarding Diana that perhaps I should break my rule of not contacting someone but instead waiting for them to make the first move, as discussed previously where Elvis Presley was concerned.

One such occasion was when I did the *Daily Star* aura reading and saw what was potentially in her future. But I hoped that perhaps the Princess or someone close to her would read the article and take heed.

Another time, however, on a rainy afternoon in London, I was taking a walk along Kensington High Street near Kensington Palace (I often stay at the Copthorne Tara Hotel nearby). I paused at the neighborhood McDonald's and decided a cup of coffee might take the chill out of the afternoon for me.

As I stood in line, a brief commotion occurred—the murmurs of people nearby, heads turning, some ladies even curtsying. And it was there, of all places in London, that I saw the Princess of Wales with her young sons, standing in line as any mother and sons might. There were security men nearby (at least I assumed them to be security since they kept watchful eyes not only on the Princess but the restaurant full of patrons as well). They needn't have worried, everyone kept a respectful and somewhat awed distance.

What I would have told her that day was that I'd been invited to tour Kensington Palace two days before and found it, from a psychic perspective, in need of what we call a thorough 'cleansing.'

As I walked through the Palace, I felt an oppressive heaviness. In the bedroom where former Queen Mary passed, for example, it was nearly impossible for me to breathe and I had to quickly leave the dark room.

To me, Kensington Palace is clearly a case of a location which is *haunted*, not *spirit visited*. A haunting, by my definition, reflects a situation where negativity invades the atmosphere. The entities are truly 'ghosts'—they are either angry or unhappy and definitely can cause destruction or depression to those around them. In many cases, they don't realize they've passed; in other cases, they realize it but refuse to leave anyway.

Spirit visited locations, on the other hand, are relatively harmless. The energy is certainly positive—the spirit is either playful, at the site to relay a message, or just there to pay a friendly visit. I can immediately tell when I enter a location whether there are any entities present or not, and then whether its negative or positive energy at the spot—in other words, whether it's haunted or spirit visited. There's no need to cleanse, or remove, spirits from a location. They cause no harm and often times leave on their own eventually.

In the case of Kensington Palace, I felt great sadness—great negativity. It was no doubt an accumulation of negativity from the last one hundred-plus years, since in addition to Queen Mary's passing, there have been other passings and tragedies at the Palace that have left their mark.

I sincerely believe this negative energy has taken its toll on the current royals. Princess Margaret, for example, has experienced a number of health problems and emotional setbacks since living there. And Diana, its most famous resident, was certainly sensitive to picking up the negativity, but perhaps powerless to overcome it on her own, leading to emotional and physical upsets.

But in the end, that day at McDonald's, my original theory won out, and I realized it would be presumptuous of me to walk up to a Princess and introduce myself . . . imposing my beliefs on her, unannounced.

Whether they are celebrated personalities or not, it truly is best that someone seek out a psychic's services, in which case, of course, we'd be more than happy to oblige.

Fast-forwarding to July and August of 1997, the romance of Diana, Princess of Wales and sometime-film-producer Dodi Fayed had begun. As fate would have it, Dodi's father, Mohamed Al Fayed, had a link to the royal family whether the family liked it or not (and they did not). Mohamed acquired the former home and possessions of the Duke and Duchess of Windsor, located in the Bois de Boulogne area of Paris, after the Duchess passed away.

He spent many years and millions of dollars renovating portions of the home for his family, while leaving the downstairs as more or less a shrine to the Duke and Duchess.

As time progressed, Mohamed made the decision to expand his family's living quarters, meaning he would dispose of most of the Duke and Duchess's belongings, allowing his family to inhabit the entire villa. Sotheby's planned an auction of the contents of the Duke and Duchess's portion of the home, and I was invited to an auction preview in Beverly Hills on August 18, 1997.

By then I had heard of the Dodi/Diana romance and as I viewed the items that warm summer night, I secretly felt that Mohamed was actually readying the home not for himself but for the new couple, should they decide to marry and live there.

The event was bittersweet for me. I couldn't help but reminisce about the Duke and Duchess while in the presence of their former belongings. I thought of the irony; how their names were once again on the lips of people worldwide, not only because of the auction but because the most talked-about current royal, Diana, was somehow linked to them and bringing them once again into prominence because of her relationship with Dodi Fayed.

And of course the greatest irony was that this was the 'marriage,' in a sense, of two royal scandals. Diana had, in her own way, certainly been at odds with the royal family. Perhaps the only source of royal scandal and irritation greater than herself had been Edward VIII's abdication of the throne so that he could marry Wallis Warfield Simpson.

And now, Diana was involved with the heir to Edward and Wallis's former home.

IN THE EARLY MORNING HOURS OF AUGUST 31, 1997, DIANA, PRINCESS OF WALES, SUFFERED EXTENSIVE INJURIES IN AN AUTOMOBILE ACCIDENT IN PARIS' ALMA TUNNEL. A TEAR IN HER LEFT PULMONARY VEIN CAUSED MASSIVE BLOOD LOSS AND DESPITE LIFESAVING MEASURES, DIANA SUFFERED CARDIAC ARREST AND WAS PRONOUNCED DEAD AT 4:00 A.M. AT THE CITY'S PITIE-SALPETRIERE HOSPITAL. KILLED AT THE SITE WERE HENRI PAUL, THE DRIVER, AND DODI FAYED. THE PRINCESS WAS 36 YEARS OLD.

NOW

When I first visited Paris following Diana's passing, there were several locations I wanted to visit in an effort to pick up any vibrations regarding the Princess of Wales' tragic passing.

Of course, the tunnel where the accident had occurred was uppermost in my mind, but I also wanted to psychically absorb the atmosphere at the Ritz Hotel, since it was at the hotel they shared their last evening and *from* the hotel Dodi and Diana left just minutes before the crash.

And I wanted to go to the Villa Windsor, the former home of the Duke and Duchess of Windsor, since Dodi and Diana had visited it for the last time on the afternoon of August 30.

Considering the circumstances of the accident, I doubted any serious spirit contact could be made with them at any of the sites . . . it was far too early (barely a few months after the tragedy). Generally, spirits who have suffered this type of trauma—such a sudden and violent passing, where they are literally "here one moment and gone the next"—understandably require an extensive period of rest and recuperation on the other side.

But I hoped that perhaps the vibrations of the locations might provide some psychic 'clue' as to the moments leading up to, and then just following, the accident. And indeed this is just what happened.

Valerie and I journeyed to Paris and London to research several writing projects and while in Paris I was asked to tape an interview for a television program. The production company sent a driver named Philippe to our hotel. His assignment was to bring us to the location for the taping—a small stretch of the city's famed Boulevard Champs Elysees.

As we rode the short distance, we asked Philippe if he could give us advice or directions about getting to the Alma Tunnel, because we planned to go there following the taping. "I'll be happy to take you there," he offered; "in fact, we can *drive through* the tunnel if you'd like."

Following the taping, we found ourselves back in Philippe's car, driving toward the tunnel. "I'll drive you through the opposite side of traffic, from the direction Dodi and the Princess were going," he said. "That way you will get a better perspective—from a bit of a distance."

"How will we know where the accident actually took place?" Valerie asked.

"It will all go by quickly," he advised, "and it's rather confusing inside the tunnel since it all looks the same. So, I'll count the pillars for you, and when we get to the spot, I'll say 'now,' in case you want to take a photo." (Which we did.)

Traffic seemed to be going very fast as we approached the tunnel. "Alma is just ahead of us," Phillipe said. Hearts pounding, we realized this was an important moment. We were about to enter a tunnel which, in the months since the crash, had become etched in the memory of people worldwide. Who hadn't seen, perhaps dozens of times, televised images of the crumpled Mercedes being loaded onto a tow truck from inside the tunnel, the rescue truck's lights flashing? And who could forget images of people stretching over a bridge wall above the tunnel, trying to catch a glimpse of what was happening below?

"Do you think going through such a dangerous tunnel is a good idea?" Valerie asked cautiously.

But there was a sense of being hurtled forward, with no turning back. "It's going to happen anyway," I warned. And I sensed the same set of circumstances surrounded Dodi and Diana. Their fate was sealed—it was 'full speed ahead' from the moment they entered the car leaving the Ritz Hotel that evening—destiny placed them there.

And then, Philippe's car sloped downward slightly and we entered the tunnel.

There was a golden glow inside ... no doubt a combination of the glare of headlights mixed with what appeared to be yellow-colored tile walls.

Everything happened at once ... several lanes of cars sped by in both directions, making the noise level high despite the heavy cement pillars in between the two directions of traffic. We could barely hear Philippe counting down to the appropriate pillar: "One ... two ... "

"This is what they were seeing—the noise of this traffic is what they were hearing," I said to Valerie.

And then Philippe called out loudly, "Now!," gesturing toward a pillar and then the wall.

As an eerie confirmation, we saw apparent remnants from the crash—a sickening series of long, black gashes on the wall. Perhaps they were skid marks or scratches from metal connecting with tile.

The instant Philippe had said "Now!" I heard another male voice, slightly familiar but not identifiable. "Unforgivable!" it said. This was a spirit voice echoing in my ear, and it repeated, "Unforgivable!"

Almost simultaneously I felt a moment of sheer torment, and the presence of a female. There were no words—only tremendous emotional pain.

But before I could sense anything further, our drive through the tunnel was over—as quickly as it had begun. Perhaps mere seconds had actually gone by. My first thought, as we emerged, was "We made it to the end of the tunnel. *They* were not so lucky."

When it was safe to do so, Philippe pulled over and stopped on a nearby road. "What did you feel?" he hurriedly asked. "Did you sense what happened?" Valerie added.

I explained about hearing the male voice, but said I couldn't actually speculate about whom it belonged to . . . clearly it was someone disturbed about the crash being 'unforgivable,' but in what sense? As for the psychic impression of the tormented female, I unfortunately sensed it was Diana, but again could not be certain.

But I did have somewhat comforting psychic feelings to relay about the last moments of Dodi and Diana. "I felt I was *inside* each of their souls as we traveled through the tunnel," I said. "They were gleeful. Dodi was about to propose marriage to Diana . . . she was relishing the sense of security and attention she felt from him. There was no sense of terror—no feeling of having their whole life flashing before their eyes. There simply wasn't time. They were just, suddenly, *gone*."

"The torment you mentioned," Valerie pressed on. "Was it physical pain Diana felt?"

"No," I reassured her. "This was an emotional torment. She'd been looking forward to seeing her beloved sons William and Harry the next day, and during those first moments following the crash, her first and only thoughts as she lapsed in and out of consciousness were, 'My boys! My boys!', for she feared they'd worry about her, or worse yet, she'd never see them again."

We sat in silence, then after thanking Philippe, asked him to leave us to find our way back to our hotel on our own. "I want to absorb the vibrations above the tunnel," I explained.

He pointed to a small gathering place nearby. "That's Place de l'Alma Square," he offered. "It's just above the tunnel. See all the people standing around?"

"What's the golden flame?" Valerie asked, referring to a sculpture in the middle of the square. "Is that a tribute to Diana?"

"I'm afraid not," he smiled. Philippe explained that the sculpture had been in the square for many years, and the flame was supposed to be a replica of the flame from America's Statue of Liberty. "It's some type of salute to Americans," he said before telling us good-bye. (I have since learned that the sculpture was a 1987 gift by the *International Herald Tribune* newspaper to honor French/American relations).

The dozens of people of all ages gathered around the bronze flame seemed to not care about the true origin of the flame. In fact, we overheard several saying, with accents ranging from British to American to German, "How nice that Paris erected such a tribute!"

The square had been transformed into a makeshift shrine. Photos of Diana, and a few of Dodi Fayed, were taped to the cement at the flame's base. Handwritten notes and tributes were also attached, or scribbled directly onto the cement and the cement wall hanging over the tunnel. And bouquets of flowers, reminiscent of those left at Kensington Palace in the days following the crash, were laid at the flame's base.

As we admired the flowers, I heard a whisper: "Too slow ... too slow," which I shared with Valerie.

"What was too slow? Are they talking about the accident?" she asked. "Are we sure they don't mean *too fast*?"

"No, I get the impression this is *after* the accident," I said, listening to the whisper. They're saying something was done too slowly after the accident."

But nothing more came forward. As I'd suspected, psychic impressions were only beginning to form and I knew longer, and indeed stronger, communications were going to be left for a later date, so we made our way back to our hotel, encouraged by even this brief effort.

Our next stop, the following day, was the Ritz Hotel, a brief cab ride from our own hotel. The cab pulled into Place Vendome, a large and elegant square featuring many designer shops, composer Chopin's former home, and of course the hallmark of the area, the Hotel Ritz, at 15 Place Vendome.

Our driver slowly drove onward, around yet another cluster of people, similar to those at the Place de l'Alma. These people were staring towards the Ritz. As we left the cab, we observed the group, and came to the conclusion that they must have been tourists, perhaps thinking they were not dressed appropriately to enter the hotel, or wondering how they'd be received if they did enter.

Or, perhaps, they had no desire to enter, simply wanting to be somewhere—anywhere—close to where Diana had once been. And a thought occurred to me: "They were gathered like this the last night she was here." It was almost as though they were still waiting for her to emerge.

We walked up the steps and through the revolving doors. Again, it was impossible to shake images of Dodi, Diana, and bodyguard Trevor Rees-Jones entering through these very doors.

From the second I entered the lobby, I was bombarded by an oppressiveness. The Ritz's interior is undeniably glamorous—but the heaviness of its vibrations were overwhelming.

"Perhaps if we have a cup of tea or coffee, we'll feel better," I suggested to Valerie.

We proceeded down the long lobby hall, passing several public rooms along the way. At the end was L'Espadon Restaurant. We'd seen a glimpse of the restaurant through glass panels which faced the lobby. We entered the restaurant's doorway, but couldn't go any further.

"It's heavy in here," I told Valerie. "I feel I could force myself to go in, but I'd be too uncomfortable to stay." "I feel it, too," Valerie confirmed.

As we stood talking, an employee from the restaurant approached us, asking if she could help. When we explained our hesitancy, she looked around, as if to see if anyone was looking, and then said, "I don't know if this means anything to you or not, but this was the last restaurant Dodi Fayed and the Princess of Wales were in. They didn't feel comfortable with all the tourists, so they didn't stay. They left to eat in their suite upstairs. Could that be what you feel?" she asked.

And of course it was. Since the woman had mentioned the famed couple, we asked if she could point us in the direction of the back entrance. It was from that entrance the couple left to take that fateful and brief last ride in the Mercedes. "No, I, um . . . there is no back entrance," the previously helpful woman said, quickly excusing herself.

Thinking it an odd response, we decided to ask another employee the same question later. In the meantime, we decided to have afternoon tea in the hotel's Bar Vendome, which we'd passed as we first entered the lobby. This room did not fare much better. We entered, sat at a table and did indeed have tea. But a heavy cloud—a black aura—hung over the room. To the hotel's credit, the finger sandwiches and pastries were excellently prepared and served, but Valerie and I could barely speak to one another. We felt heavy . . . lifeless . . . sluggish.

I have since learned this is where driver Henri Paul and bodyguard Trevor Rees-Jones passed the time while waiting for Dodi and Diana to finish their meal upstairs. It's where Jones and Paul had dinner and where, we have since learned, Paul consumed the alcohol which may have contributed greatly to the accident.

Certainly we were picking up the negative vibrations associated with these two men, who were about to meet a grisly fate after leaving the room.

We asked another employee, a security man sitting in Bar Vendome, for directions to the now infamous back door. He hesitated, then said, "There really *is* no back door . . . no back entrance. We closed it off." And with this, he left us.

We asked another hotel employee for directions to the hotel's indoor pool, telling the young woman we were working on a writing project (the pool is private and not usually open to the public). I wanted to see the pool not really because of Diana, but because it had been important in the lives of two other prominent personalities who had passed not long before.

In the early 1990s, Ambassador Pamela Harriman suffered a seizure in the pool and passed away shortly thereafter, never really regaining consciousness. And fashion designer (and friend of Diana's) Gianni Versace held a fashion show around the pool a scant three weeks before he was murdered in Miami Beach, Florida.

As we stood in the pool area, it became clear the vibrations surrounding these tragic situations had left their mark. There was a suffocating feeling to the pool area, and while it was colorfully decorated and in keeping with the elegance of the Ritz, it was not a place where I felt comfortable staying.

We next walked through an ornate drawing room leading to the shopping arcade. This time, when Valerie asked a female sales clerk for the back entrance, the woman motioned quietly and took us through a sitting area to a deserted section with a revolving wood-paneled door, leading to a small corridor. "We've boarded it up from the other side," she whispered. "We've closed it off," and with this she was gone. It didn't look right. In other words, it didn't look like the photos released in the media showing the four people huddled before leaving for their car.

But it also did not *feel* right. "This reminds me of a mortuary," I said. "The dark wood of the door reminds me of a *coffin*." Whether it was *the* back entrance or not, it was yet another disturbing section of the hotel.

"Could we just leave?" Valerie asked finally, and I was happy to oblige. We had plans for the opera that night but we didn't seem to be able to shake off our experiences at the Ritz. We settled instead for a walk and a light dinner.

Our final stop during this initial attempt to pick up vibrations in Paris led us to the Duke and Duchess's former home in the Bois de Boulogne area near the far end of the city.

I was completing the second half of my television interview and we wrapped up after lunchtime. Once again, Philippe had been assigned as our driver. He'd apparently enjoyed our expedition together in the tunnel, because when it was time for him to drive us to our hotel, he said "Or would you rather go someplace else?"

We agreed on Bois de Boulogne as our destination, but a buzzing in my right ear (often a sign of a spirit attempting to speak to you) told me it might be best to have relative quiet and privacy. I asked Philippe to deposit us about half way to the home, saying we'd walk the rest of the way, and he said he'd run errands and come back for us, in the same location, in two hours.

The walk through the woodsy area was peaceful. We came upon a police checkpoint of some sort (the area is heavily controlled by the French government and in fact, as I understand, no one has actually *owned* the Windsor Villa, instead, occupants make arrangements with the government to inhabit the home).

After passing the barricade, I felt we were getting closer to the home. I'd given psychic readings to the Windsors at the home on two occasions and Valerie asked me what I remembered about it.

"Well, first off, it's a mansion," I began. "And it's very colorful. I did the readings in what I believe was a salon. Everything was very elaborate."

"This is the street!" Valerie announced, as we approached Route du Champ d'Entrainement, reading from notes we'd made. "And there it is—number 4," she continued.

I'd have scarcely recognized it. Naturally it had been many years since I'd been there, but I also realized many changes had been made. It now resembles a mini-palace (Kensington Palace, to be exact), complete with gold and black iron gates, which I didn't remember being there previously.

The buzzing in my ear returned and we received our most satisfying spirit contact thus far in Paris. I didn't go into trance, so I recall the details. "It's the Duchess of Windsor," I told Valerie. "She's here with us now, slightly melancholy about her former home. But she says there are many more important things at the moment."

"Has she seen Diana?" Valerie asked hopefully. I answered, "She says she has not only *seen* her, she actually *greeted* her when she made the transition to the other side. The Duchess says she knew of Diana's impending crash quite a bit beforehand and she volunteered to be on the receiving committee."

"Was there a particular reason?" Valerie asked.

"She tells me there were several reasons," I told her. "She's saying, 'I confess I found the girl awkward at first, but I grew more fond of her. I came to understand her, ironically, after I passed on.' She says, 'I knew we had a kinship. All my beloved David wanted was for the title 'Her Royal Highness' to be bestowed upon me, but the Queen never granted me the title. Diana *had* the title but was stripped of it by the Queen.'"

"And she says," I continued, "'Diana's nickname as a young girl was 'Duchess,' which of course was ironically the only title I was allowed.'"

The Duchess's distinctive voice continued in my ear: 'I felt she'd need a mother here. I wish I'd been one—it's the only thing David and I missed having in our life.'

"And so she's become a sort of mother to Diana on the other side?" Valerie asked.

"Yes," I confirmed. "But she says there's more to it. She says, 'the poor dear was totally in shock when she arrived and soon afterward she fell into a deep sleep. But as she went in and out of consciousness, I knew she was devastated about not being with her boys. So I took over the task of organizing a team to attend to the situation. Her Daddy, the Earl Spencer, spent time sitting with his daughter and then visiting his grandsons. Then I took turns doing the same. And her grandmother Spencer has been a tremendous comfort. Diana used to talk to her in spirit, did you know that?' she's asking."

"Diana could communicate with her grandmother's spirit?" Valerie asked quizzically.

I told her that the Duchess said, 'not only that . . . she felt me around her when she visited this very home with Dodi Fayed!'

"That's fascinating," Valerie said. "I would never have thought that! But back to Diana's passing. Can she feel them helping her? How do they do it?"

"She says, 'we have been sending peaceful, healing energy to all three of them . . . Diana, William and Harry,'" I told her. "The Duchess says, 'I've had the chance to sit with her and hold her hand . . . to hold her and tell her, "Your grandmother Spencer, your Daddy and I will take care of your boys," and I feel she understands.'"

"That's wonderful," Valerie said. "Is she ever totally awake?"

"She says, 'Diana desperately tries to remain awake, but reality hasn't set in yet. Unfortunately, when she "comes to" a bit, she relives the accident and relives the pain of it all. But we're with her, her Daddy and I. We'll get her through it. Fortunately, David understands the responsibility I've taken on and he, as usual, supports me.'"

I laughed at the Duchess's next comment and then shared it with Valerie. "She says, 'oh, one more thing. I attended the funeral to watch after the boys. Marvelous eulogy by Diana's brother Charles . . . but a bit overly dramatic, don't you think?'"

On that note, the voice stopped. The Duchess had left us, and we made our way back to our meeting place with Philippe. I was enormously pleased . . . it was more than I'd hoped for considering the outdoor location and I knew it was soon after the tragedy to expect much of a report on Diana.

★ ★ ★

In the past year I've again begun to consider contact regarding Diana. I felt that ultimately a seance calling upon the Duchess of Windsor again would bring the best results.

Beforehand, we made a subsequent visit to Paris and sought to update the vibrations at the tunnel and the Ritz. Fortunately, the results were more pleasant the second time around.

Valerie was set to attend a one-day cooking class at the Ritz-Escoffier School, for a magazine article she was writing. I accompanied her to the hotel. "Welcome back, Mr. Kingston," the concierge said surprisingly, when we approached his desk while Valerie asked for the school's exact location.

The concierge had seen me making predictions on a worldwide satellite television program some months before, and remembered me from the last visit to the hotel. While pausing in the lobby, I felt much lighter than before. Certainly, the negativity had not disappeared, but it was tolerable.

Having been told that the easiest route to the cooking school, at 38 Rue Cambon, was to actually leave the hotel and walk around the block *behind* it, Valerie prepared to leave. "I'm going with you," I suddenly announced, "and then I'll come back and wait for you in the lobby."

We rounded the corner onto Rue Cambon and I felt a chill up my spine, which continued as we approached Number 38. "Here it is," Valerie began, and then she gasped.

"The back door!" we said simultaneously. And indeed, at long last, after the evasiveness we'd encountered from employees on our last trip, we'd found the true back entrance. There was the small guard booth we'd seen in photos (which in fact was where Valerie had to report for her escort to the cooking school) . . . there was the industrial-looking hallway where the party of four had gathered before leaving.

The hairs on my arms stood up as we waited there, and I became slightly dizzy.

Then, thankfully, the guard came to escort Valerie away. I gladly left the area, since it would have been overwhelming to stay.

I returned to wander the interior of the Ritz, where the vibrations seemed much improved from the previous year's visit, even venturing, accompanied by a helpful security guard, to the pool area once again, which had also lightened considerably.

As for the tunnel, our return trip found fewer people gathered at the flame, fewer notes and flowers. It was not that people had stopped caring; I felt they were simply trying very hard to forget. This time, we took a cab ride through the tunnel, going in the same direction Dodi and Diana had been going.

Again, I heard a male voice in spirit, this time saying, "an unforgivable *accident*," which was an important addition over the last time. By now, so much speculation had occurred—*was* it an accident, or had the entire tragedy been planned? Was it a conspiracy by the Crown itself?

As we sped through the tunnel, I saw a psychic flash of a white car, presumably the elusive one which had been so much talked about since the crash. But my sense was that, while it may have caused a distraction to the driver of the Mercedes, Henri Paul, the distraction was unintentional. I psychically "saw" the car containing people merely wanting to catch up to the Mercedes . . . to find out just who the occupants were who were so noticeably speeding through the streets of Paris.

I was struck once again by the almost-disorienting effect of the tunnel, even under the best of circumstances. Coupling this with what we now know about Henri Paul's intoxication, the environment for him as a driver would have *had* to have been devastating.

However, I came away from the tunnel with a bit less oppression, psychically, than I'd had the time before. It would appear that the city's vibrations are beginning to settle down at last.

Still filled with the vibrations of the "City of Lights," Valerie and I decided to hold our seance regarding Diana once we'd returned home to California and felt refreshed. We hoped to not only contact the Duchess or other emissaries who could report on Diana—we hoped to contact Diana herself if possible.

★ ★ ★

I chose 10:00 P.M.—a departure from our normal seance starting time of 8:30 P.M. The Princess was truly one of a kind and I felt choosing a special time would reflect that. Also, psychically speaking, 10 is a symbol of a new beginning (1 + 0 = 1), and I believed it would signal a new beginning for the Princess.

We sat in my salon, around the table where I've given countless readings over the years. On the table, we placed a gold picture frame which had been given to me by the Duchess herself. We placed a photo of the Princess nearby.

Valerie lit a red candle and we made our request for either of these two special spirits to make their presence known. A loud *crack* on a nearby wall told us *someone* was certainly approaching. "Welcome," we said in unison.

"I felt something cold breeze by my shoulder," Valerie exclaimed.

"It's her—the Duchess of Windsor," I assured her. I could see the Duchess standing, shrouded in a foggy mist, directly behind Valerie.

"Good evening, Your Royal Highness," I welcomed her, giving her the courtesy of the royal title.

The misty shape of the Duchess nodded in my direction and she outstretched her right hand, as though acknowledging my greeting.

"Welcome," Valerie said. "We hope you'll be able to answer some questions for us, Your Royal Highness. And perhaps . . . do you think it's possible we could also talk directly to Princess Diana?" she asked somewhat hesitantly.

I saw the Duchess smile, and we heard a distinct *rap* on the large circular table in front of us. "Is that a yes?" Valerie asked hopefully.

I told her, "She's apparently going to thought-project her messages to me for awhile . . . I gather that because I hear, inside my head, the answer to your question about Diana. She says, 'possibly . . . later . . . if we try hard to send her energy.' "

"That's wonderful!" Valerie said. "But of course, we're thrilled to speak to the Duchess, too."

"Interesting," I commented. "I just heard her say she's been smoothing the way for Diana in Paradise—arranging meetings for her and introducing her to what she calls 'all the right people.'"

"So the Princess is more awake now?" Valerie asked.

The Duchess told me, "Diana is awake for longer periods of time now, though she still lapses in and out of consciousness."

"To whom has she introduced Diana?" Valerie wondered.

"The Duchess—I think she'd like me to call her *Wallis* now, as I used to during our readings," I said . . . and no sooner had I spoken than a series of *cracks* were heard, first on a nearby desk, then on a window, then once again on the table.

"That's confirmation!" I smiled. "At any rate, *Wallis* says there's been a tremendous outpouring of affection for Diana in the spirit world. She says everyone has offered to help or to introduce her to the beauty of the other side—people who never knew her but knew of her good work on Earth."

I continued, "Can you imagine? She says Van Gogh (who has chosen to stay and progress in the spirit world instead of reincarnating) has offered to teach Diana painting, of the beautiful landscapes, the vivid colors."

I saw the Duchess still standing near Valerie, her lips moving, but the sound of her voice echoing directly inside my ear, as though there was a direct link from her words to my ear.

"Judy Garland sat with Diana for awhile, sweetly holding her hand," the Duchess said. "She said she'll give her singing lessons if she'd like."

"Oh, how nice," I told Valerie when I heard the Duchess begin again. "She says, 'speaking of music, pianist Oscar Levant gives wonderful concerts for us, playing beautiful George Gershwin tunes. David and I find that so romantic. Mr. Levant says he'll teach Diana piano, or rather carry on where she left off, since she *did* play.'"

I heard nothing more for a few seconds, but then I saw Elton John's face before me. Why?, I wondered, and I thought-projected the question to the Duchess.

And finally I heard the answer. Wallis told me Oscar Levant so appreciated Elton John's moving "Candle in the Wind" tribute at Diana's funeral.

"Since we're talking about celebrated people who've visited Diana, what about Gianni Versace?" Valerie asked, consulting the list of questions we'd prepared to ask the Duchess or Diana herself. Fashion designer Versace, of course, was killed only a few weeks before Diana's passing and in addition to a professional relationship, the two had been friends.

"Yes they've seen one another," I told Valerie. "But I'm hearing that Versace has barely begun recovering himself. I see Wallis smile knowingly, 'It will be awhile before either of them realize there *are* no designer clothes here—no fashion—no jewels. It took *me* awhile to adjust,' she said with a twinkle in her eye."

Valerie consulted her notes again. "We should really take a moment to ask how Dodi Fayed is. Are he and Diana together? How is he adjusting to the other side?"

For a moment it was silent. Then I heard, "Of course, he had his own welcoming committee here . . . his own family and friends to greet him. The young man is resting. The shock actually affected him more than Diana. She'd been through so much in her young life . . . she'd gained such inner strength. Dodi Fayed was rather overwhelmed in *life*, I believe," Wallis ventured. "He was intensely fascinated with the attention of the paparrazzi and with being involved with such a famous woman. Even *that* was all a bit much for him to absorb."

"But about Diana . . . " Valerie pressed on. "Has she spent time with Dodi?"

I felt a chill run through me and I sensed this was not a favorite topic for Wallis. I heard her sigh and then she said, "Yes, of course, they've seen one another. I've arranged for that to happen. And I'm sure they'll visit one another in the future. They share the mutual bond of the tragedy.

"And their marriage—*make no mistake, there would have been a marriage*—would have served a purpose, I suppose. It would have offered Diana and her boys the security they needed—private yachts, private islands—much like another well-known lady here arranged for herself. I'm talking, of course, about Jacqueline Bouvier Kennedy Onassis."

"Was there love between Dodi and Diana?" Valerie asked.

I listened. "Oh, I suppose so," the Duchess told me. "But she seems to have put this Dodi episode in perspective now and she realizes it's a miniscule part of her life."

"Has most of the trauma of the crash eased for Dodi and Diana?" Valerie asked. "Do they still relive it? Do they think it was a conspiracy as some people do?"

A brilliant flash of light shone near Valerie, then shot over toward the window, and I realized that at some point I had stopped seeing the

Duchess in any form and I was relying exclusively on the sound of her voice. But the light was strong, meaning her presence was strong.

And her answer to Valerie's question was equally definite. "So many questions," she sighed, "and rightfully so. *My* only question is (and she was barely speaking above a whisper now) why rescue efforts moved so slowly in the tunnel that night. Too slow! Too slow!"

I had a sudden, vivid recall of the voice I'd heard when standing near the Alma Tunnel. The voice had echoed the same words. Perhaps it had been the Duchess speaking to me then?

"Do you feel she could have been saved?" I asked. "I'm not a medical doctor," came the reply. "It's not for me to say, but I question—could help have arrived sooner? Could different rescue measures have been used? Could less time have been spent on rescue in the tunnel itself? People on the scene who could perhaps have helped said they didn't recognize Diana. Please! The most recognizable and photographed woman in the world?"

"Yet, in the end," she continued, "it truly was destiny. It's time to put the matter to rest in respect to family and friends who still mourn Diana. There should be no more talk of a conspiracy. It was a tragic, tragic accident."

Once again there was a bolt of light, this time near a wall with a gallery of many photos of my clients and friends. "That was so bright!" Valerie exclaimed, "like a bolt of lightning!"

"I sense she's upset," I responded. "She's agitated now. But I'm barely able to hear her. It's as though she doesn't want anyone in the spirit world to hear, particularly Diana, who I feel is fairly close by. She says, 'tragedy is ahead for the royal family. And we're doing all that we can, Earl Spencer and I, but William and Harry must be cautious of a frivolous move. Young Harry has a heavy heart.'"

There was silence while we absorbed this troubling thought.

I sent a thought to Wallis to continue, but still there was silence. "I believe she's speaking to someone in spirit—someone who's drawing close," I said to Valerie. "It's getting *awfully* cold in here!" Valerie observed.

The temperature had indeed dropped considerably. I could see not one but *two* lights now, one much fainter than the one I'd identified as the Duchess. My psychic instincts told me we were in for a marvelous treat.

"I see *two* lights," Valerie confirmed. "They're side by side ... there's a beautiful feeling with it, but overwhelming somehow. I feel almost dizzy. Could it be ... "

The fainter of the two lights came to rest on the photo of the Princess. "I have someone special for you, dear," the Duchess whispered to me. "We're going to try to do this together." A *ping* sounded on Diana's photo.

"Welcome, Your Highness," Valerie and I said in unison. "Diana— you're so welcome, please come in. We'd be honored if you could speak to us," Valerie added.

In answer, another *ping* sounded on the photo.

"I will help her to answer," the Duchess said. "I reminded her how people still love her; they still want to hear about her. When Diana passed—my, the service which was held! So many flowers at Kensington Palace! She flatters me by saying David and I paved the way for her by bringing the human touch to the monarchy."

We heard the *ping* again and almost simultaneously I heard a faint whisper, "I saw those flowers and thought, 'for me'?"

"I heard, 'for me,'" Valerie said suddenly. "Did you hear that?"

"Oh, yes," I answered. "It's the Princess of Wales, no question. And I see her doing gardening on the other side, tending to flowers ... is that right?" Another sound came in response, this time a light *tap* on the table.

I told Valerie I also was receiving a psychic image of Diana thought-projecting and visiting, in spirit, her former home at Althorp. "The poor dear forgets herself," Wallis explained. "She tries to speak to the visitors wandering the grounds, tries to comfort them ... "

We heard what sounded like a small giggle, and then I heard the faint, sweet voice of the Princess of Wales. "I mean to comfort them, but if they suddenly saw me, I'd give them a terrible fright!" It was refreshing to think Diana was regaining a sense of humor.

"I don't want to say anything wrong, or to upset you," Valerie began.

"The boys—she wants to ask about the boys," the Duchess said to me.

"Has she seen them? Has she been with them at all?" Valerie asked.

We heard the faintest whisper, "Yes!" Though I could not see her, I had a brief psychic image of Diana smiling. I heard, "But oh, to hold them again . . . to kiss them . . . "

The Duchess again took over. "Don't worry, dear . . . you'll wait for them. You'll see them again. You'll hold them again."

"I hear 'they'd be surprised to know I've gone horseback riding!'" I told Valerie. "I feel she took a fall from a horse in the life previous to her last, and it made her fearful in this recent life. She perhaps even fell off a horse then, too. But she's determined to overcome her fear." A distinct *rap* sounded on the table. "I guess that's confirmation!" Valerie smiled.

"Now, do I dare ask . . . does the Princess have anything to say about Dodi Fayed or Prince Charles?" Valerie asked.

An answer quickly popped into my mind. "I hear the Duchess saying, 'In many ways, it was a mistake—the marriage to Charles.' But I hear Diana saying, 'No—I'd have missed having William and Harry. Charles loved me in his own way, but his *heart* was elsewhere. I understand now.'"

"People may not like to hear this," I told Valerie. "But I'm being told Charles and Camilla are soul mates."

"They deserve one another," I heard, from what appeared to be a slightly bitter Duchess.

"I hope you know, Diana, how loved you were—how much good you did in your brief life," Valerie said.

Her soft voice sounded in my head. "She says, '*I* was blessed,'" I told Valerie. "She says, 'It all went by in an instant. But in the end, I wouldn't have traded a moment.'"

Again, there was a moment of silence.

"Have we lost them?" Valerie asked.

Silence.

"Is anyone still there?" she questioned.

I felt we'd lost contact with Diana, not surprisingly since this had been a shaky first attempt on her behalf.

"Thank you for coming," I said, sensing our contact with Diana had come to an end. But I heard the Duchess's voice once more. "She's resting again," the voice told me.

"This is something Wallis wants us to know," I said to Valerie. "Audrey Hepburn is spending time with Diana. In fact, she just came for her now. They're going to be working together one day, as more or less goodwill ambassadors to those less fortunate when they pass on. The poor—the hungry—they'll comfort them upon their arrival. 'UNICEF will be carried on in the spirit world,' I'm being told."

I heard one more faint bit of conversation, a whisper in my ear. I listened carefully in silence.

"Kenny? Is everything okay?" Valerie asked.

"Shh . . . it's fine," I said. "I'm listening."

All was stilled. No more lights, no more sounds, no more chills.

"They've both left us now," I announced. I felt very satisfied with our contact, knowing that a more prolonged contact with Diana may be in the future, after her much-deserved rest. That we had made contact at all was encouraging.

Regarding the Duchess's comments on the crash (that it was an accident and not a conspiracy), I will of course take her word for it, though I admit to having my own doubts on the matter.

Perhaps the last comments I'd heard the Duchess whisper to me are the most fitting closing. Her words were:

"Please try to forget this tragedy. In the end, it was fair for Diana to pass. She'd had it all—tasted it all in her wonderful young life. There is no such thing as being too young to pass or passing before one's time. We pass when it *is* our time—when it is our destiny to do so, when our mission, at least for that current life, is accomplished."

A footnote: On a holiday in London following my spirit contacts, I went to Harrods for an afternoon of shopping. A well-dressed man smiled at me; then when I returned the smile, he approached and explained that he was one of Mohamed Al Fayed's personal staff members.

"I saw you discussing Dodi Fayed and the Princess on *The Big Breakfast,* Mr. Kingston," he said (this is a popular television show in the United Kingdom). "It was fascinating."

"I have some very personal messages for Mr. Fayed . . . do have him call me," I suggested, handing the gentleman a card with my London hotel number and California home number on it.

Mr. Fayed never attempted to call, which I find unfathomable. If a loved one of mine had passed and a psychic/medium told someone close to me that they had a message about that loved one, I would move Heaven and Earth to receive the psychic message.

Now, Mr. Fayed, if you happen to read this book, there is no need to call . . . you now know it all.

THE SEX SYMBOLS

★ ★ ★ ★ ★

MAE WEST

THEN

MAE WEST WAS GLAD TO SEE YA

If you were in Los Angeles on the morning of Sunday, November 23, 1980 and glanced at the *Herald-Examiner* newspaper, that was columnist James Bacon's banner headline announcing Mae West's passing.

Nothing could have summed up Mae's love of life and people better. She truly enjoyed meeting people, and I can say from personal experience that people loved meeting and being with her in return.

I knew Mae West for most of my life; in fact some of my earliest memories include her. I first became aware of her as a friend of my mom Kaye's when we lived in Buffalo, New York. She and Kaye shared, among other things, an interest in spiritualism, or "fortune telling," as Mae called it at the time.

My mother taught me all she knew about psychic ability and I remember listening to her proudly telling Mae of what she considered to be my uncanny psychic accomplishments. This gave Mae ideas, apparently, and before long, if she telephoned Kaye and I answered, she'd say, "Now just wait a minute, dearie. I want to ask ya somethin', okay? And when I ask ya, just tell me the first thing that pops into your head without thinkin' about it, like 'yes' or 'no,' or 'good' or 'bad'—see what I mean?" And what she was actually doing was encouraging me to develop the art of clairaudio (listening to the sound of a voice and picking up psychic vibrations from it).

She started with simple questions such as "I'm thinkin' of workin' with a dark-haired man whose name starts with a C—do ya think I should do it?" But soon I was giving her lengthier answers, which I know were actually messages from the spirit world. She'd listen, then say, "You know, ya got a point there, honey. That was very enlightenin'.

Now I guess you'd better put me through to your Mama." When I think of it now, it's amazing that there I was, at 5 or 6 years old, giving psychic advice to the world's most famous sex symbol, Mae West! Yet at the time, Mae was to me simply a nice lady I talked to and saw in person.

Through the years, as my psychic gifts were expanding, Mae's involvement in spiritualism grew as well. While I was still quite young, she also sought the guidance of Reverend Jack Kelly, and, in fact, we all—Mae, my mother, and I—attended the spiritualist church where Reverend Kelly officiated.

Actually, though she asked others their advice, Mae was very psychic in her own right. She wrote, or embellished upon, most of the plays or films she ever appeared in, and believed the material she wrote came from the "Forces," as she called the spirit world. She once told me, "You see, it's like this, dearie. I need an idea for a pitchur' I want to do, so I say, 'Forces, Forces, I need some good dialogue for my new pitchur'— please help me out here.' And sure enough before long I'm gettin' wonderful ideas, so I call in a stenographer and dictate the whole thing at once—I just open my mouth and out it comes."

Mae relied on her "Forces" for advice in other matters, as well. She said that these inner psychic messages told her to eat roughage for a problem she had with colitis, at a time when doctors strictly forbade against roughage for the condition and prescribed a bland diet instead. Yet Mae, who'd sit in her dressing room nibbling a head of raw cabbage she kept beside her, cured her colon problem in this way.

Women the world over—Greta Garbo, the Duchess of Windsor, Mrs. William Randolph Hearst, Mrs. Winston Churchill, heiresses Barbara Hutton and Doris Duke—were insistent on finding out Mae's health and beauty secrets, for even as she grew older her skin was baby soft, wrinkle-free, and glowing. Her hands had nary a brown spot. Her secret can now be told—it was the result of purging herself with a daily high colonic. Her doctors were amazed, but agreed the colon-cleansing process certainly performed miracles for Mae, and again, her spirit "Forces" instructed her to begin the process.

"The Forces" also gave Mae sound advice on buying property, which increased her wealth considerably. Not many are aware that Mae's fortune was not made solely through her theatrical successes. She was, from the 1930s on, a successful land owner. She told me how she and James Timony, her lover, manager, and constant companion for years, took a drive one Sunday through a then-desolate area near Los Angeles.

"Ya see this area here, Timony?" she asked him, pointing to a strip of land, "buy it." The shocked Timony did as he was told, spending $16,000 of Mae's money for an area which would later become several blocks in the very valuable San Fernando Valley city of Van Nuys, California. Mae sold a small parcel of the land to "America's Sweetheart," actress Mary Pickford, several years later—for $180,000! The remainder became worth millions as years went by. On another Sunday drive, Mae instructed Timony to buy another parcel of land in what was to be the San Fernando Valley—it's now part of the city of Sepulveda. "The Forces" served her well, I would say!

And she later bought, then finally sold, the Ravenswood, a chic apartment building in Hollywood where she lived for over forty years. But the "Forces" correctly advised her to make a provision in the sale of the building, whereby she could remain in her sixth floor apartment, rent-free, for the remainder of her life—which she did.

It was in that apartment that I visited Mae on many occasions after moving to California myself. Visiting her was always an event. I'd enter the gold and white apartment, pass the white piano, and wait for her entrance. She was always made up, always glamorous, always "Mae West." She'd welcome me, then offer me a chocolate from the never-ending supply she kept (which she swore was not to satisfy her diabetic sweet tooth, but instead "for energy"). Next, like clockwork, she'd put on a recording and do "Frankie & Johnny" for me, and for any other guests who'd arrived, catching a glimpse of herself as she performed in one of the many wall-to-wall mirrors positioned around the room.

When we were alone, we'd discuss the spirit world, and she'd ask my psychic advice on people or projects which were important to her. Even as her career slowed somewhat , she maintained an interest in, and awareness of, show business. She was curious about other sex symbols in particular. Once, as I prepared to leave her, claiming I had a client to see, she said, "I'll bet it's that Monroe girl, ain't it?" and I realized she'd found out that I was advising Marilyn Monroe. "As a matter of fact, yes, it is," I answered her. "But tell me, Mae—what do you *really* think about Marilyn?" Hand on hip, she admired herself, undulating in front of the mirror. She raised her eyebrows, displayed that gorgeous smile, and said, "Well, she's okay—if you like carbon copies!" Yet even other glamour queens admired Mae, and in fact the first call I received on November 22, 1980, was from the glamorous Lana Turner, telling me sadly, "We've just lost Mae."

For the most part, Mae was all business. I remember watching her after performances, particularly at the Shubert Theatre in New York. An announcement in the theatre program always read, "Miss Mae West cordially invites you to remain after the performance to receive an autographed photo." After the curtain fell, a special platform was rolled onstage, on which the diminutive Mae stood, under a special (very flattering) violet spotlight, while still in full make-up and costume. Then the curtain rose again and the throngs of audience members were allowed to file past her, as she untiringly handed out the postcard-sized, pre-autographed photos to the public she loved. (Even in later years she continued carrying a stack of the photos with her when she dined in restaurants or made personal appearances).

At the theatre, she'd invite me back to her dressing room for a brief seance. The group was small—sometimes only Mae and me, sometimes also her maid or Timony, and of course many times our time was brief because the stage door man was anxious to leave. But she'd planned on the seance, wanted psychic messages about her career, and nothing would stand in her way. Her mind was always working, always planning her career moves. She'd talk about "Mae West" in the third person, as though she were a company or an institution. She'd listen to spirit's advice, then say, "Yes, that would be good for Mae West," or if I advised her against a project or situation, she'd agree and say, "You're right— Mae West would never do that." She knew her image and respected it.

There was another side to Mae, a softer and very generous side, but it was seen less frequently and she often covered it with humor. There was a Catholic church, Christ the King, at the corner near Mae's Hollywood apartment. After being driven around in her limo several times and seeing the nuns from the church near the bus stop, she told her driver one day, "We're gonna be gettin' a different car pretty soon. When we do, I want you to give this one to the girls, okay? I can't stand to see them waiting for a bus like that." And sure enough, the limo was offered to "the girls"—the good sisters of the church—shortly thereafter.

Only once in all the time I knew her did the Mae West facade crack entirely. My mom Kaye continued her friendship with Mae and came with me many times when I went to the Ravenswood. Mae often gave her clothing she no longer needed. It rarely fit and was the wrong style, but Kaye accepted it because to refuse would have hurt Mae.

Once, Kaye went into Mae's bedroom to try on a blouse at Mae's insistence. She passed by us as we stood near the door and Mae watched her intently. Suddenly her eyes filled with tears. She touched her index finger to her mouth and sighed, "You and Kaye love each other so much. You know, I'd give up everything I have to have my own mother back again. I think she'd still be alive if she hadn't gone on that strict diet of grapefruit and coffee." (To the very end Mae refused to believe that her mother had passed away from cancer).

She looked wistfully for a moment, but before I had time to comfort her, "Mae West" had returned and the mood was broken. But the image stuck with me and I know that beneath the businesswoman, beneath the real estate tycoon, beneath the glamorous if often brash sex symbol that was Mae West, there was indeed a dear, dear soul and I'm proud to say I knew her well. Mae—I'll never forget the times I came up to see ya!

MAE WEST SUFFERED TWO STROKES AND THEIR AFTEREFFECTS, THEN PASSED AWAY IN HER APARTMENT AT THE RAVENSWOOD IN HOLLYWOOD, CALIFORNIA, ON NOVEMBER 22, 1980. HER AGE WAS OFFICIALLY LISTED AT 88.

NOW

I decided it would be most fitting for this contact to take place in my home, since Mae and I had conducted many seances quietly in the intimacy of *her own* residence.

This would be a "sitting"—a small gathering (in this case, of two people) for the purposes of contacting a spirit. Valerie and I chose to be alone, in the living room. We did not know, going into the sitting, what type of contact would be made—whether we would see or hear a spirit, in this case, Mae West; whether Mae would place psychic impressions in my mind which I would then relay out loud, or whether Mae West's spirit would actually speak through me for the time being.

We placed a red glass-enclosed candle on a nearby desk. Valerie sat at the desk so that she could take notes on everything as it took place. Our only other source of illumination was a soft light attached to a painting facing the desk.

Mae used to recline on a chaise lounge while contacting spirits and dictating material to stenographers, and I felt it would be helpful for *me* to lie down on an orange velvet love seat in my living room, thus striking a position Mae had felt comfortable with, in the hopes it would encourage her to come in to us.

We sang two verses of "In the Garden," which is rather a standard hymn in the world of spiritualism. As we neared the end of the second verse, the candle flickered wildly and we knew we were beginning to make contact. (It was a cool evening, thus we had closed the sliding glass patio doors, and any windows in our immediate surroundings).

I closed my eyes and began to feel slightly lightheaded, indicating that I might be entering into a trance state. Valerie's notes take over from this point on:

Kenny began breathing heavily and mumbling slightly. A white mist seemed to actually seep in through the front door—faint and small at first but rapidly growing larger and thicker as it came fully through the door and into the room. The mist took the shape of a person and began floating toward the love seat. I watched it coming nearer, then looked down to see tiny indentations in the beige carpet, like imprints made by small feet! This has happened before during spirit contacts, but is rare and usually happens only with a strong spirit. The footprints and mist moved simultaneously and came within a foot or two of Kenny, who was stirring slightly on the love seat and breathing faster. I didn't want to speak, even to welcome the spirit, because when a psychic is beginning to go into a trance, the least noise can be disruptive and alarming. Thus I kept silent and watched.

As quickly as they'd appeared, the footprints vanished and the mist seemed to thicken and enfold Kenny. It hovered for a moment over him, then broke into tiny particles and scattered. Kenny mumbled again, rolled his head from side to side and then spoke in a distinctive feminine voice:

"I just came back from a long walk. I like to walk here on the other side as much as I did at my beach house in Santa Monica. Walkin' kept me in shape, ya know. Walkin' barefoot in the sand for a mile or two is like doin' five to ten miles on a city street."

This clearly sounded like the voice of Mae West, who had apparently chosen to come in and actually inhabit Kenny's body temporarily.

"When I met Gayelord Hauser—ya know, that nutritionist—on Earthplane, he taught me to keep my hands movin' while I walked; better exercise, he said. Funny thing, I still do it now, just automatically. Passed by Garbo walkin' around here the other day. She still does it too!"

The words were flowing quickly, and though there were many questions we'd planned to ask, Mae West, through Kenny, was strong and enthusiastic and showed no immediate sign of stopping the strong stream of communication. "Ya know, people used to tell me ya don't remember who ya were when ya pass on. Well, *I* know who I was in my last life—I was Mae West. And people here still know me by that name, though of course I've lived before, too. But Mae West was ma strongest lifetime. I see some of my old friends around. They recognize me more than I recognize them, but that's only natural. I was a phenomenon. I remember Garbo, Dietrich—they all wanted to meet me once upon a time. Now folks come up and say, 'Gee, Mae, you're looking swell.' I say, 'Thanks—I know I am,' but I'm not only concerned about my appearance anymore."

It was clear this was going to be a very easy, comfortable spirit communication. There seemed to be no struggle with words and the merger of Kenny and Mae was almost effortless. After swallowing and clearing his/her throat, the voice continued: "Ya see, I'm what we call a 'greeter' now; welcomin' new souls when they come over here. There was nothin' I liked better'n my public comin' up to me sayin' 'Hello, Miss West, glad to see ya', so now *I* go to *them*. See, they come here to the other side and they're kinda groggy and need rest. So as they're restin,' I'll sit with 'em and meditate over 'em, visualizin' 'em wakin' up strong and healthy. Then they open their eyes and it's kinda surprisin' to 'em. They'll say, 'Why, you're Mae West!' And I say 'That's right, dearie! But we're talkin' about you now, and you're welcome here!' So I greet as many as I can and give them a good start. I was pretty lucky—I was pretty well rested when I got here. I'd been sick awhile and was restin' at the Ravenswood. So I took a little rest here at first, then got on real fast with my greetin'."

There was a brief silence and Valerie had a chance to ask a question:

"You haven't said much about show business. Are you still interested in it?"

There was a brief chuckle and Mae continued:

"To tell ya the truth, I look down and see all those workin' in 'pitchurs' or on TV, but I don't think much about it anymore. Once in awhile I'll see a cute young thing—an actor or actress—plannin' for an audition or preparin' a role. I'll send, let's say, the actress, thoughts on how to play a character and suddenly she'll get an idea. She thinks she's doin' it, and I'm really tellin' her! But we do community or group entertainin' here. I still get up and do a few songs now and then, but I've been here awhile so I don't do as much as I used to—got to give others a chance to listen to songs here. We do community singin'. Nelson Eddy and Jeanette MacDonald are here—now and then they do some of their songs with us.

"Cole Porter sits down at a piano and we get some lovely tunes outta him. Now let me tell ya—this is kinda strange. He sits at what you'd think would be a piano, and goes through the motions, usin' his fingers, ya know, but ya don't actually see the piano. It ain't in front of him!

"Some people here *swear* they see a piano, like they swear they see tables, chairs, beds. I don't see any of it; they just kinda "sense" 'em and know they're there. It's not real furniture like you'd know it. Now, maybe I'm more aware because I directed pitchurs and I've always had a good eye. But other folks tell me they don't see the things either. The thing is, you don't *need* a chair, you can feel relaxed and feel the *sensation* of a chair. You want to lie down? You automatically feel the *sensation* of a bed. But it's gonna look like whatever you create in your mind—it's not really there, you kinda *imagine* it there, if ya can understand what I'm sayin'. Make up your mind you're comfortable here and you *can* be, that's what it's all about—ya create what ya want in your mind.

"Now back to entertainment. We see what ya might call 'movies' in a big group, only we call 'em 'events,' because that's what they show. It keeps us in touch with what's goin' on on Earthplane. We get a group together and images appear—no screen really, just large images dancin' around before us. Sometimes we'll just hear music here, organ music is what it sounds like and ya *know* how I always loved an organ!"

This was the first hint of the suggestive or "naughty" Mae West innuendo, and Valerie couldn't help asking, "What about sex? Do you still think about it?"

Another chuckle, in fact an out-and-out laugh emerges, then:

"Sure, dearie, I still think about it. It's one of the most important things goin' and it's pretty hard to forget. But I like to think I got a higher life now, like my aims are higher. I know this maybe sounds prudish, but I shoulda had sex for more than just fun. I shoulda had it to reproduce. I know my kids woulda been stars, or maybe I'd have had a son or daughter as a doctor—woulda been nice.

"But I don't spend too much time worryin' about what mighta been. I got no complaints here. We don't know what sickness or tiredness is. It's 'Paradiso' to me. I love it.

"Had a little problem not gettin' any sugar here. Not many people knew I was diabetic, because Paul used to shoot me up with an extra shot of insulin if I wanted an extra dessert now and then. (Though in public he always called her "Miss West," muscleman Paul Novak was, in many ways, her "husband" for over thirty years. Though technically not married to her, he was her protector, her lover, he prepared her meals and tended to her when she was ill. And most importantly, he considered it an honor to do so, and the very reason for his being on Earth).

"But they do give us little pellets here if we want them; kinda sweet, they melt in your mouth. It takes away the craving for sugar till you're over it. But we're so busy with classes, walkin', talkin', dancin'—it's a good life.

"You'll find that sweets will be replaced on Earthplane, too," she continued. "You'll buy things that look like a carrot or fruit, and they'll satisfy cravings. There'll also be a capsule or pill or maybe a pellet that you'll put under your tongue; it'll take care of diabetes by the year 2020."

There was a pause and Valerie ventured forward with a question: "Miss West, you seem so aware and knowledgeable about medicine now. Would you be able to tell us what may lie ahead in health or human developments?"

Another chuckle emerged, then the voice flowed on smoothly, "Of course I can do it because I'm even more psychic now that I used to be. So get your pad and pen ready, honey, because there's lots to tell."

The information which follows came randomly and very quickly. The words are Mae West's, taken verbatim from the spirit contact—only the dates have been re-organized *chronically* as much as possible, to allow for better continuity:

After the Year 2000

"There'll be more TV's in public places, like public squares; maybe one set per house. More time will be spent on the body, on health and on conversation. There'll be better family relationships, like back in the 1920s and '30s, with children respectin' their parents.

"Homes as you know them will become sorta extinct—there'll be more condominium-type places because homes will be too expensive. I can tell you this because I used ta be a good businesswoman and knew ma' real estate."

2010-2015

"Attitudes about teeth will change. Men will be goin' in for gold teeth like some kinda status symbol, like people go for drivin' a Rolls Royce now. The more gold teeth they got, the wealthier they'll seem, and they'll even set little diamonds in. They'll also wear headbands and feathers—fancier than a woman—like they're really 'cock 'o' the walk,' know what I mean?

"Now back to the teeth. This'll happen later, but I see a day when there'll be no more dental problems. You'll take some kind of apple-like product, bite on it, and your teeth will fall away; then you'll go to someone like a dentist and he'll put in somethin' like dentures, only more advanced. It's kinda complicated, but I've been doin' research on it. Fascinatin,' huh?"

By the Year 2015

"Sometime by or before the year 2015, *lots* of changes will take place.

"Ya see, here we don't have no air conditionin' or heatin' systems, and you won't need 'em either. You'll adjust your own body temperature through biofeedback or somethin' close to it.

"For bad backs, bad arches and varicose veins, there's gonna be a lotion to rub it all away. You'll rub it on and your bad arches or bad back will be gone, even varicose veins will be helped by the lotion. Before that, docs will discover how to take a rod of some kind with a light on it—when they use it on the veins they'll be absorbed back into the bloodstream and gone forever, better than shots or lasers like they're tryin' to use now.

"Ladies have a lot to look forward to by 2015. Facelifts will be a thing of the past. A product will come out on the market called somethin' like 'Sudden Veil Lift.' You'll put it on your face for 15 minutes, peel it off, and the skin will be tightened like a lift. But this will have long-lasting results. A lady named Julie will put the product out.

"Ladies will use more natural things than rouge or lipstick for color. Their hearts will be in better shape, too, and their circulation and their color will naturally be better.

"There won't be any more worries about dietin'—you'll be able to thought-project your weight and what you need—like programmin' yourself to what you need to be healthy."

And More by 2015

"Grocery stores are gonna be a thing of the past, too. There'll be a whole new type of store, not exactly a "health food store," but somethin' more advanced, called somethin' like 'Forever Young'—and that's how you'll feel. You'll get a bottle of somethin' to help your cholesterol, for example; a teaspoon of the liquid will just absorb your cholesterol. A teaspoon of somethin' else will fix another problem.

"You'll also buy pills in the store, lots of pills because that's what'll keep ya' goin' instead of food. There'll be a pill for breakfast, one for lunch, then maybe somethin' like K-rations—remember those?—for dinner. So, let's say you're gonna go away for three weeks, see? Ya take your K-rations with ya, plus your pills, all a different color for each meal, plus the colors will be different for different sized people.

"Now, the way you'll get the right combination of the stuff is through thought projection. You'll go to some guy, like a doctor, and he'll put his left hand on your heart and hold it there. By your thought processes and by your body sorta like 'talkin' to him, it'll tell him what's wrong. Then he'll say 'Okay, you need thirteen purple M pills, five green B's, and so on.'"

2022

"No particular health news, but you'll go into a barter-type system for money by the year 2022. Somethin' like 'scrip' will be used and banks will be almost extinct. Good since so many are foldin' anyway, huh?

"I'm tellin' ya, with all that's gonna happen, folks can expect to live to be 130 or so, and happy, and I'm not exaggeratin'. In fact, maybe I'll come back 'n join everyone on Earthplane by then!"

There was another pause at this point and Valerie took the opportunity to ask:

"When you mention 'returning'—any plans for whether you'd reincarnate as a male or female?"

"Well," Mae answered, "I can't quite pitchur myself comin' back as a man—enjoyed ma female form too much and so did a lot of other folks. I *was* a man in one lifetime, but no more for me. I got much more pleasure outta bein' a woman.

"But if we want to return—and we don't *have* to, ya know, it's a matter of choice—we can go to classes here to learn about how to get born again. They tell us about upcomin' chances, like, 'There's gonna be a young girl born soon and her life will be like such and such . . . ' then ya decide whether ya think that would be a good life for the lessons you'd like to learn next time, and kinda put in an application. But it's a long time coming yet for me. Lots to do here.

"Well, dearie, gonna go now—no more to say now . . . " and, as quickly and easily as the spirit had come, it was gone.

Kenny began breathing deeply and moving his arms about on the loveseat, rubbing his head and shifting positions. Valerie called out, "Thank you for coming!" and the white mist again formed, moved to the door and disappeared.

It was the most relaxed, most thorough spirit communication—also the most lengthy and "talkative"—that we've ever come across. Kenny coughed slightly and Valerie said, sensing he was fully back in his body, "Welcome Back."

Kenny's response, "Did we get anything good?" Valerie's reply—a very understated "Oh, yes!"

JAMES DEAN

★ ★ ★ ★ ★

THEN

It seems I was always one person removed from James Dean.

Like countless other young people in the mid-1950s, I watched as his magic filled the screen in *East of Eden*. He had a relaxed energy, yet the sensitivity—the charisma—shone through.

However, I was destined not to meet him, no doubt in part because his young life was cut short. Instead, I found my life intertwined somehow with several of his friends and co-workers—those whose lives he had touched deeply—and it is upon these people who knew him well in life that I will rely for this section of the book. In each case, without exception, the people who spoke of him over the years recalled him fondly: he was a troubled young man, his passing was a tragedy, but "oh, the talent . . . the gift . . . he was wonderful," they all agreed.

Not long ago, I met the fine actor Martin Landau through a mutual business acquaintance. We spent perhaps an hour sharing stories and beliefs about the great talents of Hollywood, New York, and indeed the entertainment world in general. When I discussed the work being done on this book, and named some of the great performers we planned to make contact with, including James Dean, Landau spoke glowingly of many of them, Dean in particular. "Now there was an actor," he reminisced. "What a tragedy—what possibilities he had for the future! We'll never know the great roles he might have brought us as time went on!"

Several years ago I spoke before a gathering of the Motion Picture Mothers, an organization which boasts, as members, the mothers of some of the true greats of Hollywood. These women have gathered for many years for social, cultural, and civic-minded events. During a luncheon prior to my lecture, I was seated next to Julie Holdridge, the charming mother of Cheryl Holdridge, who had once been married to

Lance Reventlow (a friend of Dean's). She naturally spoke of her daughter and her marriage to Lance, and then spoke of Lance's untimely ending (in a plane crash). She compared the tragedy to James Dean's, in that both were so young and full of life, yet they possessed, in her opinion, almost a fascination with "death," bringing themselves close to the point of passing with their daredevil stunts with race cars and fast driving. "So sad," she said softly. "So sad."

The very talented Broadway actress and Academy Award-winning film star Mercedes McCambridge came to me for a psychic reading sometime around 1970. Following the reading, we chatted a bit and I found her delightful and a true professional. In fact, I was hosting a radio show in Southern California at the time and just before she left that evening, I asked Ms. McCambridge if she would, as several other performers had done, tape a brief "promo" for my show (basically introducing me and asking listeners to stay tuned for my program). She rehearsed the spot several times that very moment in my home and then, on my recording equipment, produced a tape which I brought with me to the radio station the next time I was on the air.

But earlier, during our brief conversation following her reading, our talk had somehow become focused on stars we'd admired and lost, and she mentioned Dean, for whom she'd developed a particular fondness while working on the *Giant* set with him. She mentioned his brooding sensitivity, but most of all his talent and the great future she'd felt would be ahead for him following the release of that film (tragically, it was released *after* his passing). She also, ironically, told me how she and her husband had been only a short distance from Dean's accident site within hours of his passing (they'd been, if memory serves me, on a driving trip up north and had stopped somewhere in the Bakersfield area overnight). I remember the look on her face—disbelief, that so quickly and so close by, such a special young man had lost his life.

Another client, the Oscar-nominated young actor Sal Mineo, had psychic readings with me many times. I saw him often at my home and also at my studio in Los Angeles. The studio was located above the Coronet Theatre, where Mineo was directing the play *Fortune and Men's Eyes* starring a very young actor, near the beginning of his career—Don Johnson. This was one of the most talked-about productions in L.A. theatre, due in large part to the totally nude scenes involving Johnson (and Mineo, when he would replace Johnson in his role). The play was the talk of the town and many mentioned how Mineo had a "bigger *appeal*" than Johnson! Sal naturally got a "kick" out of this type of review!

In spite of his shocking involvement in the play, I found Mineo, both before, after, and during that period, to be quite sensitive. He spoke, during our times together, quite wistfully of Dean, with whom he'd worked in *Rebel Without a Cause*. It was clear Mineo idolized Dean.

Dean's passing had naturally upset Mineo greatly and also instilled a fear in him that he, too, would pass tragically. This fear was not totally unfounded, for not only had Dean passed, but also, from the same film, young Nick Adams, whose supposed suicide occurred in 1968. (Oddly, I had been invited to a party at the Bel Air home of Hollywood trade paper owner Tichi Wilkerson Kassel one night, but was unable to attend. The next day, friends who had attended told me what a great evening I'd missed, where one of the highlights had been the musical entertainment by Nick Adams. That evening, at a newsstand in the San Fernando Valley, I saw a very lonely and dejected-looking Adams standing alone. I felt compelled to talk to him, yet chose not to. Within a day or two, his body was found in his home).

Sal Mineo and I discussed his fear of a similarly tragic ending, and unfortunately, the fear was only compounded by a most unpleasant experience we shared sometime around late 1975 or very early 1976.

I returned to my home after participating in a seminar on the psychic world and felt flushed with a fever. I decided to visit a doctor, but received a telephone call just before I left for the appointment. The caller was a comedian who had branched into personal management for performers. We had met once when he did his stand-up act to open my one-man night club performance.

He suggested we meet as soon as possible to discuss some business, because he had great plans for me, but needed to discuss my signing a contract with him almost immediately. My sixth sense told me to wait, and I told him so, not only because I was unsure of him but also because I felt ill. He was quite persistent, and perhaps because I did feel ill and feverish, I agreed, in a haze, to stop off to see him at his office while I was out that day.

As I sat with him, feeling by now quite ill (the doctor had confirmed that I had some type of infection and should go home to bed), he urged me to sign a contract with him at once. I was eager to return home and some of his ideas sounded promising, but I told him I would have to bring the contract to my attorney. "Oh, no, you need to sign this right away," he insisted. "This is very important and we cannot waste time." By now I was thinking, "Anything, to get me out of here and home in my bed," and I reluctantly signed.

When I *was* safely home and in bed, I telephoned the man and asked to be relieved from the contract I'd just signed. "Oh no," he said firmly. "This is binding and I'm holding you to it."

When I had rested for a day or so, I called my attorney. He told me he'd look at the contract, but that no one had held a gun to my head and forced me to sign (if only words could be considered a "gun"!), so he thought it was legal.

Shortly afterwards I received a call from a very powerful woman who was booking guests for several top television shows. I told her of my predicament and she said, "You never should have signed with the man, but let me call him. Believe me, *I'll* get him to release you!" Not five minutes later, the former comedian called. "Kenny, you know," he began suavely, "I've been thinking. If you're unhappy, I'd be glad to release you from the contract. I'll bring it over to you tonight, okay?"

Sal Mineo was due at my home that evening for a reading, so I suggested that the man arrive shortly after the reading. At its conclusion, I told Sal that the man would be arriving, and explained the situation. Being his compassionate self, he was angered by the treatment I'd received. As he was leaving, he encountered the manager on his way in.

"How are you, Mineo?" the manager asked. "By the way, I didn't care for your show." (Meaning *Fortune* . . .)

Sal understandably took this as a personal insult. "And I don't care for what you did to my friend Kenny," he responded angrily. The man told him it was none of his business, to which Sal answered, "Kenny's my friend, and I'm making it my business."

With pure hatred on his face, the manager said, "You know, Mineo, I hope you have a violent death." Now caught up in the heat of the moment, and yet with no true malice in his eyes, Sal replied, "Maybe the same time I pass, you'll pass, too."

Unfortunately, my dear client Sal was most accurate in his prediction. He was found a short time later (on February 12, 1976) in his West Hollywood garage, having been knifed to death. I read the account in the newspaper the following day and, remembering his premonition, checked the obituary column. To my shock, I found the name of the comedian-personal manager, who had succumbed to a heart attack— the same day Sal Mineo was murdered!

I have always hoped, and somehow psychically felt, that Mineo and Dean have found each other in friendship again on the other side. Perhaps this, or other revelations, will come forward as we begin the "NOW" section pertaining to James Dean.

> JAMES DEAN PLANNED TO PARTICIPATE IN A CAR RACE IN SALINAS, CALIFORNIA ON OCTOBER 2, 1955. HE LEFT FOR THE AREA TWO DAYS EARLIER, BUT NEVER REACHED HIS DESTINATION. HE SUSTAINED FATAL INJURIES WHILE DRIVING HIS RACE CAR TOWARD SALINAS, CRASHING NEAR CHOLAME, CALIFORNIA. THE TIME WAS APPROXIMATELY 5:45 P.M.—THE DATE WAS SEPTEMBER 30, 1955. JAMES DEAN WAS 24 YEARS OLD.

NOW

Often, it's easiest for a spirit to make its presence known at the site of its passing—the last place where this soul was "alive" on Earth. The site of a passing is bound to be especially memorable for the soul—whether the memory is of the trauma involved, the pain, the struggle, or perhaps the peace and happiness from a final release of all Earthly concerns.

In the case of a violent passing such as a murder or an accident, the spirit's recollection is particularly strong and often they return to the scene time and again to try and make some sense of the event. When a psychic/medium returns to the scene and calls on that spirit, it often gives the spirit a wonderful opportunity to have a final "say"—to tie up loose ends or to communicate messages which they were deprived of communicating in "life," due to the suddenness of their passing.

Whatever the reason for coming together, the very joining of psychic and spirit at the site of a passing is sure to generate a tremendous amount of energy and we felt that it would be most appropriate to tap into that energy for our contact with James Dean. To further enhance our possibility for success, I wanted to attempt the spirit contact on the exact anniversary of the accident and at the exact time of day.

I asked Valerie to research basic information regarding James Dean's fatal car accident. I wanted to re-trace his steps as accurately as possible; the goal was to follow in his footsteps by putting myself on the route he took those last few hours of his life. I was sure the strongest amount of spirit energy would be found near the accident site, but I also felt certain that Dean's spirit might communicate all along the way leading up to the site, and that he might actually *wish* to relive the accident, painful though it might be at times, as a method of finally releasing it, for spirits do carry memories of their previous lifetimes with them to the other side, and often have to work at dealing with their feelings about these lifetimes as part of their growth process in Paradise.

I asked two other gifted psychics, the husband and wife team of Doris and Bill Freebury, to accompany Valerie and me on the trip. The Freeburys join me regularly in giving psychic readings at my twice-monthly spiritualist meetings in California's San Fernando Valley, and I know they are both dedicated and capable of bringing in spirits. The four of us would certainly be a formidable team as we sought to recreate every aspect of Dean's last hours. The number four was also significant because Valerie informed me that there had been four in Dean's traveling party, as well—Dean and his mechanic Rolf Wutherich traveled in Dean's race car and Dean's driving teacher Bill Hickman and Sandy Roth, a photographer ready to chronicle the race, followed behind in Dean's other car.

Valerie was able to obtain an accurate account of the roads driven on the trip, and to our surprise, Dean began his final day by leaving his home in Sherman Oaks—*my* home base and the very city from which we'd *planned* to leave, even before knowing of Dean's association there!

The night of September 29, Valerie announced that although she'd found Dean's last home address, she was unsure of its exact whereabouts and wanted to make a quick "dry run" of the area, to save us the necessity of searching for the home the following morning. According to her notes, the home had burned to the ground some years ago and a more modern home had since been built, but it would still seem like a good place to begin our journey, and thus Valerie drove to the neighborhood. What happened that night as she drove alone gave us a clue that we were *already* in tune with James Dean and would be guided along our route. Valerie's account follows:

"James Dean lived on a street named Sutton in Sherman Oaks and I'd driven by a section of Sutton in the neighborhood many times. I'd noticed that the street was fairly short, however, and wanted to make sure that the section we wanted—the 14600 block—was the section I'd seen before. To my dismay, I discovered that it was not. I pulled over and thought, "Okay, now what? Sutton must be one of those streets which go for a block or two and dead end, only to pick up again somewhere else.

"I continued to drive and again found a block of Sutton, but it, too, was not long enough to extend to the 14600 block. I'm sure I was driving erratically, starting and stopping, and the next thing I knew the car stalled. I waited for a moment, then was fortunately able to start the engine once more.

"I was frustrated; it was getting late and I felt like giving up, yet I knew how important it was to find the home. I said, 'Mr. Dean—and it seems strange calling you that because you were so young when you passed—but I don't know what else to call you, Mr. Dean. We want to do justice to finding your former home site and taking your route, but I'm lost and need your help.' I'd continued driving as I said this and the *very next* street I came to was the correct stretch of Sutton! I almost felt I was *driven* to the spot by someone else, and I felt it was Dean himself."

The Freeburys arrived to pick us up in their blue Cadillac at 10:30 the next morning. This was not the time Dean had originally left; he'd left his home much earlier in the morning, but spent time in Hollywood at Competition Motors, where he'd purchased the car he would use in the race and where he'd recently left it for tuning up. This is the car Dean would drive to Salinas. He also made several other stops in the Hollywood area, some of them at places which no longer exist. His entire morning was spent at various Hollywood and San Fernando Valley locations and we agreed that to simplify the matter we would begin at his former home. We decided to begin at 10:30 A.M. because, even though Dean actually left the area much later after completing his errands, he was obviously driving at sometimes incredible speeds. Though we would not go to the site of all of his errands, there was still no way for us to drive at a safe speed along the highway route (a distance of at least 160 miles), make the stops Dean made closer to the accident and still arrive at the site by approximately 5:45 P.M., unless we left early.

Doris Freebury and I sat in the back seat with a tape recorder to capture our impressions; Bill Freebury drove and Valerie sat next to him armed with another tape recorder, maps and notes, allowing her to act as our "navigator."

We quickly reached our first stop—the home site on Sutton. According to past accounts, Dean's home had resembled a log cabin. A fire destroyed *that* home many years ago and in its place a more modern home was built. But for all its modernization, Sutton remains a very serene street and a very peaceful feeling soon came over us. The neighbor next door to Dean's former home was sprinkling his lawn in the morning sun; another neighbor walked a dog. This was very much a comfortable, upper middle class residential street; it was not hard to imagine that it had no doubt been even more so in 1955, when Dean lived there.

Bill turned off the car engine for a moment and we sat quietly, each asking James Dean's spirit to come in to us, accompany us, and hopefully *guide* us, on our journey.

We were each experiencing a wide range of emotions—peacefulness, calm, excitement, anticipation—but certainly not fear, and we were grateful. If Dean were with us, and it was too early to be sure, at least he was not approaching the re-enactment of his journey with fear or dread. If he had been, surely one of us would have felt it.

The first part of the trip found Dean heading on nearby Sepulveda Boulevard, toward the Ridge Route (the Ridge Route is basically nonexistent now, having been essentially replaced by Highway 405—a many-laned metropolitan freeway which leads into Highway 5, another bustling thoroughfare).

Bill started the engine, and we drove off, turning onto Sepulveda and at approximately 11:00 A.M. we switched both tape recorders on as we began our trip. What follows is a combination of a description of the journey and most importantly a transcript of our psychic version of the final "JAMES DEAN ROUTE":

Traffic was progressing very well for 11:00 A.M. as we left Sepulveda and entered the 405 freeway. Valerie noticed a silver Mercedes driving to the left of us. Dean's car had been silver as well—a Porsche.

"Look, there's a silver car coming from behind us into the right lane, too!" she observed. A moment later Doris said excitedly, "There's a silver car in front of us now, too—we're totally surrounded by silver cars! This must be a definite omen!" (We felt we were being guided, or "escorted," by Dean).

"Yes, it was a silver car somebody was driving with Dean that day," Kenny remarked. "Wait—isn't that interesting? I said 'somebody was driving!'" (After all, the natural assumption has always been that *Dean* was driving the car, with his mechanic Rolf in the passenger seat).

"I hope we find out more about that," Valerie encouraged. "In the meantime, James Dean's first stop after leaving the Valley area was a restaurant named Tip's—oh, that must be it on the left of the freeway just up ahead!"

We pulled off the freeway near the city of Newhall/Valencia. However, we felt no strong psychic "pull" after getting out and standing in the parking lot. "I'm not getting anything," Kenny said. "I don't either," Doris agreed, "except a sense of prolonging, as though he were pro-longing getting to the final destination." (This seemed logical, since Dean would have barely begun his trip when he stopped in the Newhall area—why stop so soon?)

The waitress inside informed us that this was not the original Tips Restaurant, where Dean had actually stopped. *That* location was farther up the street and now bore a different name. "You're close," she said, "and though *this* restaurant kept the old name, the actual *old* building is up the street. It's kind of confusing, isn't it? But that's what's been done."

"That explains why we didn't feel anything too strongly here," Kenny reasoned. "Do you want to go to the other location—is it important—or should we just go on?" Valerie asked.

"Let's go on," Kenny suggested, and Doris and Bill agreed.

We turned back onto the roadway and continued now on Highway 5 going north.

"I feel good. I have a sense of anticipation," Kenny claimed. "I do, too" Doris said, "I feel excited about this," as though sensing Dean's own excitement that fateful day.

"It will be awhile now before the next important landmark occurs," Valerie pointed out. "That will be near a place called Wheeler Ridge, where Dean got a speeding ticket. We'll cross the Kern County line and then near the Grapevine"(a particularly treacherous stretch of freeway), "he got a ticket for supposedly going 85 miles per hour."

We continued in silence a few moments, then Kenny said, "I'm getting claustrophobic. My ears feel closed; I feel the urge to speed. I feel Dean decided to hurry at this point. He wanted to get to the next restaurant for some reason." Kenny began breathing rapidly, "I'm getting uncomfortable," he continued. "I'd like to go as fast as I can, to 'get it over with,' whatever that means."

There were hills on both sides of the road we were traveling; we could not see the oncoming lanes of traffic and the truck speed limit was only 35 miles per hour, yet Doris and Kenny felt an urge to rush on. Valerie had been periodically watching the map, without alerting anyone to the group's exact location, and a quick look proved that we were fast approaching the site where Dean received his ticket, and Kenny's psychic feelings confirmed this.

"Everything's closing in on me. I feel I'm going to be pulled over," Kenny announced somewhat anxiously. "I'm out of control—the car's driving itself, yet I'd like to go much faster . . . "

"There's the sign for the Grapevine—it's one mile ahead. We are right now very close to where he was getting the ticket," Valerie said.

"I'm using the cruise control," Bill said, "but otherwise I'd want to 'kick it up' more and go even faster."

"I feel like I want to fly," Valerie said excitedly. "How fast are we going?"

"Almost seventy," Bill answered, but it feels . . . "

"Like we're just crawling?" Valerie asked.

"Yes, like we're creeping," Bill agreed.

"Something wasn't quite right here," Doris announced. "He thought about turning back at this point. He knew something was wrong, but didn't know why he felt he had to go on. He had a moment when he felt he might pass if he continued ... "

Doris' voice drifted and Kenny became silent. It appeared they were being at least partially taken over by some spirit influence and both were nearly approaching a trance state.

We drove on in silence, until passing an area near Lake Isabella, where we joined Route 99 toward Bakersfield/Fresno. This was past the point where Dean received the speeding ticket. "Awhile back," Doris said, "after he got the ticket, he felt excited but sad. He thought about returning home that day, to his cat." He'd apparently left a pet Siamese cat with a friend, we found out after our trip. "He was hurrying and wanted to speed, not just to test the car for the race but to 'get it over with' and get home again."

After journeying on Highway 99 a few miles, Valerie consulted her notes. "Dean exited on Union Avenue, leading into Bakersfield. That's the next offramp, Bill."

Union Avenue indeed seemed to lead into Bakersfield, but the stretch was a long one, taking us several minutes and bringing us first into an open country road, then a farming area. Kenny and Doris looked at one another and almost simultaneously said, in voices sounding nearly drunken or drugged, "We feel a spirit vibration with us." Doris continued, slurring slightly, as though being pulled into a trance state, "The spirit says, 'I'll continue to go with you. I'm reliving this ... '"

Just then, to our right, near the intersection of Highways 99 and 223, we saw what seemed to be a plane crash, with the plane in flames and a conglomeration of fire engines and people gathered around. At a distance, it appeared to be a major disaster and we all gasped in horror. Yet as we drew closer, the light reflectors used by film companies plus several cameras and microphones could be seen in use on the field near Union Avenue.

As we drove up next to the site, a large billboard loomed in front of us, with the words, WE ARE IN PREPARATION FOR FILMING THE MOVIE *JOY RIDE*. THANK YOU, WARNER BROTHERS, in bold, black letters.

"Thank God," Kenny said, "but that could be an omen, you know. 'Joy Ride'—wasn't that what Dean was taking, in a sense?"

Before we had time to debate *that* omen, three others appeared: a silver car was being towed into town (Dean's silver car was towed away from the accident); we also passed two companies who'd perhaps somewhat morbidly capitalized on the tie-in with portions of the titles of Dean's films—the *Rebel* Tire Company and a few doors away, the *Eden* Rock Motel.

To psychics, the mere fact that we noticed these words represents another case of an omen or "sign"—positive encouragement that the spirit world is approving of the venture. To the average person driving through Bakersfield that day, the silver car, the tire company or the motel might have gone unnoticed. But when a carload of spiritualists is tracing James Dean's route and asking for encouragement, the sights are indeed uplifting and helpful. We stopped for a quick cup of coffee, then felt a sense of excitement and anticipation as we continued out of Bakersfield.

Highway 99 leaving the town took on an entirely different feeling, however. We had been told by our waitress in Bakersfield that several hundred automobile accidents generally take place on this particular stretch of Highway 99 over any given four-to-five-year period, thus we were forewarned that perhaps it would be treacherous driving. A two-lane highway, it looks much like it must have in the 1950s when Dean traveled it, and a sense of peace, yet heaviness, hit us as soon as we had driven a mile or so. The feeling was tranquil, yet as Kenny perhaps best explained, "This road makes one feel like you could leave it and go into Paradise."

Our journey took the form, at this point, of much give and take, and will be transcribed in script form for the time being:

Doris: Dean's really excited now. He's gone through different moods as we've driven along, from being depressed to being elated. Now he's reliving the last moments, but he's happy to be with us. He says that when he passed, he truly 'went home,' and that whatever his life was like on Earth, life in the spirit world has meant more to him—he has been happier and more at peace. He's also studying law, and may try to guide someone here on Earth once he's studied enough. He may also reincarnate as a lawyer next time.

Kenny: I sense skid tracks were once here. And somewhere up ahead, on Highway 46, there was a change in drivers. Dean did not continue driving the car.

Bill: I agree; but I feel the other male, the mechanic, hadn't been driving long before the accident. Dean might have been alive if he'd kept driving ...

Kenny: (interrupting) Oh, brother! Oh, brother! You know who's in this car? Pier Angeli. Welcome, Pier!

All: Welcome, Pier!

Valerie: She was an actress, wasn't she? And didn't she spend time with Dean? Weren't they dating or am I wrong?

Kenny: He drove his motorcycle to the church where she was getting married to singer Vic Damone, and he sat outside in front during the cermony. Dean was in love with her.

Valerie: Did she kill herself—do I remember that?

Kenny: Yes. Oh my God, yes, she committed suicide. This is too much! She's coming with us, in spirit, at least part of the way today. She's spending time with Dean now in the spirit world.

We turned from Highway 99 onto Highway 46, the last highway Dean ever drove, and our journey continued. Our next planned stop would be the combination gas station, store, and coffee shop called Blackwell's Corner. It would no doubt have gone through time as a simple oasis in the midst of nowhere, except that it was the last place James Dean stopped, presumably for a light snack, and in one moment's time, Blackwell's Corner became immortalized.

As we approached Blackwell's,

Kenny said:	I pick up Cary Grant here. Why?
Valerie:	Oh, that's right! I hadn't thought it was important to mention, but I read that the film *North by Northwest* was filmed nearby. Oh, there's more! Dean stopped for a snack at Blackwell's, but he also stopped because he saw Lance Reventlow's car in the parking lot. (In addition to being a friend of Deans' and a fellow race car driver, Reventlow, oddly enough, was the son of heiress Barbara Hutton and stepson of Cary Grant).

After driving in relative silence for perhaps a few minutes, we first spotted a huge sign, and soon afterwards a fairly small building, and pulled into the parking lot surrounding the building. We'd arrived at Blackwell's Corner.

The building begins its tribute to Dean very early; the first thing visible when entering the store is a large, battered and faded poster of Dean. "So this is where ... " Valerie began. A young woman behind the counter, anticipating the question, answered, "Yep, this is where James Dean stopped for the last time. The original coffee shop burned to the ground back in the sixties, though, in case you're interested." The answer almost appeared memorized, and less than thirty seconds later the reason became clear: while the four of us browsed in the tiny store, several other people entered and immediately approached the same clerk: "Was this really the last place James Dean stopped?," they also asked.

The coffee shop was closed for the day, but after listening to us explain our mission, the clerk, who now identified herself happily as Sonya Hill, quietly unlocked the door leading from the store to the cozy restaurant and ushered us in. It was a virtual "shrine" to the late star. Posters, photos, theater lobby cards were everywhere; the menu even boasted a photo of Dean, with the claim "James Dean's Last Stop" emblazoned on the cover. Kenny tested his newfound psychic theory (that Dean had not been driving the car at the time of the accident) on Sonya. Her eyes grew larger and she answered: "You know, no one is really around who worked here that day, but there are a couple of people who worked in the coffee shop during that time period, and I heard someone around here say that *they* thought he might not have been driving."

Suddenly Sonya and another young employee became very interested in our project, and especially in the psychic aspect of it. (This may have been enhanced by the fact that just before entering the coffee shop, two or three young people came up to Kenny and said, "We've always wanted to meet you. We see you on television and listen to you on the radio all the time!"). Sonya suggested, "Would you like a copy of the final speeding ticket James Dean received? I could make a copy for you. We have one in the display case over there" (pointing toward another cluster of Dean memorabilia). We quickly answered that we'd like the copy very much, and she hurried off.

The copy revealed yet another omen: On the ticket, Dean's place of business was listed as "Warner Brothers"—at the film site for *Joy Ride* which we'd passed before entering Bakersfield, the sign had announced that it was a "*Warner Brothers*" production!

Perhaps the heavy dose of Dean photos and items displayed everywhere, plus the knowledge that Dean had actually been in the spot where we were standing, added to the feelings we experienced, but when Sonya and her friend left us alone in the coffee shop, we felt overwhelmingly that Dean was with us; his energy seemed to swirl around us and engulf us. It was full of anticipation, yet there was a heaviness about it. Kenny summed it up best, "He's making me feel what his spirit has felt many times since: 'This is it—I never walked on the Earth again; this was the last time I got out of my car fully 'alive'. To leave this place, in my mind, means to go toward 'death'. It's not a bad thing, just very heavy—very overwhelming. Feel it with me—feel it with me.' "

And, after being told what Dean felt about going on, we realized that *we* needed to go on, in order to maintain our time schedule, which was geared for arriving at the accident site prior to 5:45 P.M. It was now 4:45.

Back in the car, on Highway 46, we felt a sense of destiny somehow; there was a powerful sense of awareness that these next several miles were the last Dean ever traveled. Kenny began quietly singing a hymn, "In the Garden," and soon we were all joining in . It was comforting, yet eerie. "I feel peaceful and happy now," Kenny said, "as though Dean was either unaware of what lay ahead, or he was not afraid. But I also feel we're singing this hymn because the other side was calling up his spirit at that time—on the day of the accident, spirits were gathering to help him make the transition to the other side."

The details of the accident quickly played themselves out as we continued our trip:

Doris: He didn't get proper care. It may not have been anyone's fault, but rather it was a matter of not having the proper type of equipment, like we have now in trauma centers. He was in deep shock, but not dead, when they reached him, I feel. He probably would have had a chance for survival if the equipment had been different; the way things were, he didn't.

Bill: I agree; he wasn't killed instantly at the accident site. He's saying, 'I thought to myself Oh my God, of all the places to have an accident, way out here!' In other words, had the accident been in or nearer a town where there was a lot of activity, with ambulance facilities nearby . . .

Kenny: You can survive with a broken neck, can't you? Because I'm feeling a broken neck.

Bill: Yes; he could have had a broken neck, but he was alive.

The road became particularly hilly at this point, prompting Kenny to say, "This is frightening; like a suicide area here." Valerie agreed, "It is; that was just a little hill we went over, but I could see that if you accelerated a little and were therefore going too fast, it could really be dangerous."

Just then we came upon the intersection of Highways 46 (the road we traveling) and 41. "This is the intersection where the accident happened. Right here! Right here!" Valerie nervously announced. In fairness to the situation, research had explained that the roads had been widened and lights added for night driving, yet the intersection still had a menacing quality about it. Imagining how the area had looked prior to these improvements gave a better understanding of what Dean and the others involved in the accident faced that day.

We were early, and thus decided to drive on to the James Dean memorial statue site, where a plaque had been erected many years ago. "It's supposed to be just up the road near a grove of trees," Valerie read from her notes. "Does anyone know east or west or north or south at this point?" (for the area is quite desolate). "There's supposed to be a sign for the town or area of Cholame, then a grove of trees and a post office; we're looking for a metal sculpture. Wait—there's a restaurant and a post office—and a group gathered; we'd better pull over."

And indeed we and perhaps 30 others had found the memorial site: children, young people in their twenties and thirties, people in their sixties. They'd brought picnic gear—baskets and coolers, and it appeared they'd camped out, waiting for this moment. "I want to find out where they're from," Kenny declared.

The answers surprised us. A pair of 27-year-old twins, Patrick and Christopher Missling, had come from Germany—they'd timed their vacation around the anniversary date. They'd discovered Dean four years ago after seeing his photo in a magazine. At first they thought it was an ad for jeans, but they quickly discovered his significance as an actor, and have followed his career, posthumously, ever since. They seemed to be very intelligent young men, with one of them studying to become a lawyer in his hometown of Munich.

Two teenage sisters, Delia and Beatrice Pacheco, drove from their home just a few miles from the accident site to lay flowers at the monument. It was not their first trip to the site, but they felt the need, they said, to return again this year.

A gentleman perhaps in his late fifties, Chuck Meeker, also lives fairly close by, near Fresno, and made the trip (again, a repeat trip), to commemorate the day. Meeker and his wife have been Dean fans for many years, and have included trips to his hometown in Indiana and to the former film location of *Giant*, in Marfa, Texas, in their vacation plans prior to this. He informs us that from his extensive reading about Dean, Dean's last words to his companion Rolf were (as they saw the oncoming car being driven by a local young man, Donald Turnupseed), "I see him; he's stopping for us," indicating that Dean realized that an accident could be forthcoming, but felt the other car would be able to prevent the collision.

Kenny tested his theory (based upon what Dean's spirit had told him along the route) that Dean had not been driving. Meeker's response:" I can't imagine Dean turning over the car to Rolf just because he got a ticket earlier." "But he may have had trouble with the car and asked Rolf, his mechanic, to drive it and give his opinion, or to test the speed. What do you think of that?" Kenny pressed on. "Yes, if he'd been having trouble with the car . . . you know, now you're making me think about this, and I've read everything I could read about this for years!" Meeker replied. "Thank you, spirit!" Kenny quietly said as he walked on to another group of people.

There were many similarities in those gathered—everyone is a Dean admirer; all have gathered to experience these moments as Dean had nearly 40 years ago. There was a sense of almost morbid excitement about the gathering; yet there also seemed to be a deep respect, and Kenny observed, "He's pleased; enormously pleased with this. 'They haven't forgotten!' he says."

Clearly those gathered around the memorial site had not forgotten. In fact they had read about and actually studied Dean's life and career. There was one debate: over the actual time of the accident. Various accounts have listed it at anywhere from 5:30 P.M. to 5:59 P.M., and indeed each person asked seemed to have a different theory. But from 5:30 on, as the time unquestionably grew nearer to the accident, the tension built, and then groups began leaving the statue to make the short trek back to the actual accident site. We had planned to leave also and retrace the road taken at the moment of impact. Thus, we drove back on Highway 46, passed the intersection by perhaps a half mile, and turned around to head back. Our tape recorded account continues from this point:

Valerie:	The first thing I notice is that sun is really strong in my eyes. It's hard to see. That could definitely have been a contributing factor.
Doris:	As we're doing this, I just feel that there's—almost like a letdown.

Kenny: Yes, very much right now. I feel it, too.

Doris: Isn't that strange? I think it's James Dean thinking,
                    'now that it's almost over, nobody will talk to me
                    anymore, at least for another year.'

Kenny: Excuse me, what time is it, Bill?"

Bill checked his watch, as did all four of us, and we found that it was
exactly 5:45 P.M. "I feel that it's over—the accident's over," Kenny continued. "He's nearly gone."

We drove just past the intersection and parked near the ravine
where Dean's car had landed after rolling over repeatedly. It's hard to
imagine that this area had changed much at all since the time of the
accident. It is desolate; basically all that exists is dirt, grass, a telephone
pole, and a barbed-wire fence. While sitting in the car, we watched the
assortment of fans walking in the grassy ravine. One young man even
went so far as to lie prone in the ravine, apparently attempting to mimic
the exact position he must have envisioned Dean had been found in at
the time of the accident.

Kenny: I think it could very well be the case that Dean
                    was testing the car and had some reason to ask
                    his mechanic to drive. The mechanic wouldn't
                    be foolish enough to say he caused the accident
                    or was driving afterward, if he didn't have to.

Bill: Oh, no, of course not ... I sure can see the sun—
                    where it could have be a contributing factor for
                    everyone.

Valerie: Plus he had a silver car—that wasn't easy to see
                    in the sun.

One by one, as we each spoke, our voices became heavy—sleepy, as
though perhaps we were picking up the lack of "life" which would have
been left in Dean at this time. The speech was almost slurred—definitely heavy and strained:

Bill: I still don't feel he was killed instantly, though.

Doris: I don't either; though they may never admit
                    that. It might make someone responsible.

Kenny:	The law student back there doesn't understand why nothing was ever done with Donald Turnupseed, the driver of the other car. But he said he was a local boy, and a veteran with a young, pregnant wife, and perhaps he was protected by the town somehow.
Valerie:	The girls with the flowers back at the memorial said, when we asked about Turnupseed, 'You mean the guy who killed James Dean?' There's a lot of anger there.
Bill:	Just the same, if Dean came down off that hill behind us going over 100 miles per hour, as someone back at the memorial suggested, it would be hard for anyone else to judge his speed as he approached.
Kenny:	Dean's last words were supposed to have been, 'They'll see us and they'll stop'? I still feel there was more involved than Dean simply thinking the other person would stop. Someone didn't tell the full story after the accident ... I can feel Dean's car rolling as I'm talking ... it's rolling. (Shaking his head as he speaks.)
Doris:	Which side of the car did the mechanic get thrown out of?
Valerie:	According to my notes, the left ...
Doris:	Then he was driving!
Valerie:	That's not what my research said, but ... that's what Kenny, and now you, have said.
Kenny:	Now, wait ... if James Dean was thrown out to the right ...
Valerie:	On the passenger side, with his foot on one of the pedals, is what I read ... and Rolf was found in what looked like a 'push up position' on the left side, as though he'd landed on his stomach

and tried to push himself up off the ground before he perished.

Kenny: Where Bill is (the driver).

Valerie: Yes; Dean was found, so they said, with his head and body over the passenger side, with his foot trapped under the pedals.

Kenny: All these things are speculative. As soon as I said to the man back there—what was his name, Meeker? As soon as I said, 'Who said Dean was driving?' He said, 'I've got to go home and read tonight, because for all the reading I've done these years, it's possible I'm wrong.' There should be no question in anyone's mind.

Bill: I also feel, though, that even a good driver, either Dean or Rolf, couldn't get out of the way . . . couldn't avoid another car . . .

Doris: I don't feel they were going over 100 miles per hour.

Valerie: No, I agree with you. I almost see him shaking his head.

There was silence for a moment and we decided to move on again, traveling on Highway 46 away from the accident, as the ambulance carrying Dean would have done. Unbelievably, just as we drove past the memorial site one more time, and continued on toward the town where Dean had been carried, an ambulance passed us going in the opposite direction. What were the odds that we would see an ambulance at all on this particular stretch of road, at just this time? Again, we felt sure it was an omen that the spirit world was with us strongly.

Valerie: You know, we seemed to have a drive and determination earlier today as we drove. Now we seem peaceful, yet hollow. We're so quiet.

Bill: Empty . . .

Doris: I feel it's already happened, he's relived it, and he's sad and empty now because . . .

Kenny:	Another year ...
Doris:	Yes, another year before he feels anyone will talk to him. He's afraid they'll have forgotten.
Kenny:	Then I stick to 5:45 as the accident time, because we wouldn't feel so heavy and empty unless we were reliving the impact. He's reminding me that we established that he is studying law on the other side. That seems important for him to tell people. And one of the young men at the memorial site is also studying law ...
Doris:	Isn't that strange? I do feel that young man is someone Dean will guide, oddly enough. How unusual to find him there—of course, Dean no doubt guided us toward finding the young man.
Valerie:	Now, back to the accident ...
Kenny:	He didn't want to leave his house in the morning ...
Doris:	He delayed and delayed ...
Valerie:	Does anyone feel whether he made this portion of the trip, to the hospital, alive or not? The ambulance came this way.
Kenny:	My feeling is he was still alive in the ambulance..(pauses, closes his eyes and appears to transport himself back to that time) . . . He's going over ...
Doris:	(Also transported back to that day) Yes ...
Kenny:	He's struggling, but still alive.
Doris:	In a coma or slipping . . . they may think he's dead, but he's aware.
Kenny:	His mother is going to be at the end of the tunnel to greet him.
Valerie:	Does Dean have any messages?

Kenny: He's guiding actor Luke Perry.

Valerie: In what way?

Kenny: He wants him to do a remake ...

Valerie: Of?

Kenny: (Listening) Just a minute ... I'm saying right now
                that it's *East of Eden*. He also says Perry should
                take his work more seriously ... don't try to be
                'another James Dean'—be himself.

Bill: I can't help but back up Kenny's theory that
                Dean was still alive right here.

Kenny: But there's a peacefulness ... no pain. Whatever
                the body releases through shock or whatever,
                that's what the body is releasing. What do you
                feel, Doris?

Doris: Same thing. He was at peace. It might have been
                the endorphins released by his own body, but
                there was no pain.

Valerie: (Reading from notes) He was pronounced 'dead
                on arrival' at the hospital. Could he have passed
                at the accident site?

Kenny: I feel not. At this moment he was still clinging to
                life.

Just then we passed several handmade crosses embedded in the
ground along the roadside. Undoubtedly there were erected to commemorate the site where other accidents had occurred, as is the
custom in many areas, yet it was a most spiritual and eerie sight while
discussing Dean's progression from life to 'death'.

Kenny: In addition to the crosses, I see a small bridge
                off to the right up ahead. It looks like the
                Golden Gate Bridge. When Dean is reborn, he'll
                be reborn in San Francisco, he tells me.

Dean: He is trying to help the young man from
                Germany with law before he (Dean) reincar-
                nates, which is really bizarre.

Kenny:	The young man is going to be much stronger after today.
Doris:	I'll bet he's going to be shocked about James Dean, too.
Bill:	After the accident, a whole hour may have gone by before they got to the hospital, judging by how much time we've taken driving, not to mention the time they spent at the scene.
Doris:	Yes, and I don't see the equipment like they have now to take care of people, either. He could have survived.
Kenny:	Not negligence, they just weren't equipped. (Again slipping into a semi-trance and reliving Dean's feelings of long ago) Oxygen has left his body ... lot of blood lost ... very low blood count.
Doris:	I do see internal bleeding, but I still feel they could have saved him. He might have been thrown from a distance into the steering wheel, not impaled by it, as someone at the memorial site claimed.
Kenny:	Most of the nurses and doctors were mesmerized that it was James Dean ... they could have written down anything on the report. And their overall thinking was, 'It's sad, but the man is dead.'
Valerie:	(Looking into the back seat) Someone pulled my hair! (In truth, no living person had done so, and we could only assume that Dean or another spirit, in a moment of playfulness, had done it).
Doris:	When he passed over, he wanted to talk to his loved ones here, but no one could hear him. It was very frustrating.
Kenny:	That's why we should do prayerwork for those in spirit, not just on the anniversary of their passing ...

Valerie:	Our conversation is turning to what you feel when you've passed over. Is that significant?
Kenny:	He's slipping ...
Bill:	This is where it happened ...
Doris:	He's trying to separate ... separate from his body ...
Kenny:	(Breathing heavily and rasping) Slipping quickly ...
Doris:	I feel the same thing ...
Kenny:	(Deep exhale, then speaking quietly): I feel he's gone.
Valerie:	Gone?
Kenny:	Gone now, yes. There could still have been a chance with the proper machines, but too much brain damage had taken place. By the time they reached him, it was basically too late for that.
Doris:	I feel there was something lacking; a syringeful of something he needed. He's showing me a syringe ... maybe they didn't have the proper medication or the proper equipment ...
Kenny:	Maybe coming out to him in the ambulance they didn't know exactly what condition he was in ... they didn't bring everything. I'll bet when they heard it was James Dean that threw every nurse in the hospital into a panic.
Doris:	And I wonder, too, if in those days they did not have the radio equipment they have today.
Kenny:	(Moving his head slowly from side to side) Do you feel him floating now?
Doris:	Yes, I do.
Valerie:	I was going to say I felt lightheaded.
Kenny:	But I feel 'up' now, like I've released him.

Bill and Doris:	Yes, I do, too.
Doris:	He's happy. He says he's a rebel *with* a cause now, and he's laughing. He says it's different now.

We noticed yet another silver car as we continued our journey. "It's four miles to the 101 Freeway, and I can't wait!" Valerie exclaimed. "The sun has been in my eyes all this time—it's so strong. This also means it's four miles to where the hospital was, so we're saying Dean passed just in back of us, about 5 miles from the hospital, right?"

Kenny:	About five miles, right—he almost made it. But the brain damage . . . the injuries . . .

Perhaps it is truly best that Dean did not survive the accident, if it would have meant living with the injuries we psychically felt he sustained. And fortunately his legion of fans worldwide remember him in their own special way—as the rebellious, strong, and handsome young man. For all the fear his spirit expressed that he would not be remembered, indeed his memory lives on, perhaps stronger than ever today.

The memorial site was *clearly* proof that Dean had not been forgotten, and a description of the location seems a fitting tribute to close our section on James Dean.

A shiny, brasslike sculpture, perhaps six feet high, stands against a tree. It is simple in structure—one band of metal across, bearing Dean's name, birthdate, and date of passing, and a post on either side embedded into the ground below. But the tree, which had been named the "Tree of Heaven" by locals many years before the accident, is large and impressive, and the entire area is enclosed by a small cement fence to which two plaques are attached. The plaques are worth quoting. The artist, a Japanese man named Seita Ohnishi, dedicated the metal tributes to the site on July 4, 1983, and titled one plaque "A Small Token" :

"This monument stands as a small token of my appreciation for the people of America from whom I have learned so much. It celebrates the people who have over the years courageously followed the path of truth and justice while expanding the limits of mankind with their boundless pioneering spirit. It also stands for James Dean, and other American rebels who taught us the importance of having a cause. To all those who helped this stranger from Japan realize his dream of erecting this monument, I express my heartfelt thanks—the Hearst Family, which graciously made its land available for this monument, Bill Bast and Mrs. Sanford Roth (James Dean's closest and best friends) who shared their memories with me, and the people of this community who warmly extended their kindness and cooperation, and naturally to all the James Dean fans who have carried his torch throughout the years—Thank You."

And on another plaque next to the previous one, where a small sparrow is also sculpted into the metal, another message, called "Tribute to a Young Man" and dated September 30, 1977:

"His name was James Byron Dean. He was an actor. He died just before sundown on September 30, 1955, when his Porsche collided with another car at a fork in the road not 900 yards east of this tree, long known as the "Tree of Heaven." He was 24 years old. Aside from appearing in several Broadway plays, he starred in three motion pictures, *East of Eden*, *Rebel Without a Cause* and *Giant*. Only *Eden* had been released before his death.

"Yet before he was in his grave James Dean was already a legend. Every day somewhere in the world—at the cinema or on television, James Dean lives on. Cinema is no longer just celluloid—every day we find reminders that the drama of James Dean is the theme that we live. He was a youth, yearning for one precious touch of a warmth between parents and their offspring, he was an individual struggling in this huge land of infinite promise and many races. He was a rebel searching for that cause we must all possess, this young man seemingly ordinary yet possessing a talent—an individuality— that were unique in their combination, has come to personify a generation awakened.

Many are those who feel strongly that James Dean should not be forgotten. There are some things, like the hatred that accompanies war, that are best forgotten. There are others, like the nobler qualities of man, to which this young actor directed our attention, that should be preserved for all time. James Dean is all the more with us today because his life was so fleeting. In Japan, we say that his death came as suddenly as it does to cherry blossoms—the petals of early Spring always fall at the height of their ephemeral brilliance. Death in youth is life that glows eternal."

MARILYN MONROE

★ ★ ★ ★ ★

THEN

I was living high atop Pacific Heights in San Francisco in 1954 when my friend, Broadway and film star Clifton Webb, called from Beverly Hills to say he needed a special favor. Clifton wanted to arrange an appointment for his friend, a "Mrs. DiMaggio," who was living in San Francisco at the time and wanted to have a psychic reading from me as soon as possible. DiMaggio was a fairly common name in the area, so I merely made an appointment for later that evening, as a favor to Clifton, then chatted briefly with him about other matters and concluded our conversation by saying, "Tell your friend to be at my home at nine o'clock this evening."

However, on that foggy evening, Mrs. DiMaggio was late in arriving, something few clients are guilty of. At 9:15 P.M., my houseman suggested giving up the wait for the woman. "No, I feel she will still come," I insisted, and told him he could turn in for the evening.

I was not surprised, therefore, when a few moments later I heard the chime of the doorbell.

When I opened the door, a beautiful blonde in a black coat with white ermine trim and a white transparent kerchief on her head stood before me, struggling somewhat for air as she whispered, "I'm Mrs. DiMaggio."

Of course, I immediately recognized her as screen goddess Marilyn Monroe, who had just recently married baseball great Joe DiMaggio and was living in San Francisco.

An instant rapport developed between us, and I asked her why she was so out of breath. Marilyn told me she had taken a cab to the area, but walked the last few blocks, because the story had broken in the newspapers that morning that she was undergoing psychiatric treatment and she didn't want to ruin *my* reputation. *That* was the essence of Marilyn Monroe.

Our client-psychic relationship quickly developed into a friendship as well, beginning with that evening. Whenever Marilyn needed detailed psychic advice, she would see me in person, and she did this God knows how many times.

But often we would discuss matters over the phone as well, for Marilyn was a great user of the telephone, an obsession she was thrilled to learn I also shared.

Marilyn suffered from insomnia, and once she found out I was a "night person," who often stayed up late working, she'd call at any hour, feeling she'd found a fast friend and likely candidate to welcome her calls.

"Hello you, it's me," she'd whisper into the phone, and this soon became our code. Even if I was not home, she'd leave a similar message with my answering service to avoid having to answer fan-type questions from the operators. She'd say, "Tell you that me called" or "Just say, 'Hello you—it's me.'" Though they were baffled and some perhaps recognized the world-famous breathy whisper, no operator ever questioned Marilyn, and she delighted in our secret phrase. Her use of the phone gave her a "high"; she loved the energy she felt it gave her, and often talked her way out of bad moods by using the phone.

I spent several delightful evenings while living in San Francisco at DiMaggio's, a popular restaurant owned by members of Joe DiMaggio's family. Frequently on hand at the restaurant was Joe himself. Each time, as I walked past the quaint shops along Fisherman's Wharf on my way to the restaurant, I knew that it wasn't the atmosphere at DiMaggio's which attracted me or the many tourists who clamored for a table there. I'd been invited by a very special blonde "cook" who wanted to have some fun for the evening, and without knowing it, the tourists were waiting for the same lady.

On these special evenings, a glowing Marilyn would meet me at the restaurant's backdoor. We'd chat briefly, then while I was led to a special table set up in the kitchen, she would whip up a special meal. It was never complicated—Marilyn was not very expert at cooking—but she would delight at the steak and diced potatoes or egg dishes she'd fix for me (with the aid of the regular chef).

The most amusing part of these evenings would be the many tourists lined up at the bar or dawdling over their dinner because they'd heard Marilyn was in San Francisco after doing a picture, and they knew she sometimes came into the restaurant when she was in town. They were so terribly eager for a glimpse of the gorgeous beauty, who was, even then, unbeknownst to them, just a few feet away—at work in the kitchen!

In fact, once or twice when I was arriving, again through the back-door, I saw Marilyn giving the final turn to something on the grill—her sole contribution to the complicated meal the chef was preparing. She would say, "When this is delivered to the table, just have the waiter tell the person it's the 'Marilyn special'!"

She took great joy in knowing that tourists were lined up at the front door for a chance at dining in a restaurant where Marilyn had dined. Of course the bartender regaled the tourists with tales of when Marilyn had last been in the restaurant, and hinted that perhaps "she just might come in this evening—we never know!" Yet in truth, Marilyn never entered the main room on the evenings I was there; on those evenings, that was Joe's domain and she didn't want to detract from his involvement. Besides, she was deliriously happy playing the part of housewife, with the kitchen being her home. I was, in her eyes, a friend who'd stopped by her home that evening, and Marilyn truly loved those moments.

Some of Marilyn's happiest days were spent with Joe DiMaggio, and I've always maintained that she would still be alive today if they had stayed married. Marilyn desperately wanted to be happily married. She also had a fierce desire to have children and often spoke despondently to me about her inability to have "little people," as she called them. She suffered several miscarriages during her life and each one left her feeling empty and a failure.

Eventually I moved to Southern California, and Marilyn and Joe settled in the same area, Beverly Hills, soon afterward, to be closer to Marilyn's work, as her involvement in films grew stronger.

My visits with her continued, through phone calls and in-person sessions. I saw her through extreme highs and extreme lows. While her marriage to DiMaggio at first made her happy, soon differences arose and some of her saddest days were spent during and just after their divorce.

Yet one of the most difficult and longest-lasting struggles Marilyn encountered had nothing to do with the men in her life at all. What Marilyn fought against, sometimes on a daily basis, was a then-mysterious emotional disease which, each time it reached its peak, could keep her a prisoner in her own home for days at a time.

Sadly, when Marilyn was gaining a worldwide bad reputation for her lateness and inability to appear on a set or at a party, what the world *didn't* know, and what I am revealing here for the very first time ever, was that my dear client was not drinking or under heavy medication; nor was she merely pulling a "star" tantrum. She was suffering—suffering terribly—from a little-understood (at the time) disease we now know as agoraphobia.

Long before she told me about it, I suspected it had been developing inside her. Psychically I sensed the fear she was holding within. On one or two occasions I asked Marilyn how she'd spent the last two or three days, and she turned pale, and said evasively, "I was in my bedroom." "Tell me about it, Marilyn," I'd urge, and she'd say she hadn't bathed, washed her hair, or gotten dressed. She simply locked herself in her own private, safe room, fearing the outside world—fearing the responsibility of being "Marilyn Monroe."

I had sensed she was having difficulty because two of my other clients, also glamorous sex symbols, Greta Garbo and Marlene Dietrich, battled the same problem sporadically, though in less severe form than Marilyn. I found many similarities with all three ladies; in thoughts, words, and actions they all shared a terror of dealing with the "outside world."

The first time Marilyn discussed this fully with me, she said tearfully, "Kenny, I *want* to be on time, I really do. I *try* to get ready, but sometimes I'm almost paralyzed with fear. I spend hours getting ready because I'm afraid to go out. I sometimes just can't face people."

I asked her if she disliked people and she said, "Oh no, I *love* people—but I don't like what they do to me! I love being an actress, but sometimes I'd just like to be a person instead!"

When I asked Marilyn if certain times bothered her more than others, she cried, "It can happen *any* time! Sometimes I can't leave the house, and other times I get up the courage and leave the house, but just keep circling the block once I get where I'm going because I'm too afraid to go in. I don't know how to be 'me' anymore. It's just not safe."

I knew this was true, because once I arrived at her home and she greeted me looking, quite honestly, dreadful. "I've been in my room," she said, and I knew she'd been under a siege of staying housebound again. "Come back in an hour, okay?" she pleaded. And with tremendous effort, Marilyn pulled herself together, quickly cleaned herself up, applied some makeup, and emerged an hour later the image of a confident, glamorous movie star. No one would have suspected the agony she had experienced in the previous days.

Yet, when we got into the car on our way to a friend's party, she asked me to circle the person's home repeatedly. "They think I want to make an entrance or be dramatic"—she sighed—"but it's just so frightening!" Thus it continued off and on—sometimes while working she could leave the safety of her home, only to find another "safe harbor" in her dressing room at the studio, where she would again fight to remain.

Finally, during a phone call, I convinced Marilyn we should begin work on her problem. I'd had great success working with private clients who shared Marilyn's fear, and felt confident I could have equal success with her. Unfortunately, because it was so deep-rooted, it was to be a lifelong battle for Marilyn. At times, she would go through almost a remission period, in a sense, exhibiting no symptoms for months at a time. Then, unfortunately, perhaps because she became overconfident and discontinued working on the problem, the symptoms would recur. My only hope in revealing Marilyn's secret is that the many sufferers of agoraphobia today may find some small amount of comfort and help in my description of the techniques we used. And for that reason, I'm sure Marilyn is pleased.

We began with a visualization technique used by many of us who believe in psychic phenomena. I asked Marilyn to see herself surrounded by what is called the "white light of protection"—an imaginary ray of light which you visualize as encompassing your entire body. The white light represents purity, and we in the psychic field feel it prevents any negativity from entering.

I asked Marilyn to repeat, "I, Marilyn, place the white light around the top of my head, my eyes, nose, and mouth, but never touching my body.

The white light of protection continues around my neck, my shoulders, and my chest—never touching my body."

We continued, mentioning every part of Marilyn's anatomy. "It is surrounding my arms, my waist and my hips," she'd repeat. "The white light circles my legs, my feet, and my toes, yet it never touches my body." She would conclude with, "This white light totally protects me and keeps me from all harm." This technique is a powerful tool, since it suggests protection yet keeps the body totally untouched or invaded by any outside forces. It was very rewarding to hear Marilyn's voice grow stronger as she visualized herself safe.

I've also believed strongly in meditating for many years and have suggested that my clients follow the simple method which I use involving the burning of a tall, nonscented dinner-style candle for approximately five minutes at a time. The candle is used primarily to focus one's attention and also to draw attention from the spirit world, asking for their guidance. Through *my* spirit guides, I was given various colors which symbolize certain problem areas, and with this in mind, I suggested Marilyn burn a light blue-colored candle to release depression and fear, and following that a rose-colored candle to bring in peace and contentment. (Complete colors of candles are included at the back of the book).

Marilyn was to blow the first candle out after five minutes, get the smoke in the palms of her hands, then later light the second candle. The meditation is used to visualize your problem being solved; thus I told Marilyn to say, "I am strong and brave. I see myself walking into a room and not being afraid." This was merely going beyond the power of positive thinking.

I also gave her affirmations or positive sayings to repeat, and often she'd call me on the telephone and her first words after "Hello" would be "My mind is peaceful and contented—I love and approve of myself. I am free to be me!" (one of her favorite affirmations).

Another simple technique we worked with found Marilyn writing the word "fear" on a piece of paper, then scratching it out and replacing it with the word "faith."

I recall one time during the early stages of the battle with agoraphobia when Marilyn thought she'd already beaten the problem. She called me excitedly, saying, "Let's drive to Palm Springs tomorrow—just you, Clifton, and me!" We'd discussed such a trip several times, but never actually made final plans to go.

Not wanting to discourage her, but fearing it was too early to hope for recovery, I said I'd pick her up the following day and together we'd pick up Clifton and head out of town.

The next day, as we got about halfway to Palm Springs, I glanced at Marilyn and saw that she was perspiring and her face was growing pale. "Are you all right?" I asked. "No!" she said. "I have to go back—I can't go on!" Just then we passed a hot dog stand along the roadside and I suggested we pull over for a cup of coffee. Marilyn eagerly agreed—anything to stop our progress. Clifton grumbled, but agreed as well, so out we went to the hot dog stand. Marilyn had a wonderful knack for going unrecognized if she wore little or no makeup, and the scarf over her platinum hair hid her from view. She relaxed considerably while we sat drinking our coffee.

Then the moment arrived when we had to face the prospect of continuing our journey. I tried to keep a cheerful attitude and said, "Okay, you two, back in the car and on we go!" I no sooner started the engine than Marilyn panicked and said, "We have to go home!" "But, Marilyn," I reasoned, "we're halfway on our journey. It will take just as long to go home as to continue to Palm Springs." "No, we *must* go home; I have to be home," she insisted.

By now Clifton was becoming agitated as well, perhaps because his friend Marilyn was agitated, and he said, "Kenny, we *should* go home. Let's go home." No doubt a few glances at Marilyn's pale, tense face had convinced him that danger *might* lie ahead.

I turned the car around and within an hour we were "safely" home in Los Angeles again.

The above exercise was repeated again on two separate occasions, yet the closest the three of us ever got to Palm Springs together was that hot dog stand!

The illness perhaps reached its greatest peak during Marilyn's filming of *The Misfits*. Yet sometime afterward I felt we were making progress once again. Then, in mid-November, 1960, Marilyn rang me up, sobbing into the telephone. "I killed him! I killed him!" she gasped. "Marilyn, what are you saying?" I asked her.

"It's Gable, Kenny—he's gone and I think I caused it!" Marilyn felt her chronic lateness on *The Misfits* set made Gable angry, and the frustrations caused by her delays brought on his fatal heart attack.

I told her that psychically I didn't feel that was true, but she couldn't be consoled at that moment. Marilyn had respected Gable greatly and loved working with him. She was devastated with guilt that her lack of control over her fear could have, in her mind, caused his passing.

Of course in the days and weeks following Gable's passing, the news media grasped the notion of Marilyn's lateness and accused her of the very thing she'd been worried about, but I knew they were only after good copy for a story.

Finally, after several months, I said, "Marilyn, we'll contact Gable in spirit and settle this once and for all."

"Oh, could we really *do* that?" she squealed with excitement. Then: "But won't he be angry with me? Maybe he won't speak to me," she said.

I assured her that I felt Gable was eager to communicate, and during my next visit with Marilyn, instead of a reading we held a brief seance in memory of Clark Gable.

As I suspected, his spirit came in quickly, much to Marilyn's delight. Gable reassured us that his heart attack was not caused by stress. He said he'd been on a crash diet, and the strain of the sudden weight loss program had been too much for his heart.

"Do you really think that he meant it?" Marilyn asked when the seance had ended. "Marilyn, the spirits don't lie," I reprimanded her. "You're right—you're right!" She smiled. "I feel so much better!"

Much of 1961 found Marilyn happy again, yet toward the end of the year and the early days of what was to be her last year, 1962, her personal agony began again. Marilyn desperately sought to be taken seriously as an actress and felt she was not accomplishing that goal. To pacify herself and take her mind off her career, she decided to buy a home.

"Come with me," she asked me one evening. "I want you to see what I want to buy." We headed for the city of Brentwood and an area off San Vicente Boulevard. There are twenty-five streets named Helena in this area; Marilyn asked me to turn onto "Fifth Helena."

I felt uncomfortable as we drove to the end of the cul-de-sac. "There it is!" she said, pointing to a small residence to the left of our car. "You like it, don't you?" she asked expectantly, like a child seeking approval. "Let's go inside, Marilyn," I suggested, hoping the outside, with its trees hanging down and casting ominous shadows, would be forgotten once we went indoors. But my sense of doom did not leave. As much as I hated to disappoint Marilyn, and I knew I would, I strongly suggested she not buy the house, though I suspected she wouldn't listen to me in this insistence. I felt negativity surrounding the house.

"But I love it!" she insisted. "When I've changed things around and had it fixed up, it will be wonderful," she promised.

Something told me psychically Marilyn would find greater depression there, so I tried to convince her the house would be "too damp and dark."

Then, when she told me that she would have to borrow money to make the down payment on the house, which seemed odd considering the films she'd made over the years (although we'd discussed many times the fact that her money was being mishandled), I suggested, "Perhaps this is an omen that you shouldn't buy yet, Marilyn." However, none of my arguments persuaded her and this was one time my client and friend refused to listen to spirits' advice.

Marilyn bought the house and began repairs and remodeling, which occupied much of her time, in addition to her plans for beginning work on a new film, *Something's Got to Give.*

We spoke less frequently during this time, until her illness again surfaced full force and caused so many delays and absences from the set that 20th Century Fox soon afterward dismissed her from her contract. This was a definite low point in her career and we discussed it in detail, though I told her I felt she'd be reinstated. Marilyn doubted me, but said she hoped I was right. "I want to work." She sighed.

On August 1 an exuberant Marilyn called me. She'd been reinstated by the studio and was looking forward to resuming the filming of *Something's Got to Give.* "Let's go to the beach!" she urged—one of her favorite places to relax. "Oh honey," I told her, "I can't. I have clients today. You're strong now—you know you are—go alone."

"Do you think I can? What if someone recognizes me?" she asked. "Wear no makeup, don't wear dark glasses, wear a sloppy joe sweater, and put a kerchief on your head and you'll be fine," I encouraged her. "I'm going to do it!" she giggled.

A very excited Marilyn called me that evening. "I did it! No one recognized me. I had the most wonderful time!" She laughed happily. We chatted a bit longer and she said, "I love everyone right now, Kenny. And you know, love is the one immortal thing about us; without love what else can life mean?"

These words will echo through my ears for the rest of my life, for they were the last words Marilyn ever spoke to me while she was alive.

> MARILYN MONROE'S NUDE BODY WAS FOUND IN THE EARLY MORNING HOURS OF AUGUST 5, 1962, BY HER HOUSEKEEPER, MRS. EUNICE MURRAY, IN MARILYN'S BRENTWOOD, CALIFORNIA, HOME. CAUSE OF PASSING WAS LISTED AS "POSSIBLE ACCIDENTAL OVERDOSE."

NOW

I've communicated many times with Marilyn's spirit since her passing in 1962. She's appeared at seances on any number of occasions, and I felt confident she would appear once I began work on this book.

The most recent contact occurred during a nightclub engagement in Hollywood. The Hollywood Roosevelt Hotel is one of the older hotels in the "glamour capital" of the world. Within its walls is the Cinegrill, a cozy nightclub which was once the watering hole and gathering place of Ernest Hemingway, Humphrey Bogart, Robert Benchley, Dorothy Parker, and my former client Marilyn.

The Cinegrill still plays host to celebrity audiences today and offers entertainment by stellar names from around the world. In fact, it is one of the few remaining nightclubs in Hollywood reminiscent of its heyday. I've had the pleasure of headlining in the room on several occasions.

During my most recent engagement and while beginning work on this book, I stayed in a suite on the tenth floor of the hotel. While showering one day prior to going downstairs to a rehearsal in the Cinegrill, I heard a soft voice whisper, "I'll be down there." I quickly turned off the water, but the voice was gone. It sounded like Marilyn, but at that point I couldn't be sure.

I asked my cowriter Valerie to join me in the nightclub for the rehearsal, which was merely a chance for me to familiarize myself with the stage and the world predictions I would make for the first time that evening. I also made a strange request of Valerie. "Don't wear perfume," I requested, and I refrained from wearing any scent as well. Then I'd be certain that any fragrance would be coming directly from spirit. (Spirits often use the sense of smell as a means of making contact, and though it doesn't happen often, I wanted to be prepared to be as receptive as possible to the slightest scent, in case Marilyn chose to reveal herself in that way).

The concierge let us into the Cinegrill, where the lighting and sound technicians were waiting. Following the run-through of my perform-ance, all technicians left and we heard the click of the door as they shut it behind them on their way out.

We turned off the lights in the room and found our way to one of the intimate tables in the center of the room. Our only source of illu-mination came from a few pinpoints of light streaming in around the edges of the curtains in the nightclub. The Cinegrill sits directly on Hollywood Boulevard, facing the former Grauman's Chinese Theater (now called Mann's) and the cement courtyard famous for its hand and footprints of the film immortals of yesteryear and today. The faint hum of traffic and tourists could be heard, but we determined that it was not easy to cause any disturbances as we tried to contact a spirit.

We felt a slight chill in the room, as though the windows had just been opened, though we knew all windows and doors were tightly shut. The chill was a sure sign that a spirit was trying to enter, and we were eager to make contact.

I believe music helps raise the vibrations on any occasion; it is espe-cially important prior to spirit contact. I suggested we sing two of my favorite hymns, "In the Garden" and "Only Believe." However, midway through the first hymn, the cool air grew stronger. It was actually a strong breeze now, though again, no doors or windows were open. The breeze enveloped us and goose bumps rose on our flesh.

"Hello you, it's me!" we heard, barely a whisper, but it came from the direction of the stage just in front of us. "It's me! It's me!" the voice echoed.

The air felt as though it were charged with electricity at that moment. A tiny dot of light, resembling a tiny spotlight, formed on the stage, faint at first but growing brighter. A beautiful perfumed scent filled the room, yet as I mentioned previously neither of us had worn any fragrance.

"Is that you, Marilyn?" I asked. Again we heard, "It's me! It's me!" and in the middle of the spotlight a shape began taking form. "Welcome Marilyn," we said. "Come in." The spotlight expanded into a white glow. Slowly a white gown appeared, next we saw golden hair, and finally an angelic, glowing face.

This was a happy Marilyn—more like the carefree Marilyn I had seen on a number of playful occasions on Earthplane. Again we greeted her with "Welcome Marilyn," then added, "you look wonderful—very happy."

"I am happy." She smiled. "I'm studying philosophy and psychology." She giggled. "I'm making up for the education I didn't have before. I wanted to be an intellectual. You know, I married Arthur Miller because he was an intellectual—I found that very sexy." Marilyn had told me during a session on Earthplane that she married Miller, an exceptionally gifted writer, for "all the wrong reasons," and I assumed this was what she meant at this moment.

"Oh yes, Kenny dear," she continued, "he was nice enough to me, but he was not the right man for me. I could never be 'smart enough' with Arthur." I was suddenly reminded that Marilyn had also mentioned wanting to have brilliant babies, and she felt Miller was the perfect candidate to father them. Her miscarriages of his children disappointed her greatly.

"Marilyn," I said to the luminous vision before me. "I'm writing a new book and this is your chance to speak to your many admirers—to go on record with anything you want to say."

The figure roamed about restlessly now, leaving the stage and floating even closer to the table where we were seated.

"Not on purpose! I didn't do it on purpose," I heard.

I assumed she meant the fateful evening of August 4, because her spirit had told me repeatedly that her passing was not a suicide. Marilyn then confirmed it: "I didn't kill myself! Happy—I was happy! I was working again. I was starting a new picture!"

"Tell us what happened, then, Marilyn," Valerie urged.

"Kenny knows." She sighed. "I was just so tired—I never meant to take so many pills. It was an accident."

"What about the stories that the Kennedys were involved?" Valerie asked.

Again the form of Marilyn became restless, gliding away from us slightly, toward a corner of the room. Tiny sparks of light followed her moving form, then seemed to connect with it when the movement had stopped.

"They weren't part of it!" we heard, referring to the question about the Kennedys' alleged involvement in her passing. "It was an accident," she insisted.

"But about the Kennedys . . . " Valerie continued.

The form moved slightly, sparks flying loose from it and then stopping again as Marilyn said, "Bobby Kennedy was never very attractive to me. He was a means to an end, know what I mean?"

Valerie asked, "It was John F. Kennedy you really wanted?"

Marilyn giggled. "He was surely more appealing! He was sexy!"

I pressed on: "Do you want to tell our readers whether you slept with John or Bobby Kennedy?"

Marilyn seemed to be avoiding our question. Suddenly her form returned to the stage and we heard, "There's another blonde in Hollywood today who could tell you more about Jack Kennedy."

"Who is she, Marilyn?" we asked.

A smile filled the facial area of the glowing form before us, and the head seemed to be shaking as though Marilyn was saying, "No, I won't tell."

Then: "She may even talk one day about the apartment on Rossmore"—an exclusive street in Hollywood—"and what happened the night of the presidential nomination!"

Marilyn seemed to be enjoying the guessing game and it was obvious she would not tell us who the mysterious blonde was.

The vibrations in the room seemed very upbeat and contented, and it seemed her spirit was in no hurry to leave, so we continued, "Is there anything else you'd like people to know, Marilyn?"

"Sex" was the next word we heard, in a low whisper. "What about sex?" we asked.

"I loved it!" She laughed. "Only now we don't have it here. No need for it—we can have that satisfied, happy feeling with another person without it."

I knew that in life Marilyn had been upset by rumors she'd had a lesbian love affair with her acting coach, Natasha Lytess, and felt this might be a good chance to discuss it.

"You know we were never like that, Kenny," she said in response to my question about the affair. "She was my friend—she helped me. I asked you once if you thought I was a lesbian because I looked at other women, but that's all I ever did was look." (True, Marilyn had confessed fearfully one time that she worried about herself because she found she was looking at other women's bodies and faces. I told her, "You love the human anatomy, don't you, Marilyn? Then it's only natural you're fascinated by the size and shape of everyone, male or female. Maybe you're just looking at the competition," I teased her. This seemed to pacify her and we never discussed it again.)

Marilyn's spirit moved about once again, excitedly, then came to rest as we heard, "Sex doesn't matter here, but I'm coming back *next* time as a boy!" This was not the first time Marilyn's spirit had told me of plans to reincarnate as a male, and I realized she was still serious about her plans.

"Men used me before, as Norma Jean and Marilyn," she said. "But I learned to use them, too. I loved sex. I learned to give Marilyn Monroe's body to get Marilyn Monroe something in return."

"Will you be good at being a male?" Valerie asked. "I'll be very good"—she laughed—"because I'll be very sensitive. I'll treat women the way they should be treated—with respect and dignity."

"When are you returning, Marilyn?" I asked.

Her only frown of the session so far appeared, and a sense of heaviness and urgency filled the room. "I won't be coming back for quite a while," she told us. "I'm watching over her."

We waited for Marilyn to continue, but silence followed. "Who, Marilyn, who are you watching over?" I asked.

"Melanie Griffith!" she cried. "She needs help! Men will use her, too, like they used me. I want to help her to be strong. She still loves him deeply—Don Johnson—but he could hurt her badly if she isn't careful."

"What will you do for her, Marilyn?"

"Watch over her—protect her—and their little boy. I can help her. She can talk to me if she wants to. I'll be there. Even though they're divorced, I'll help them get back together one day. They belong together, like Joe and I did."

Why Melanie Griffith? I wondered, though comparisons had been made when Melanie appeared in the film *Working Girl*.

"Sure, we're alike," Marilyn giggled. "She does a great imitation of my voice! But she can't take her clothes off all the time in pictures. She can't keep choosing sexy roles. I want to help so she'll be taken seriously." (This was one of Marilyn's greatest disappointments; she longed to be seen as a serious actress and worked long and hard to prove herself capable).

"Melanie will do some dramas, then a comedy or two. But I want her to do a play with Don Johnson. Know what it is? *Bus Stop*. I wish I'd done it onstage, even after the film version. But the best part is, Melanie will always be a good mother, too"—she sighed—"like I wanted to be."

A satisfied feeling filled the room; Marilyn seemed pleased with her plans. "Who have you seen on the other side, Marilyn?" I asked.

"Oh, lots of friends, Kenny. I just saw Monty Clift, and oh, yes! Rudolph Valentino! I always loved him in films, you know!"

Indeed, Marilyn had told me once on Earthplane that she'd visited Valentino's former home, Falcon Lair, many years after his passing. "Too bad he died so young," she told me then, "we'd have been great together!"

"How is Valentino?" I asked. "He's gorgeous," she laughed.

The glow of Marilyn began to dim slightly, and we could no longer see her as clearly. A different feeling invaded the room—it was still charged with energy, but began to feel warmer. "Are you leaving us, Marilyn?" I asked. "Is there anything else you want to say?"

Suddenly there was a feeling of tension in the air.

"Okay, I'll tell you! I never—*not ever*—had an affair with Robert Fitzgerald Kennedy! He was a family man!" Marilyn cried out.

The words hung heavily in the air, but before we could say anything, Marilyn's image fused into a pulsating glow of white light. I heard faintly, "No underwear here, Kenny! But then that's not new!" This made me laugh, and relieved the tension of the moment before, as I recalled the fact that Marilyn never wore undergarments while "alive," if she could possibly avoid them. It's long been my belief that those in the spirit world create the image of clothing mentally, and that rather than wearing traditional clothes, most see themselves bathed in a simple flowing garment. Apparently, Marilyn had chosen to recall fondly her days on Earthplane and did not create the need for wearing underwear in the spirit world, either!

We waited for more from my dear former client, and remained silent to allow her to continue, but we were faced with silence instead.

It was clear our communication was coming to an end, and nothing more would be heard from Marilyn for the time being. A faint beam of light was all that remained of her now and the room felt less "alive," as we said, "Thank you for coming, Marilyn. Come again."

The light moved swiftly toward us, swung around me, and enveloped me momentarily, then faded to a soft, pulsating dot and disappeared. I felt a strong warmth surge through me and knew I'd just been given the equivalent of a spirit "hug."

The "spell" was broken—Marilyn was now gone. The temperature in the room returned to normal. Silence and darkness filled the fabulous Cinegrill once again. Yet left behind was a sense of happiness and contentment—two words I was pleased to associate with my dear friend and client Marilyn.

AND THEN . . .

★ ★ ★ ★ ★

I was asked many times during interviews pertaining to the writing of this book if I planned to attempt contact with world-famous (or rather *infamous*) criminals—Al Capone or Jesse James, for example. I agree; it would have been fascinating to delve into the current lives of these troubled souls.

But spirit communication is a privilege, to be used not abused, and this applies not only to the psychic/medium but perhaps most importantly to the spirit. Those who have murdered, stolen or otherwise harmed others must first atone for their crimes before being allowed to communicate.

On rare occasions, such as that with Hitler, a spirit is allowed to communicate briefly as part of the atonement process, for certainly someone who's been so evil faces hatred or rejection even now. If the spirit is still entirely evil, the psychic/medium could end up ordering it out shortly after it has made itself known, which would be demeaning to the spirit, and rightfully so. Only if some possible good can come from the communication—if the spirit can express its remorse somehow, or possibly teach a lesson to others—is a formerly evil soul allowed access to a psychic/medium.

In some cases spirits of criminals, even if they are in the process of reforming, are unreachable because they're more or less in "exile." Whether this is a self-imposed exile or not even I haven't determined. It could be that the spirit is now quite embarrassed or ashamed of its actions, for all the members of the Supreme Court put together could not judge the spirits half as harshly as they learn to judge themselves, once they're able to separate themselves from their earthly life and evaluate the impact of that life. It may take a great deal of time to come to this awakening, but it's powerful and sometimes painful when it occurs.

It could also be that very few, if any, other spirits want to deal with a formerly evil person on the other side, because their vibration is highly unpleasant. Or it's possible that with no more entourage around them—no one to hide behind or do their bidding—these evil spirits are shown to be the powerless souls they really are.

Some spirits were unable to be reached for this book because they're still too weak. There is definitely an adjustment period on the other side, where the first goal is to rest, relax and recuperate, with spirit communication being of much less importance.

I was most desirous of contacting former First Lady Jacqueline Kennedy Onassis for this book. But because she had been so ill just prior to her passing, her spirit was a classic example of one who needed the recuperation time.

Because of her great strength of character while she was alive, though, I attempted to reach her nonetheless. I thought that if *anyone* could recover quickly, it would be her. And indeed we were rewarded with a brief contact, held at an intimate late-night seance in my home.

I first attempted the contact for a feature article in *Experiences Magazine*, the publication sponsored by my psychic hotline.

After quite a long stretch of silence, when I sensed she was summoning the strength to communicate, I heard what appeared to be her soft, gentle whisper. Not surprisingly, the contact revealed that she was preoccupied with the welfare of her children (this was before John, Jr.'s tragic plane crash).

"I so wish I could hold and kiss my children," she sighed. "I hope they realize that I'm with them often, watching over them and trying to protect them from the insensitivities of the world."

For a brief moment, she mustered the strength to physically materialize, and seance attendees saw her dressed in a flowing orange garment. Her spirit appeared somewhat fragile yet she looked contented and at peace.

"Were you bitter about your early passing?" I asked. She shook her head. "No—I needed the rest. I was so tired," she confided.

As quickly as she'd physically materialized, she disappeared from sight. But her breathy voice remained, almost a whisper in my ear.

One of our participants asked about son John and she said sadly, "If he and his wife Carolyn don't have a child, I'm sorry to say tragedy or separation is ahead for them."

She had advice for daughter Caroline as well. "She should concentrate on writing, especially a novel she has in mind." She added proudly, "It could become a best-seller!"

She spoke lovingly of her grandchildren, especially Rose (Caroline's daughter). "Whether she's aware of it or not, she's being visited by her beloved great-grandmother Rose Kennedy," Jackie revealed.

"We are both around that dear child, but Rose will be a guiding force in her namesake's life. I for one would like to see her take piano lessons. I think she could become an illustrious concert pianist."

With this proud statement, the voice stilled and our brief spirit encounter was over.

Then, following the July 16, 1999 plane crash which killed John, Jr., his wife Carolyn and her sister Lauren, I attempted once again to contact the former First Lady. But during another late-night sitting—this time with just Valerie and myself present—we were unable to receive a physical or verbal contact from Jackie. We sensed she was immersed in the project of welcoming and comforting her son (this was thought-projected to me).

We left her to the privacy of this all-important mission, but we couldn't help wondering: was the accident the 'tragedy' she'd spoken of in the earlier contact? If John, Jr. and Carolyn *had* had a child, or if Carolyn had been pregnant at the time of the flight, would they have taken the chances they took (the late-night flight, with John self-piloting)? Or would they have taken a commercial flight instead?

I'm comforted by the thought that Jackie's wish from the earlier contact had indeed become a reality: I'm sure she *did* have the opportunity once again to hug and kiss her beloved son John.

I experienced another brief contact with a spirit in the process of resting and recuperating—this time due not to an illness but to a drug overdose instead.

The spirit was promising young actor River Phoenix. I thought perhaps enough time had elapsed since young Phoenix passed away on Halloween night in 1993, on the pavement outside the popular nightclub The Viper Room on Hollywood's famous Sunset Strip.

While standing on the spot where Phoenix collapsed I only briefly felt his presence. He was still weak and actually still 'drugged' in a way. His spirit was attempting to come out of the hazy effects of the drugs he'd taken. I could only hear faintly a voice tell me he was trying to reach actor Johnny Depp (owner of The Viper Room). He seemed anxious to apologize for any negative publicity the club may have received as a result of that ill-fated evening of his passing.

I also sensed a warning to actors Leonardo DiCaprio and Jason Priestly. "*Don't* follow my example!" a faint voice whispered. "No one helped me . . . but *I'm* trying to help you! *Don't* follow my life—*don't* follow Robert Downey, Jr.'s life! *Learn* from us!"

This was all I heard and then the drugged-like sensation returned. I'm sorry to say River Phoenix has a long road of recovery ahead of him. Hopefully recovery will be easier for the talented performers he mentioned, should they slide into any alcohol or drug-related problems.

We also attempted to reach former television "Superman" George Reeves, because though his 1959 passing was listed as a suicide, I have always felt psychically that it was a murder. I wanted to confirm this through a spirit contact with Reeves.

But whether murder or suicide, Reeves' spirit was silent when we attempted to reach him, and I felt a heaviness and lethargy, indicating that though he's awakened on the other side, he is not yet ready to talk about so important a matter. This is normal in the case of such a traumatic passing.

(Incidentally, the person I feel was involved in the murder was a famous face as well, and just passed onto the other side fairly recently. I suspect these two will have a meeting, or confrontation, in the spirit world, and there will be even more to tell regarding this mystery in the future!)

Another murder victim I had hoped to reach for an in-depth contact was former Beatle John Lennon. There was so much to ask him: has he been able to forgive the man who shot him—Mark David Chapman?

What were his feelings that December night as his soul so quickly and violently left his body? What does he think of the music world today?

But again, in a situation as tragic and sudden as this, a soul must be allowed to rest. It is, I am certain, a total shock to be on Earthplane one moment, then experience the pain and terror of a murder, and find yourself on the other side. It is the unexpectedness of this that even catches those on the other side unaware at times. Generally our loved ones are there to meet us, and have been planning or looking forward to our crossing over for this glorious "reunion." In many cases, when someone is ill, one or more of their loved ones will hover around them at home or in the hospital, watching over them during their final days of illness and preparing them for their journey, by sending comforting rays to them.

When a person's life is taken so brutally, however, the loved ones in spirit may not be alerted to it at first (a passing of this type may be part of one's destiny or part of an overall master plan, but not everyone is alerted to it). In these cases, a committee or "greeter" may be assigned to a spirit—a friendly soul or group of souls sent to comfort and guide the newcomer until its loved ones have been notified and are ready to provide comfort themselves.

I would imagine this to be the case with John Lennon, for as we sat at an empty Hollywood Bowl one early evening (where the Beatles had performed nearly 35 years before), I was given a glimpse of Lennon shortly after his passing. He was more or less in a sleep state—eyes closed, surrounded by people who, as far as I could tell psychically, had not been closely involved with him in "life."

I did have one more psychic impression while sitting at the Hollywood Bowl—that of urgency around Lennon. There was a tension surrounding me in the night air as I closed my eyes and saw Lennon with outstretched arms. In spite of the urgency or desire to communicate, his spirit was unable to successfully come in to me, and again I felt a weakness and also a confusion around him at that time.

Then one day recently—quite some time after the Hollywood Bowl attempt—I was reading a newspaper account of the knife attack on former Beatle George Harrison, whose home was invaded by an intruder.

Quite unexpectedly, as I was reading, I heard a male voice with an English accent. It seemed as though this person was reading the story over my shoulder.

"I had to help him out," the voice said. "Couldn't let it happen again. He couldn't go the way I did."

This seemed like a clue. Could it be John Lennon, who didn't want to see another Beatle murdered?

I telepathically sent a question to the voice. "If you *are* John Lennon, first, you're welcome. Please continue to communicate in whatever way you're comfortable."

I heard a loud rap against the wall near where I was seated and I took this as confirmation of Lennon's identity. I heard a buzzing in my right ear which was quickly followed by the voice again, and I realized Lennon was apparently most comfortable—or most capable—of communicating in this method.

"I turned his body around . . . " I heard, followed by a laugh. "The doctor in that report says it was 'just by chance' the wound wasn't more serious. Chance, nothing! I maneuvered him around so the knife wouldn't penetrate any vital areas!" (according to the news account, the knife just missed a major vein).

Again I sent thought-transference to Lennon: "How is it that you were with him during the attack? Were you there ahead of time?"

I heard another loud crack against the wall, and then, "I'd been spending time with George lately . . . felt he needed protection. Before that I spent time with Paul, helping him cope with the loss of Linda." (McCartney's wife passed from cancer in 1998). "And I'm leading him to a future love."

I sent him another thought, asking what else he'd been doing . . . how he was feeling . . . what might be ahead for his fellow Beatles.

But there was silence. I waited. Still nothing. As quickly as the spirit had made its presence known, it had vanished. I suspect Lennon will be watching over his fellow Beatles for quite some time to come, and that this might actually be part of his own recovery process.

I'm sure in time he'll have much to say to his former wife Yoko and his sons Sean and Julian, but in the meantime I encourage his many fans to remember him with love and kind thoughts. But now is the time to put aside the tears or mourning. Such activity is, of course, expected and absolutely understandable when someone's passing is relatively fresh. But after a period of mourning, repeated tears hold a spirit Earthbound. They see us crying and feel badly knowing the tears are for them. They feel helpless because they're unable to physically console us. They tend to be torn between moving on and adjusting to the other side and staying near us, feeling guilty and hoping their spiritual presence might be of comfort.

There have been other times, frankly, when I haven't tried to contact a spirit yet they've made their presence known. These haven't been full-fledged spirit contacts, but not for any particular reason. The spirit wasn't weak or incapable of contact; they just didn't feel the *need* for a lengthy discussion.

Two such cases are screen legend Clark Gable and comedy genius Groucho Marx. I had several brief contacts from Gable while taping television interviews in the Hollywood Roosevelt Hotel suite he once occupied with wife Carole Lombard. It seems the ideal location for many film crews who want to film in Southern California and know I gave psychic advice to Gable on Earthplane. On these occasions I've been told by Gable that he and Lombard are together again on the other side and still very much in love.

My most recent contact from Gable occurred quite unexpectedly when I opened my mail and received an invitation to the wedding of Gable's son, John Clark Gable (from Gable's marriage to Kay Spreckels Gable).

I'd spoken to John Clark once or twice and he'd mentioned his relationship with a young woman named Lexe. The invitation to John Clark and Lexe's wedding was bittersweet—it was to take place on February 1— Clark Gable's birthday.

As I touched the colorful invitation, I felt a strong male presence (and a familiar one, since I'd encountered Gable's spirit several times before). This contact was brief but meaningful. Gable made it known he was sending love to his son and that he was very much aware of the impending marriage. He also told me he intended to be present at the Malibu wedding. I was personally unable to attend but I'm sure "the

King," Clark Gable, was a man of his word even in the spirit world, and he kept his promise.

In the case of Groucho Marx, I came upon his spirit in a surprising way. A television crew from CNN was taping me in several haunted locations throughout Hollywood. One such location was the famed Laugh Factory, a comedy club which has launched or furthered the careers of many comics.

The crew was pleased to record me getting the psychic impression of a spirit near the men's room door . . . feeling a cold breeze in another spot. And then I stopped and said, "Upstairs . . . the second story. Do you know who's there? Groucho Marx!"

The club's publicist gasped. "That's amazing!" she said. "I've uncovered some historical information on this location—it was used as office space for Groucho Marx and his staff! Right where you're pointing—upstairs—that was his personal office!"

Those gathered around asked me what Marx was telling me. "Mostly, he's just saying he's pleased with the club," I told them. "And one more thing. He's watching over comedian Byron Allen," I said, surprising even myself with this revelation.

"He's coming into the club for an appearance soon!" the publicist exclaimed. "Then tell him Groucho likes his style," I smiled. "He's guiding him."

It wasn't a lengthy contact—barely more than a 'hello.' But many times the point of a spirit contact is merely a 'hello'—an acknowledgment of approval from the other side.

I wanted to bring you, dear Sweet Spirits, screen legend Marlene Dietrich, particularly to see what she thought of her own personal *Mommie Dearest* situation with daughter Maria Riva (who wrote a "tell all" book about her mother's life). But in this case she had not been gone long enough. During my attempted contact, my former client Garbo came in again. I asked if she had seen her onetime rival and if indeed Dietrich was still resting. Garbo told me that first, she feels no animosity toward Dietrich now, and any sense of rivalry is gone. But secondly, she told me, "Too soon . . . too soon. She is seeing no one yet," confirming my belief.

And there are other reasons why spirits are elusive. Sometimes it's simply a matter of the timing being off. A spirit might be very busy when a contact is attempted, for there is, as we've seen, much studying, guiding, and visiting to be done, and we can't *command* a spirit to come to us; it must be by mutual agreement.

As spirits grow and progress, they exist on different plateaus, much as there are different environments or neighborhoods on Earthplane. Those on an extremely low plateau (such as the criminal) are not capable of rising high enough to be allowed to work with a psychic/medium. Those who have evolved to a very high plateau may almost be "beyond" this activity, meaning that they have removed themselves so far from Earthly concerns and have grown so much wiser that they would only return in spirit to help a loved one in need, or to convey particularly meaningful or necessary information (a warning, an answer to a monumentally urgent question, etc.).

In some rather shocking instances (such as with billionnaire Howard Hughes) there can be no spirit contact because there is no *spirit*—the person is still alive and very much on Earthplane.

And I will go even farther to say that at the time of writing this book, I can only draw the conclusion, based on several attempts to contact him, that rock legend Jim Morrison (of *The Doors*) is not on the other side.

According to published reports, Morrison passed away in Paris on July 5, 1971, and is buried in that city's Pere La Chaise Cemetery. But during many visits to Paris I was not only unable to contact him in spirit, I was unable to even get a sense of spirit energy surrounding him.

I could reach no spirit emissary to reach him on my behalf . . . I heard no spirit voice, however faint, which answered to his name . . . there was simply no response and no information about a spirit named Jim Morrison.

While at the cemetery viewing his grave, I felt *nothing*—emptiness. In fact, the word "empty" flashed like a neon sign over the grave.

Based on all of this, I conclude that there is every likelihood he is *alive*, and that those in the spirit world are helping keep his secret. I have the psychic impression of a man who wanted to disappear—to exist no more as the wild—and wildly popular—musician he once was.

I've been told that there were mysterious and unexplainable instances surrounding his passing. But perhaps the biggest mystery is just where Jim Morrison might be—*today*.

And of course, in the case of other spirits, one other instance can account for lack of contact—reincarnation. If a spirit has chosen to be reborn, they are naturally back on Earthplane, living another life as another person, and thereby totally unreachable. They're as 'alive' as you and I. One example is movie great Humphrey Bogart. My last attempt to contact him proved futile and I was told by my spirit guides that Mr. Bogart's spirit is now living the life of a young boy in the Boston, Massachusetts area.

Whether I'm at a dinner party or giving an interview, it would seem that many of my conversations deal with celebrities, politicians or those in social prominence. But am I name dropping? No. These are, in many instances, my friends. They're part of the community in which I'm involved.

I must admit that I've lived a charmed life in many ways—a happy childhood, a happy adulthood. The people I discuss are people I've known or those in whose circles I've somehow traveled.

I consider it commonplace, for example, that last Christmastime, as I got out of my car in a shopping center, I encountered Jayne Meadows (Mrs. Steve) Allen as she emerged from one of the stores and headed for her car. We discussed career business for a moment, then, since we are old and dear friends, the topic turned to holiday preparations, decorations and family gatherings.

Several months before, while browsing in one of Southern California's more elegant department stores, I spotted Academy and Emmy Award-winning actress Patty Duke, whom I did not know. I felt compelled, however, to introduce myself and my "ghostwriter" Valerie Porter to Miss Duke. We felt perhaps it would be fascinating to include the talented actress in a future book we'd planned, which would include transcripts of psychic readings given to celebrities.

From the beginning, there was an instant bond of sorts. It began with me saying, "Patty, I've always enjoyed your work. Let me introduce myself." Miss Duke said, "You don't have to introduce yourself, Kenny.

I've always enjoyed your psychic work." This was further proof of the camaraderie I've enjoyed as part of the show business community.

What should be comforting to us all is the camaraderie which still exists, and grows even stronger, in Paradise. During our spirit contacts, we've seen examples of old friends and lovers being reunited, and even former rivals coming closer in some instances. It's only natural that we gravitate toward one another on the other side.

While I've mentioned well-known figures in this book because of their universal appeal and because it is easier for the general population to identify with these celebrated names, this should only offer each of you encouragement that you and your friends and loved ones will gravitate toward one another, also.

It should also offer hope that you, too, can make contact with your own community of spirits. You may be doing it already, without being aware of it. Don't always dismiss an instance as a dream or your imagination—you may be receiving visits from spirit. *Follow* that scent or that light—*pursue* that whisper or the mist you see out of the corner of your eye. Believe and know with all your heart that you can indeed make contact with your loved ones. That bond is never really broken.

I've brought spirits in to my audience members in nightclubs, at lectures, and in private readings, and through these methods I've hopefully brought some of my knowledge into their lives as well—knowledge of the world I believe in and love so strongly—the spirit world.

I'm often asked who is the most important person I've ever read psychically, and I always say quite honestly that though my life has been touched by great and the near great, the most important person is— "the next person," for I love my work and look forward to each new relationship with spirit.

I've done the best I could in bringing you spirits for this collection of contacts. I know there are more to come and I hope in the not-too-distant future *I'll be talking to* even more of your personal favorites and mine.

CANDLE MEDITATION CHART

Meditate with the following color candle for your specific problem. The candle should be a long, tapered, nonscented one, thus providing no distractions. Burn it for only five minutes at a time and use only one color at a time. You may burn the candle at any time of the day or night, and as many times as you wish, or you may go on to another color immediately following the color you just burned. As you have the candle lit, visualize your problem being solved. Be creative—see all that you desire coming to you—in fact, it is already yours. Then blow out the candle and hold your hands over the smoke. Rub the smoke into the palms of your hands, releasing your thoughts about the problem and making your final connection with the candle. Try to think no more of your problem until you feel the desire to meditate again. Let the forces take over and help you solve your situation:

White ....Health (of yourself or a loved one)

Green ....Financial situation

Blue ....Release depression and fear

Red..........................To make contact with a spirit

Rose ....For peace and contentment

Orange ....To find a lost possession, or to draw things to you—like a magnet

Pink ....Aid in work or career matter

Yellow ....Love life—to find or improve love